Architect's Pocket Book

D1428080

Architect's Pocket Book

Charlotte Baden-Powell

Second edition

ELSEVIER

Architectural
Press

AMSTERDAM • BOSTON • HEIDELBERG • LONDON • NEW YORK • OXFORD
PARIS • SAN DIEGO • SAN FRANCISCO • SINGAPORE • SYDNEY • TOKYO
Architectural Press is an imprint of Elsevier

Architectural Press
An imprint of Elsevier
Linacre House, Jordan Hill, Oxford OX2 8DP
30 Corporate Drive, Burlington, MA 01803

First published 1997
Reprinted 1998, 1999
Second Edition 2001
Reprinted with amendments 2002 and 2003
Reprinted 2004, 2005

Every care has been taken in the preparation of this book but neither the author nor the
publishers can be held responsible for any errors or omissions, or for any results arising
from such errors or omissions by any person or body using this book

British Library Cataloguing in Publication Data
Baden-Powell, Charlotte, Architect's pocket book – 2nd ed.
   1. Architecture
  I. Title
     720

Library of Congress Cataloguing in Publication Data
Baden-Powell, Charlotte,
  Architect's pocket book/Charlotte Baden-Powell – [2nd ed.]. p. cm.
  Includes index
  ISBN 0 7506 4764 7
  1. Architecture – Great Britain – Handbooks, manuals, etc. I. Title

  NA 2590 B3 2001
  721'.02'1 – dc21

ISBN 0 7506 4764 7

For information on all Architectural Press publications
visit our website at www.architecturalpress.com

Working together to grow
libraries in developing countries

www.elsevier.com | www.bookaid.org | www.sabre.org

ELSEVIER   BOOK AID International   Sabre Foundation

Composition by Tek-Art, Croydon, Surrey
Printed and bound in Great Britain

Contents

Preface

'I *know* it's somewhere – but where?' . . .
. . . any architect, any time

The inspiration for this pocket book was the front section of the *Building Technician's Diaries* which were published in the 1960s and 70s. These small airmail paper pages were densely packed with useful information for the architect, surveyor and builder. Obviously concise, often rule-of-thumb but nevertheless marvellously useful. These diaries are no longer available and are of course wildly out of date. So it seemed to me that there is a need for a new small and more complete compendium which can sit beside the drawing board/computer and also be carried easily to site.

It is aimed primarily at the smaller practice and is particularly suitable for small works. The subjects range from general arithmetic and geometric data through building regulation requirements, the sizes of furniture, fittings, joists, materials, U-values, lighting data and much more.

The choice of what to include is necessarily subjective and is the result of running my own practice for 38 years. The subjects have been gleaned either from much more comprehensive works and the more imaginative and useful aspects of manufacturers' literature. I have deliberately not included anything about costs or legal matters as these change too frequently for the book to be of any lasting value. The choice of contents is inevitably subjective and I would be interested to hear from readers of any items which they would have liked to be included. The blank pages at the end of the book are provided for personal additions.

Every effort has been made to ensure that the information given is accurate at the time of publication. When compiling the book I found many things were incomplete, out-of-date or plainly wrong. The user should be aware that the information is concise, in order to suit the small size of a pocket book. Also that legislation is frequently changing and that the British Standards and Building Regulations are being constantly superseded. If in doubt, or further more detailed explanation is required, consult the source given at the bottom of the page, with the addresses and telephone numbers at the back of the book. Where no reference is given, this is because I have compiled the information from several sources.

This book is not a construction manual, it contains no typical detail drawings, but is instead a collection of information needed before such drawings are prepared.

The second edition contains 30 new pages of subjects ranging from Party Wall Awards and green issues to industrial processes. The new drawings include information about setting-up perspectives, wheelchairs, traditional doors and windows, colour spectrum, etc. Additions have also been made to the original text. Names and addresses have been updated and email and websites added.

The aim of the book is to included information from a wide range of sources. Facts which one knows are somewhere - but where? I like to think that this is the book I should have had to hand, both as a student and while running my private practice. I hope you do too.

Acknowledgements

I am greatly indebted to the following people for their help and advice:

Choice of contents	John Winter (architect)
	Bill Ungless (architect)
Geometric data	Francis Baden-Powell (architect)
Structural data	Howard Hufford
	(structural engineer)
	David Cook (geotechnical engineer)
Water byelaws	Graham Mays (Water Research
	Centre secretary)
Electrical wiring	Brian Fisher (electrical contractor)
Lighting	Martin Wilkinson
	(lighting consultant)
Joinery	James Toner (building contractor)
General reference data	Peter Gunning (quantity surveyor)
Typography	Peter Brawne (graphic designer)

I should also like to thank the many helpful technical representatives of the manufacturers listed at the back of the book.

My thanks are also due to:

Mari Owen, my secretary, for so patiently struggling with typing, re-typing and endlessly correcting a difficult text;

Neil Warnock-Smith, my Publisher, for his support and enthusiasm for the original idea for the book;

Michael Brawne, Professor of Architecture and my husband, for his wise words, help and encouragement throughout.

1
General Information

Climate maps

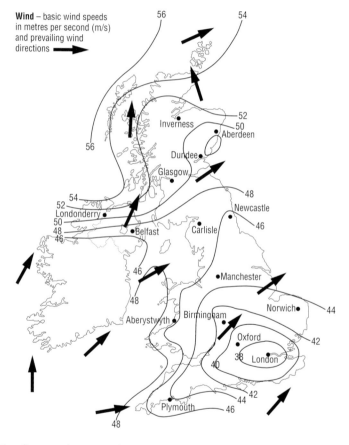

Wind – basic wind speeds in metres per second (m/s) and prevailing wind directions ➡

The figures show maximum gust speed likely to be exceeded on average only once in 50 years at 10 m above the ground in open country. To convert metres per second to miles per hour multiply by 2.24.

	8°C
	6°C
	4°C
	2°C
	0°C
	−2°C

Temperature – average for January

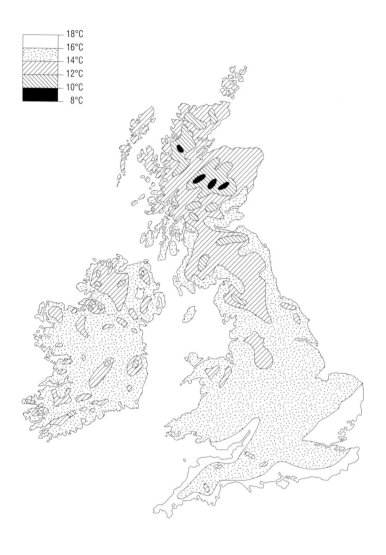

Temperature – average for July

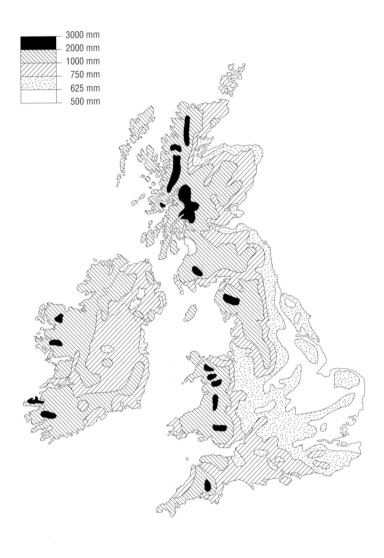

	3000 mm
	2000 mm
	1000 mm
	750 mm
	625 mm
	500 mm

Rain – annual average

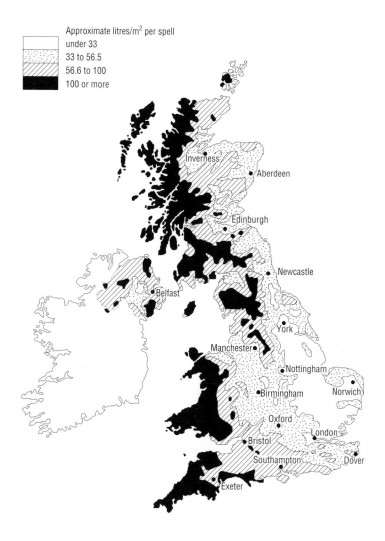

Approximate litres/m² per spell
under 33
33 to 56.5
56.6 to 100
100 or more

Rain – wind driven

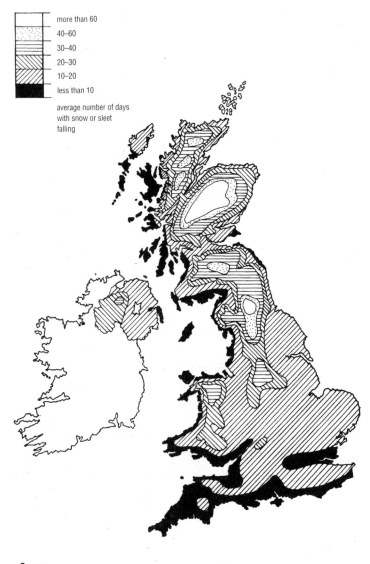

more than 60
40–60
30–40
20–30
10–20
less than 10

average number of days
with snow or sleet
falling

Snow

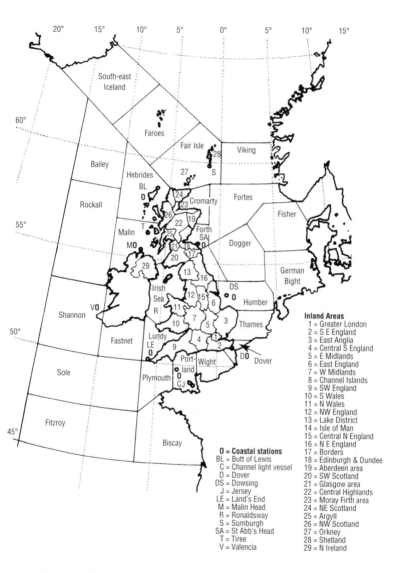

20° 15° 10° 5° 0° 5° 10° 15°

60°

South-east
Iceland

Faroes

Fair Isle

Viking

Bailey

Hebrides

28

S

27

Cromarty

Fortes

BL
O

24

23

Rockall

Fisher

26

19

55°

T

22

Forth

Malin

25

SA
O

MO

21

17

Dogger

20

German
Bight

29

13

16

Irish
Sea

12

15

DS
O O

Humber

11

6

R

Shannon

VO

10

7

5

3

Thames

Fastnet

Lundy
LE
O

4

2

Plymouth
O
CJ

9

Port-
land
O

Wight

DO Dover

Sole

Biscay

50°

45°

Fitzroy

Inland Areas
1 = Greater London
2 = S E England
3 = East Anglia
4 = Central S England
5 = E Midlands
6 = East England
7 = W Midlands
8 = Channel Islands
9 = SW England
10 = S Wales
11 = N Wales
12 = NW England
13 = Lake District
14 = Isle of Man
15 = Central N England
16 = N E England
17 = Borders
18 = Edinburgh & Dundee
19 = Aberdeen area
20 = SW Scotland
21 = Glasgow area
22 = Central Highlands
23 = Moray Firth area
24 = NE Scotland
25 = Argyll
26 = NW Scotland
27 = Orkney
28 = Shetland
29 = N Ireland

O = Coastal stations
BL = Butt of Lewis
C = Channel light vessel
D = Dover
DS = Dowsing
J = Jersey
LE = Land's End
M = Malin Head
R = Ronaldsway
S = Sumburgh
SA = St Abb's Head
T = Tiree
V = Valencia

Sea areas, inland areas & coastal stations
used in weather forecasts by the Meteorological Office

Metric system

The **Système International d'Unités (SI)**, adopted in 1960, is an international and coherent system devised to meet all known needs for measurement in science and technology. It consists of seven base units and the derived units formed as products or quotients of various powers of the base units.

Note that base and derived units, when written as words, are always written with a lower case first letter, even if the word is derived from the name of a person.

SI Base units

metre	**m**	length
kilogram	**kg**	mass
second	**s**	time
ampere	**A**	electric current
kelvin	**K**	thermodynamic temperature
candela	**cd**	luminous intensity
mole	**mol**	amount of substance

SI Prefixes (showing the nine most common)

mega	**M**	× 1000 000
kilo	**k**	× 1000
hecto	**h**	× 100
deca	**da**	× 10
deci	**d**	÷ 10
centi	**c**	÷ 100
milli	**m**	÷ 1000
micro	**μ**	÷ 1000 000
nano	**n**	÷ 1000 000 000

SI Derived units

celsius	**°C**	=	K	temperature
coulomb	**C**	=	As	electric charge
farad	**F**	=	C/V	electric capacitance
henry	**H**	=	W/A	inductance
hertz	**Hz**	=	c/s	frequency
joule	**J**	=	Ws	energy
lumen	**lm**	=	cd.sr	luminous flux
lux	**lx**	=	lm/m^2	illuminance
newton	**N**	=	$kg/m/s^2$	force
ohm	**Ω**	=	V/A	electric resistance
pascal	**Pa**	=	N/m^2	pressure
siemens	**S**	=	$1/Ω$	electric conductance
tesla	**T**	=	Wb/m^2	magnetic flux density
volt	**V**	=	W/A	electric potential
watt	**W**	=	J/s	power
weber	**Wb**	=	Vs	magnetic flux

SI Supplementary units

radian	**rad**	=	unit of plane angle equal to an angle at the centre of a circle the arc of which is equal in length to the radius
steradian	**sr**	=	unit of solid angle equal to an angle at the centre of a sphere subtended by a part of the surface equal in area to the square of the radius

Metric units

Length
kilometre	**km**	=	1000 metres
metre	**m**	=	length of path travelled by light in vacuum during a time interval of 1/299 792 458 of a second
decimetre	**dm**	=	1/10 metre
centimetre	**cm**	=	1/100 metre
millimetre	**mm**	=	1/1000 metre
micron	**µ**	=	1/100 000 metre

Area
hectare	**ha**	=	10 000 m^2
are	**a**	=	100 m^2

Volume
cubic metre	**m^3**	=	m $\times$ m $\times$ m
cubic millimetre	**mm^3**	=	1 /1000 000 000 m^3

Capacity
hectolitre	**hl**	=	100 litres
litre	**l**	=	cubic decimetre
decilitre	**dl**	=	1/10 litre
centilitre	**cl**	=	1/100 litre
millilitre	**ml**	=	1/1000 litre

Mass or weight
tonne	**t**	=	1000 kilograms
kilogram	**kg**	=	1000 grams
gram	**g**	=	1/1000 kilogram
milligram	**mg**	=	1/1000 gram

Temperature

Kelvin (K)   The kelvin belongs to a group of seven SI base units used as a quantitive unit of thermodynamic temperature. It is named after Lord William Thompson Kelvin, a Scottish physicist (1824–1907). In 1848 he suggested a scale of temperature, now called kelvin, in which the zero point is *absolute zero*, the temperature at which the motions of particles cease and their energies become zero. The units of kelvin and degree celsius temperature intervals are identical (thus 1 °C = 1K), but the point of absolute zero in celsius is minus 273.15K, thus 0 °C = 273.15 K.

It is now customary for temperature and temperature intervals to be described in degrees celsius (°C) although colour temperature of light sources is measured in degrees kelvin (K).

Celsius (°C)   The celsius scale is a scale of temperature on which water freezes at 0° and boils at 100° under standard conditions. It was devised by Anders Celsius, a Swedish astronomer (1701–44). He originally designated zero as the boiling point of water and 100° as freezing point. The scale was later reversed.

Centigrade   A temperature scale using the freezing point of water as zero and the boiling point of water as 100°. The scale is now officially called celsius (see above) to avoid confusion in Europe where the word can mean a measure of plane angle and equals 1/10 000 part of a right angle.

Fahrenheit (°F)   A scale of temperature still used in the USA which gives the freezing point of water as 32° and boiling point as 212°. Named after Gabriel Daniel Fahrenheit, a Prussian physicist (1686–1736) who invented the mercurial barometer. The Fahrenheit scale is related to the Celsius scale by the following relationships:

temperature °F = (temperature °C × 1.8) + 32
temperature °C = (temperature °F − 32) ÷ 1.8

Imperial units

Length

mile	=	1760 yards
furlong	=	220 yards
chain	=	22 yards
yard (yd)	=	3 feet
foot (ft)	=	12 inches
inch (in)	=	1/12 foot

Area

square mile	=	640 acres
acre	=	4840 square yards
rood	=	1210 square yards
square yard (sq yd)	=	9 square feet
square foot (sq ft)	=	144 square inches
square inch (sq in)	=	1/144 square foot

Volume

cubic yard	=	27 cubic feet
cubic foot	=	1/27 cubic yard
cubic inch	=	1/1728 cubic foot

Capacity

bushel	=	8 gallons
peck	=	2 gallons
gallon (gal)	=	4 quart
quart (qt)	=	2 pint
pint (pt)	=	1/2 quart
gill	=	1/4 pint
fluid ounce (fl oz)	=	1/20 pint

Weight

ton	=	2240 pounds
hundredweight (cwt)	=	112 pounds
cental	=	100 pounds
quarter	=	28 pounds
stone	=	14 pounds
pound (lb)	=	16 ounces
ounce (oz)	=	1/16 pound
dram (dr)	=	1/16 ounce
grain (gr)	=	1/7000 pound
pennyweight (dwt)	=	24 grains

Nautical measure

BS nautical mile	=	6080 feet
cable	=	600 feet
fathom	=	6 feet

Conversion factors

	Imperial to SI		SI to Imperial		
Length	1.609	mile	kilometre	km	0.6215
	0.9144	yard	metre	m	1.094
	0.3048	foot	metre	m	3.281
	25.4	inch	millimetre	mm	0.0394
Area	2.590	sq mile	sq kilometre	km^2	0.3861
	0.4047	acre	hectare	ha	2.471
	0.8361	sq yard	sq metre	m^2	1.196
	0.0929	sq foot	sq metre	m^2	10.7639
	645.16	sq inch	sq millimetre	mm^2	0.00155
Volume	0.7646	cubic yard	cubic metre	m^3	1.3079
	0.02832	cubic foot	cubic metre	m^3	35.31
	16.39	cubic inch	cubic millimetre	mm^3	0.000061
Capacity	28.32	cubic foot	litre	l	0.03531
	0.01639	cubic inch	litre	l	61.0128
	16.39	cubic inch	millilitre	ml	0.06102
	4.546	UK gallon	litre	l	0.21998
	28.4125	fluid ounce	mililitre	ml	0.0352
Mass	1.016	ton	tonne	t	0.98425
	0.4536	pound	kilogram	kg	2.20458
	453.6	pound	gram	g	0.002205
	28.35	ounce	gram	g	0.03527
Density	16.0185	pound/ft^3	kilogram/m^3	kg/m^3	0.06243
Force	4.4482	pound force	newton	N	0.22481
	14.59	pound f/foot	newton/metre	N/m	0.06854
Pressure, stress					
	4.882	pound/ft^2	kilogram/m^2	kg/m^2	0.2048
	107.252	ton f/ft^2	kilonewton/m^2	kN/m^2	0.009324
	47.8803	pound f/ft^2	newton/m^2	N/m^2	0.02088
	6894.76	pound f/in^2	newton/m^2	N/m^2	0.000145

	Imperial to SI		**SI to Imperial**		
Energy	3.6	kilowatt hour	megajoule	MJ	0.27777
Heat	1 055.0	Btu	joule	J	0.000948
Heat flow	0.000293	Btu/h	kilowatt	kW	3415.0
Heat transfer	5.67826	Btu/ft^{2}h °F	watt/m^2 °C	W/m^2 °C	0.17611
Thermal conductivity	0.144228	Btu in/ft^{2}h °F	watt/m °C	W/m °C	6.93347
Cost	0.0929	£/sq foot	£/sq metre	£/m^2	10.7639

Approximate metric/Imperial equivalents

Length

1.5 mm	≈	$1/16''$
3 mm	≈	$1/8''$
6 mm	≈	$1/4''$
12.5 mm	≈	$1/2''$
19 mm	≈	$3/4''$
25 mm	≈	$1''$
100 mm	≈	$4''$
600 mm	≈	$2'0''$
2000 mm	≈	$6'8''$
3000 mm	≈	$10'0''$

Temperature

°C		°F	
100	=	212	boiling
37	=	98.6	blood heat
21	≈	70	living room
19	≈	66	bedroom
10	=	50	
0	=	32	freezing
−17.7	=	0	

Heat transfer

1 Btu/ft²h °F ≈ 10 watt/m² °C

Lighting

10 lux	≈ 1 lumen/ft²

Area

1 hectare	≈ $2^{1}/2$ acres
0.4 hectare	≈ 1 acre

Weight

1 kilogram	≈ $2^{1}/4$ lbs
28 grams	≈ 1 ounce
100 grams	≈ $3^{1}/2$ ounces
454 grams	≈ 1 lb

Capacity

1 litre	≈ $1^{3}/4$ pints
9 litres	≈ 2 gallons

Pressure

1.5 kN/m²	≈ 30 lbs/ft²
2.5 kN/m²	≈ 50 lbs/ft²
3.5 kN/m²	≈ 70 lbs/ft²
5.0 kN/m²	≈ 100 lbs/ft²

Glass thickness

2 mm	≈ 18 oz
3 mm	≈ 24 oz
4 mm	≈ 32 oz
6 mm	≈ $1/4''$

Greek alphabet

Capital	Lower case	Name	English transliteration
A	α	alpha	a
B	β	beta	b
Γ	γ	gamma	g
Δ	δ	delta	d
E	ε	epsilon	e
Z	ζ	zeta	z
H	η	eta	ē
Θ	θ	theta	th
I	ι	iota	i
K	κ	kappa	k
Λ	λ	lambda	l
M	μ	mu	m
N	ν	nu	n
Ξ	ξ	xi	x
O	o	omicron	o
Π	π	pi	p
P	ρ	rho	r
Σ	σ (ς)*	sigma	s
T	τ	tau	t
Υ	υ	upsilon	u
Φ	φ	phi	ph
X	χ	chi	ch, kh
Ψ	ψ	psi	ps
Ω	ω	omega	ō

*ς at end of word

Geometric data

Measurement of plane and solid figures

π (pi)   = 3.1416

Circumference
circle   = $\pi \times$ diameter
cone   = $\pi \times \frac{1}{2}$ major axis + $\frac{1}{2}$ minor axis

Surface area
circle   = $\pi \times$ radius^2, or 0.7854 $\times$ diameter^2
cone   = $\frac{1}{2}$ circumference $\times$ slant height +
                          area of base
cylinder   = circumference $\times$ length +
                          area of two ends
ellipse   = product of axes $\times$ 0.7854 (approx)
parabola   = base $\times \frac{2}{3}$ height
parallelogram   = base $\times$ height
pyramid   = $\frac{1}{2}$ sum of base perimeters $\times$ slant height
                          + area of base
sector of circle   = ($\pi \times$ degrees arc $\times$ radius^2) ÷ 360
segment of circle   = area of sector minus triangle
sphere   = $\pi \times$ diameter^2
triangle   = $\frac{1}{2}$ base $\times$ perpendicular height
triangle
(equilateral)   = (side)^2 $\times$ 0.433

Volume
cone   = area of base $\times \frac{1}{3}$ perpendicular height
cylinder   = $\pi \times$ radius^2 $\times$ height
pyramid   = area of base $\times \frac{1}{3}$ height
sphere   = diameter^3 $\times$ 0.5236
wedge   = area of base $\times \frac{1}{2}$ perpendicular height

Nine regular solids

Various types of polyhedra have exercised the minds of mathematicians throughout the ages, including Euclid, whose great work *The Elements* was intended not so much as a geometry text book but as an introduction to the five regular solids known to the ancient world. This work starts with the equilateral triangle and ends with the construction of the icosahedron.

The five so-called *Platonic* solids form the first and simplest group of polyhedra. They have regular faces, all of which touch one another and the lines which make up any of the vertices form a regular polygon.

Further variations of the regular polyhedra, unknown in ancient times, are the *Kepler-Poinsot* star polyhedra. In all four cases the vertex figures spring from pentagrams. These polyhedra can be formed from the regular dodecahedron and icosahedron.

Kepler (1571–1630) found the two stellated dodecahedra, and Poinsot (1777–1859) discovered the great dodecahedra and the great icosahedron.

Five platonic solids

| TETRAHEDRON four triangular faces | CUBE six square faces | OCTAHEDRON eight triangular faces | DODECAHEDRON twelve pentagonal faces | ICOSAHEDRON twenty triangular faces |

NETS

PLANS

The Kepler–Poinsot star polyhedra

SMALL STELLATED DODECAHEDRON	GREAT STELLATED DODECAHEDRON	GREAT DODECAHEDRON	GREAT ICOSAHEDRON

NETS

72°

This solid may be built up with pyramids fixed to an icosahedron

PLANS

Source: *Mathematical Models*

Golden section

The **golden section** or **golden mean** is an irrational proportion probably known to the ancient Greeks and thought to be divine by Renaissance theorists. It is defined as a line cut in such a way that the smaller section is to the greater as the greater is to the whole, thus:

AC : CB = CB : AB

The ratio of the two lengths is called *phi* Φ.

$$\Phi = \frac{\sqrt{5} + 1}{2} = 1.61803 \ldots$$

For approximate purposes it is 1 : 1.6 or 5 : 8. Φ is the ratio of line lengths in any pentagram.

The **golden rectangle** is one in which Φ is the ratio of one side to the other.

This is implicated in the mathematics of growth as demonstrated in the **Fibonacci series** 0, 1, 1, 2, 3, 5, 8, 13, 21, 34 . . . where each number is the sum of the preceding two. This ratio of successive numbers progressively approximates more nearly to the golden rectangle.

The **Fibonacci spiral** is a curve that increases constantly in size without changing its basic shape. This is demonstrated by using squares increasing in the Fibonacci scale i.e. 1, 2, 3, 5; from which diagram can be seen three nearly golden rectangles.

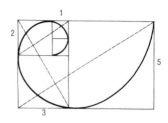

Leonardo Fibonacci (c.1170–1230) was an Italian mathematician who introduced arabic numerals to Christian Europe. He travelled extensively, particularly in North Africa where he learnt the decimal system and the use of zero. He published this system in Europe but mathematicians were slow to adopt it.

Le Corbusier used the Fibonacci series in his system of proportion 'Le Modulor'.

To draw a golden rectangle :

Draw a square ABCD. Halve the base line at E. From this point draw a line to corner C and with radius EC drop an arc to find point F.

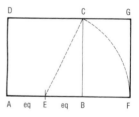

The golden rectangle is AFGD as also is BFGC.

The angle between the diagonal and the long side of a golden rectangle is approximately 31.45°.

Paper sizes

International paper sizes

The basis of the international series is a rectangle having an area of one square metre (A0) the sides of which are in the proportion of 1 : $\sqrt{2}$. This is the proportion of the side and diagonal of any square. All the **A** series are of this proportion, enabling them to be doubled or halved and remain in the same proportion which is useful for photographic enlargement or reduction. A0 is twice A1 which is twice A2 and so on. Where larger sizes of A0 are needed the A is preceded by a figure, thus 4A is four times A0.

The **B** series are sizes intermediate between any two A sizes. This series is used mostly for posters and charts. The **C** series are envelopes to suit the A sizes.

DL or long sizes are obtained by dividing the A and B series into three, four or eight equal parts parallel to the shorter side so that the proportion of 1:$\sqrt{2}$ is not maintained. In practice, the long sizes should be produced from the A series only.

The dimensions of these series are of the *trimmed* or *finished* size.

	mm	inches		mm	inches
A0	841 × 1189	$33^{1}/_{8}$ × $46^{3}/_{4}$	B0	1000 ×1414	$39^{3}/_{8}$ × $55^{5}/_{8}$
A1	594 × 841	$23^{3}/_{8}$ × $33^{1}/_{8}$	B1	707 ×1000	$27^{7}/_{8}$ × $39^{3}/_{8}$
A2	420 × 594	$16^{1}/_{2}$ × $23^{3}/_{8}$	B2	500 × 707	$19^{5}/_{8}$ × $27^{7}/_{8}$
A3	297 × 420	$11^{3}/_{4}$ × $16^{1}/_{2}$	B3	353 × 500	$13^{7}/_{8}$ × $19^{5}/_{8}$
A4	210 × 297	$8^{1}/_{4}$ × $11^{3}/_{4}$	B4	250 × 353	$9^{7}/_{8}$ × $13^{7}/_{8}$
A5	148 × 210	$5^{7}/_{8}$ × $8^{1}/_{4}$	B5	176 × 250	$6^{15}/_{16}$ × $9^{7}/_{8}$
A6	105 × 148	$4^{1}/_{8}$ × $5^{7}/_{8}$	B6	125 × 176	$4^{15}/_{16}$ × $6^{15}/_{16}$
A7	74 × 105	$2^{7}/_{8}$ × $4^{1}/_{8}$	B7	88 × 125	$3^{1}/_{2}$ × $4^{15}/_{16}$
A8	52 × 74	$2^{1}/_{16}$ × $2^{7}/_{8}$	B8	62 × 88	$2^{7}/_{16}$ × $3^{1}/_{2}$
A9	37 × 52	$1^{7}/_{16}$ × $2^{1}/_{16}$	B9	44 × 62	$1^{3}/_{4}$ × $2^{7}/_{16}$
A10	26 × 37	$1^{1}/_{16}$ × $1^{7}/_{16}$	B10	31 × 44	$1^{1}/_{4}$ × $1^{3}/_{4}$

	mm			inches	
	mm		inches		
C0	917 × 1297		$36^1/_8$ × $50^3/_8$		
C1	648 × 917		$25^1/_2$ × $36^1/_8$		
C2	458 × 648		18 × $25^1/_2$		
C3	324 × 458		$12^3/_4$ × 18		
C4	229 × 324		9 × $12^3/_4$		
C5	162 × 229		$6^3/_8$ × 9		
C6	114 × 162		$4^1/_2$ × $6^3/_8$		
C7	81 × 114		$3^3/_{16}$ × $4^1/_2$		
DL	110 × 220		$4^3/_8$ × $8^5/_8$		

Source: *Whitaker's Almanack*

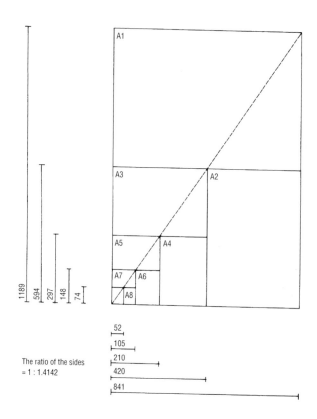

The ratio of the sides
= 1 : 1.4142

Paper sizes – **A** series

International A series paper and envelopes

Sizes most commonly used for correspondence

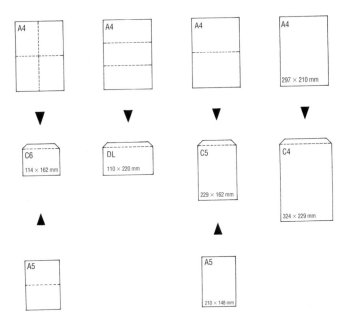

The second dimension of an envelope denotes the position of the opening flap.

Imperial paper sizes

Imperial sizes are still used for some printing and drawing papers, the most common of which are listed below:

	inches			mm		
Quad Double Crown	60	×	40	1524	×	1016
Antiquarian	53	×	31	1346	×	787
Quad Crown	40	×	30	1016	×	762
Double Elephant	40	×	27	1016	×	686
Imperial	30	×	22	762	×	559
Double Crown	30	×	20	762	×	508
Double Foolscap	27	×	17	686	×	432
Cartridge	26	×	12	660	×	305
Royal	20	×	25	508	×	635
Crown	20	×	15	508	×	381
Post	19	×	$15^1/_4$	483	×	387
Foolscap	17	×	$13^1/_2$	432	×	343

Drawing conventions

Demolition

removal of part

infilling opening

removal of area

making good after forming opening

Steps, ramps, slopes

direction of RISE ramp, stair or steps

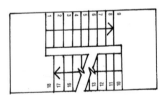

dogleg staircase

direction of FALL, natural drainage

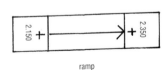

ramp

direction of FALL, slope

FLOW direction of watercourse

Landscape

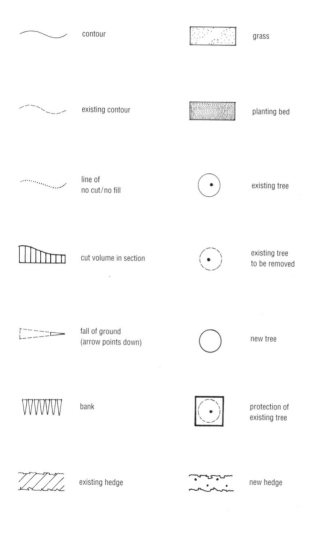

contour	grass
existing contour	planting bed
line of no cut/no fill	existing tree
cut volume in section	existing tree to be removed
fall of ground (arrow points down)	new tree
bank	protection of existing tree
existing hedge	new hedge

Drawing conventions – continued

Masonry

brickwork

blockwork

stonework

Timber

any type sawn

softwood machined all round

hardwood machined all round

Site-formed materials

mulch

concrete

asphalt macadam

topsoil

granular fill

plaster render screed

subsoil

hard fill

Manufactured materials

board, layer, membrane,
sheet – small scale

glass sheet

quilt – large scale

sheet etc – large scale

blockboard

insulation board

plywood

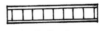
veneered blockboard

insulation quilt

Doors

	hinged leaf
	hinged leaf (alternative)
	hinged leaf normally closed
	hinged leaf normally open
	hinged leaf opening 180°
	hinged leaf opening both ways
	pair of hinged leaves
	sliding leaf
	revolving leaves
	sliding/folding leaves end hung
	sliding/folding leaves centre hung

Windows

F	fixed light
	side hung (arrow points to hinge)
	top hung
	bottom hung
	horizontal pivot
	vertical pivot
	vertical pivot reversible
	horizontal hinge projecting out (H window)
	horizontal sliding
	vertical sliding
	slide and tilt
	tilt and turn

Source: BS 1192 : Part 3 : 1987   *Recommendations for symbols and other graphic conventions*

Perspective drawing – method of setting up

1 Draw the plan to a scale and set it at the angle at which it is to be viewed.

2 Establish the position of the *Observer* on plan, preferably so that the building falls within a 30° cone. Any wider angled cone will produce a distorted perspective. The centreline of this cone is the *line of sight.*

3 Draw a horizontal line through the plan. This is called the *picture plane*, which is set at 90° to the line of sight. The further the picture plane is from the Observer, the larger the drawing will be.

4 Draw two lines parallel to the visible sides of the building – from the Observer to the picture plane – to determine the *vanishing points* (VP). As this building is orthogonal, these lines are at right angles to one another.

5 Draw the *horizon* where the perspective drawing will be. Draw vertical lines from the picture plane VPs to establish the VPs on the horizon.

6 Draw lines from the Observer to the three lower corners of the plan, cutting the picture plane.

7 Where these lines cut the picture plane at A, B and C, draw vertical lines up to find the three visible corners of the building.

8 Draw a vertical line from one of the two points where the picture plane cuts the plan to establish a *vertical scale line*. Mark this line to the same scale as the plan to determine the bottom and top edges of the building relative to the horizon. The horizon should be at about 1.6 m for normal eye level.

9 Connect these marks to the appropriate vanishing points to complete the outline of the building.

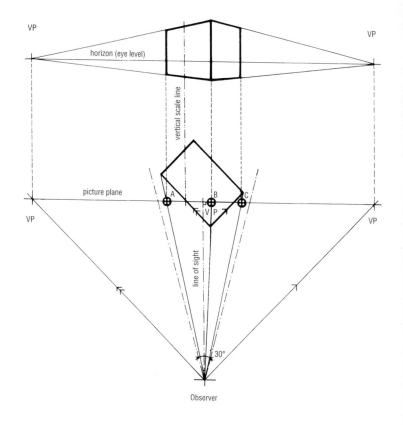

Perspective drawing – method of setting up

CI/SfB Construction index

CI/SfB is a library system used by the building industry and is suitable for the smallest or largest office.

CI = Construction Index

SfB = Samarbetskommitten för Byggnadsfrägor – a Swedish system of the late 1940s.

CI/SfB notation has four divisions:

0	1	2 & 3	4

Table 0	=	Physical environment
Table 1	=	Elements
Tables 2 and 3	=	Constructions and Materials
Table 4	=	Activities and Requirements

The current CI/SfB edition was issued in 1976 and, according to RIBA Information Services, is still widely used although the scheme is long overdue for revision.

CI/SfB Tables

Table 0   Physical environment

0   Planning areas
01   Extra terrestrial areas
02   International, national scale
     planning areas
03   Regional, sub-regional scale
     planning areas
04
05   Rural, urban planning areas
06   Land use planning areas
07
08   Other planning areas
09   Common areas relevant to
     planning

**1   Utilities, civil engineering
     facilities**
11   Rail transport
12   Road transport
13   Water transport
14   Air transport, other transport
15   Communications
16   Power supply, mineral supply
17   Water supply, waste disposal
18   Other

2   Industrial facilities
21–25
26   Agricultural
27   Manufacturing
28   Other

**3   Administrative, commercial,
     proactive service facilities**
31   Official administration, law
     courts
32   Offices
33   Commercial
34   Trading, shops
35–36
37   Protective services
38   Other

4   Health, welfare facilities
41   Hospitals
42   Other medical
43
44   Welfare, homes
46   Animal welfare
47
48   Other

5   Recreational facilities
51   Refreshment
52   Entertainment
53   Social recreation, clubs
54   Aquatic sports
55
56   Sports
57
58   Other

6   Religious facilities
61   Religious centres
62   Cathedrals
63   Churches, chapels
64   Mission halls, meeting houses
65   Temples, mosques, synagogues
66   Convents
67   Funerary, shrines
68   Other

**7   Educational, scientific,
     information facilities**
71   Schools
72   Universities, colleges
73   Scientific
74
75   Exhibition, display
76   Information, libraries
77
78   Other

8   Residential facilities
81   Housing
82   One-off housing units, houses
83
84   Special housing
85   Communal residential
86   Historical residential
87   Temporary, mobile residential
88   Other

9   Common facilities, other facilities
91   Circulation
92   Rest, work
93   Culinary
94   Sanitary, hygiene
95   Cleaning, maintenance
96   Storage
97   Processing, plant, control
98   Other, buildings other than by function
99   Parts of facilities, other aspects of the physical environment, architecture, landscape

Table 1   Elements

(--) Sites, projects, building systems

(1–) Ground, sub-structure
(10)
(11) Ground
(12)
(13) Floor beds
(14)–(15)
(16) Retaining walls, foundations
(17) Pile foundations
(18) Other substructure elements
(19) Parts of elements (11) to (18), cost summary

(2–) Primary elements, carcass
(20)
(21) Walls, external walls
(22) Internal walls, partitions
(23) Floors, galleries
(24) Stairs, ramps
(25)–(26)
(27) Roofs
(28) Building frames, other primary elements
(29) Parts of elements (21) to (28), cost summary

(3–) Secondary elements, completion if described separately from (2–)
(30)
(31) Secondary elements to external walls, external doors, windows
(32) Secondary elements to internal walls, internal doors
(33) Secondary elements to floors
(34) Secondary elements to stairs
(35) Suspended ceilings
(36)
(37) Secondary elements to roofs: rooflights etc
(38) Other secondary elements
(39) Parts of elements (31) to (38), cost summary

(4–) Finishes, if described separately

(40)
(41) Wall finishes, external
(42) Wall finishes, internal
(43) Floor finishes
(44) Stair finishes
(45) Ceiling finishes
(46)
(47) Roof finishes
(48) Other finishes to structure
(49) Parts of elements (41) to (48), cost summary

(5–) Services, mainly pipe and ducted

(50)–(51)
(52) Waste disposal, drainage
(53) Liquids supply
(54) Gases supply
(55) Space cooling
(56) Space heating
(57) Air conditioning, ventilation
(58) Other piped, ducted services
(59) Parts of elements (51) to (58), cost summary

(6–) Services, mainly electrical

(60)
(61) Electrical supply
(62) Power
(63) Lighting
(64) Communications
(65)
(66) Transport
(67)
(68) Security, control, other services
(69) Parts of elements (61) to (68), cost summary

(7–) Fittings

(70)
(71) Circulation fittings
(72) Rest, work fittings
(73) Culinary fittings
(74) Sanitary, hygiene fittings
(75) Cleaning, maintenance fittings
(76) Storage, screening fittings
(77) Special activity fittings
(78) Other fittings
(79) Parts of elements (71) to (78), cost summary

(8–) *Loose furniture, equipment

(80)
(81) Circulation loose equipment
(82) Rest, work loose equipment
(83) Culinary loose equipment
(84) Sanitary, hygiene loose equipment
(85) Cleaning, maintenance loose equipment
(86) Storage, screening loose equipment
(87) Special activity loose equipment
(88) Other
(89) Parts of elements (81) to (88), cost summary

(9–) External, other elements

(90) External works
(98) Other elements
(99) Parts of elements, cost summary

*   Use only **(7–)** if preferred

Table 2   Constructions

A*	Constructions, forms	N	Rigid sheets for overlapping
B*		O	
C*		P	Thick coating work
D*		Q	
E	Cast in situ work	R	Rigid sheets
F	Blockwork, blocks	S	Rigid tiles
G	Large blocks, panels	T	Flexible sheets
H	Section work, sections	U	
I	Pipework, pipes	V	Film coating & impregnation
J	Wirework, meshes	W	Planting, plants, seeds
K	Quilt work, quilts	X	Components
L	Flexible sheets (proofing)	Y	Formless work, products
M	Malleable sheets	Z	Joints

*   Used for special purposes e.g.: resource scheduling by computer

Table 3   Materials

a*		p	Aggregates, loose fills
b*		q	Lime & cement binders, mortars, concretes
c*			
d*		r	Clay, gypsum, magnesia & plastic binders, mortars
e	Natural stone		
f	Precast with binder	s	Bituminous materials
g	Clay (dried, fired)	t	Fixing & jointing materials
h	Metal	u	Protective & process/property modifying materials
i	Wood		
j	Vegetable & animal materials	v	Paints
k		w	Ancillary materials
l		x	
m	Inorganic fibres	y	Composite materials
n	Rubbers, plastics etc	z	Substances
o	Glass		

*   Used for special purposes e.g.: resource scheduling by computer

Tables 2 and 3 are positioned in the third division of the label, either separately or together as required,

e.g. | | | Ff | | = precast blocks

Table 4   Activities, requirements

Activities, aids

(A)   Administration & management activities, aids
(Af) Administration, organization
(Ag) Communications
(Ah) Preparation of documentation
(Ai) Public relations, publicity
(Aj) Controls, procedures
(Ak) Organizations
(Am) Personnel roles
(An) Education
(Ao) Research, development
(Ap) Standardization, rationalization
(Aq) Testing, evaluating

(A1) Organizing offices, projects
(A2) Financing, accounting
(A3) Designing, physical planning
(A4) Cost planning, cost control, tenders, contracts
(A5) Production planning, progress control
(A6) Buying, delivery
(A7) Inspection, quality control
(A8) Handing over, feedback, appraisal
(A9) Other activities, arbitration, insurance

(B)   Construction plant, tools
(B1) Protection plant
(B2) Temporary (non-protective) works
(B3) Transport plant
(B4) Manufacture, screening, storage plant
(B5) Treatment plant
(B6) Placing, pavement, compaction plant
(B7) Hand tools
(B8) Ancillary plants
(B9) Other construction plant, tools

(C)   *Used for special purposes*

(D)   Construction operations
(D1) Protecting
(D2) Cleaning, preparing
(D3) Transport, lifting
(D4) Forming, cutting, shaping, fitting
(D5) Treatment, drilling, boring
(D6) Placing, laying & applying
(D7) Making good, repairing
(D8) Cleaning up
(D9) Other construction operations

Requirements, properties

(E)   Composition
(F)   Shape, size
(G)   Appearance
(H)   Context, environment
(J)   Mechanics
(K)   Fire, explosion
(L)   Matter
(M)   Heat, cold
(N)   Light, dark
(P)   Sound, quiet
(Q)   Electricity, magnetism, radiation
(R)   Energy, side effects, compatability, durability
(S)
(T)   Application
(U)   Users resources
(V)   Working factors
(W)   Operation, maintenance factors
(X)   Change, movement, stability factors
(Y)   Economic, commercial factors
(Z)   Peripheral subjects: presentation, time, space

Sources: RIBA Information Services, NBS Services

Uniclass

CI/SfB is being superseded by a new system called **Uniclass** (Unified Classification for the Construction Industry). It was developed for the Construction Project Information Committee (CPIC) and the DoE Construction Sponsorship Directorate. The project was led by consultants from the National Building Specification (NBS) and is based on principles set out by the International Standards Organisation (ISO). The Construction Products Table is based on the work of Electronic Product Information Co-operation (EPIC).

It was designed for organizing information in libraries and projects, but can also be used for structuring files in databases. It is a faceted system which allows tables to be used independently or in combination with each other. It can be integrated with other information systems such as the Common Arrangement of Works Sections (CAWS), Civil Engineering Standard Method of Measurement (CESMM) and the Building Cost Information Service (BCIS) Standard Form of Cost Analysis.

Uniclass consists of 15 tables:

A Form of information
B Subject disciplines
C Management
D Facilities
E Construction entities
F Spaces
G Elements for buildings
H Elements for civil engineering works
J Work sections for buildings
K Work sections for civil engineering works
L Construction products
M Construction aids
N Properties and characteristics
P Materials
Q Universal Decimal Classification

Source: RIBA Publications

2
Planning

Planning and other permissions

Planning permission

Definitions

Original House: The house as it was first built, or as it stood on 1 July 1948 if it was built before that date.

Highway: All public roads, footpaths, bridleways and byways.

Special Area: Conservation Area, National Park, Area of Outstanding Natural Beauty and the Norfolk and Suffolk Broads.

Volume: Measured from external faces.

Summary of consents
needed for work to dwellings and related property

1 Dividing off part of a house for use as a separate dwelling.
2 Use of a caravan in a garden as a home for someone else.
3 Dividing off part of a house for business or commercial work.
4 Providing a parking place for a commercial vehicle or taxi.
5 Building something that goes against the terms of the original planning permission.
6 Work which might obstruct the view of road users.
7 Work which will involve a new or wider access to a major road.
8 Additions or extensions to a flat or maisonette, including those converted from houses, excluding internal alterations which do not affect the external appearance.

House extensions

9 An addition which would be nearer to any highway than the nearest part of the original house unless there is at least 20 m between the extended house and the highway.

10 Covering more than half the area of land around the original house with additions or other separate buildings.

11 An extension to a terrace house or a house in a Special Area larger than 10 per cent, or up to 50 m³, whichever is greater, of the volume of the original house.

12 An extension to any other kind of house larger than 15 per cent, or up to 70 m³, whichever is greater, of the volume of the original house.

13 An extension which is larger than 115 m³.

14 An extension which is higher than the highest part of the roof of the original house.

15 An extension where any part is more than 4 m high (except roof extensions) and is within 2 m of the property boundary.

16 Any roof extension, loft conversion or dormer window in a Special Area

17 Any extension to a roof slope which faces a highway.

18 Roof extensions which would add more than 50 m³ to the volume of the house or 40 m³ to that of a terraced house. This allowance is not in addition to, but must be deducted from, any other allowances set out above.

Separate new buildings
on the land around the house

19 Any building (or structure) to be used other than for domestic purposes or which exceeds conditions set out in 9 and 10 above.

20 Any building more than 3 m high, or 4 m high if it has a ridged roof.

21 Any building in the grounds of a Listed Building or in a Special Area which would be more than 10 m³.

22 A storage tank for heating oil larger than 3500 litres or more than 3 m above ground.

23 A tank to store liquefied petroleum gas (LPG).

Building a porch

24 With an area measured externally of more than 3 m^3.

25 Higher than 3 m above ground.

26 Less than 2 m from a road.

Erecting fences, walls and gates

27 If a house is a Listed Building.

28 If over 1 m high where next to a road or over 2 m elsewhere.

Planting hedges or trees

29 If a condition was attached to the planning permission of the property which restricts such planting or where the sight line might be blocked.

Erecting a satellite dish or antenna

other than normal TV or radio aerials

30 If the size exceeds 700 mm in any direction (900 mm in some outlying areas) or 450 mm if attached to a chimney.

31 If it projects above the roof or chimney to which it is attached.

32 If it is in addition to another antenna already installed, whether or not this has planning consent.

33 If it is installed on a chimney or on the wall or roof slope facing a highway in a Special Area.

New cladding

34 Cladding the outside of the house with stone, tiles, artificial stone, plastic or timber in a Special Area.

Driveways

35 If a new or wider access is made onto a major road. Approval of the highways department of the local council will also be needed if a new driveway crosses a pavement or verge.

Planning permission is not required for

Sheds, garages, greenhouses, domestic pet houses, summer houses, swimming pools, ponds, sauna cabins or tennis courts, unless they contravene the conditions described in 9, 10, 19, 20 and 21 above.

Patios, hard standings, paths and driveways unless used for parking a commercial vehicle or taxi.

Normal domestic TV and radio aerials – *but* see under Erecting a Satellite Dish or Antenna above.

Repairs, maintenance or minor improvements such as redecorating or replacing windows, insertion of windows, skylights or rooflights – *but* see the next section on Listed Buildings and Conservation Areas, where consents may be needed.

Other permissions

Listed Buildings

A Listed Building includes the exterior and interior of the building and, with some exceptions, any object or structure within the curtilage of the building, including garden walls.

Listed Building Consent is needed to demolish a Listed Building, or part of one, or to alter or extend it in any way inside or out which would affect its architectural or historic character.

Check with the council first. It is a criminal offence to carry out any work without consent. No fees are required.

See also p. 50.

Conservation areas

Consent is needed to demolish any building in a Conservation Area with a volume of more than 115 m³, or any part of such building. Consent may also be needed to demolish gates, walls, fences or railings. No fees are required.

National Parks, Areas of Outstanding Natural Beauty and the Broads (Special Areas)

Generally permissions to carry out building work in these areas are more limited, so check with the appropriate body first.

Trees

Many trees have Tree Preservation Orders which mean consent is needed to prune or fell them. Trees are often protected in Conservation Areas. These normally exclude fruit trees or small decorative trees with trunks less than 100 mm in diameter. Six weeks' notice is needed before any work may be carried out.

Building Regulations approval

All new building must comply with the Building Regulations.

Rights of way

If a proposed building would obstruct a public path then consult with the local authority at an early stage. If they agree to the proposal then an order will be made to divert or extinguish the right of way. No work should proceed until the order has been confirmed.

Advertising

Displaying an advertisement larger than 0.3 m^2 outside a property may need consent. This can include house names, numbers or even 'Beware of the Dog'. Temporary notices up to 0.6 m^2 relating to local events may be displayed for a short time. Estate Agents' boards, in general, should not be larger than 0.5 m^2 on each side and may be banned in Conservation Areas.

Wildlife

If the proposed new building will involve disturbing roosts of bats or other protected species, then English Nature (EN), the Countryside Council for Wales (CCW) or Scottish Natural Heritage (SNH), whichever is appropriate, must be notified.

Source: *Planning – A Guide for Householders*

Planning appeals

Considering an appeal
It is possible to appeal against a Local Planning Authority (LPA) which has refused Planning Permission, whether outline or full; or if they have given permission but with conditions which seem to the Appellant to be unreasonable; or if a decision has not been made within the time laid down, which is normally 8 weeks. However, before lodging an appeal, the Appellant should consider modifying the scheme to suit the LPA. Generally if such a scheme is presented within 1 year of the refusal date, no extra planning fee is requested. Appeals should be a last resort. They take time and cost money. Most appeals are not successful. Proposals should fit in with the LPA's development plan for the area. Permission is unlikely to be given for development on green-belt land or on good quality agricultural land, or for access to main roads. Inspectors judge appeals on their *planning merit*. They are unlikely to be swayed by personal considerations.

Making an appeal
Appeals must be lodged within 6 months of the date of the decision. The Secretary of State (SoS) can accept a late appeal, but will do so only in exceptional circumstances. Appeals are normally decided on the basis of *written representations* and a visit to the site by the planning inspector. However, where the Appellant or the LPA do not agree to this procedure, then the inspector can arrange for a *Hearing* or a *Local Inquiry*. Forms, whether for appealing against Planning Permission, Listed Building Consent or Conservation Area Consent, should be obtained from the Planning Inspectorate in England and Wales, the Scottish Executive (SEIRU) in Scotland and the Planning Appeals Commission in Northern Ireland.

Written representation
The appeal form, with documents and plans, should be sent to the Planning Inspector (PI) with copies of all papers also sent to the LPA. The LPA will send their report to the PI, copies of which will be sent to the Appellant, who is allowed to make

comments. The PI may contact *interested people* such as neighbours and environmental groups for their comments. When the Inspector is ready, a site visit is arranged. This may be an *unaccompanied* visit if the site can be viewed from public land or an *accompanied* visit when the site is on private land and where both the Appellant and the LPA are present.

Hearings
Hearings are less formal and cheaper than a local inquiry and legal representatives are not normally used.

Local inquiry
This procedure is used if the LPA and the Appellant cannot decide on a written representation and the PI decides a hearing is unsuitable.

Written statements made by the LPA and the Applicant are sent to the PI with copies to one another.

Details of the inquiry must be posted on the site, and the LPA will inform local papers and anyone else likely to be interested.

Statements or representatives may be asked for from the Ministry of Agriculture, Fisheries and Food (MAFF) where the proposal involves agricultural land, or the Health and Safety Executive (HSE) where the proposal involves the storage of dangerous materials. All witnesses or representatives may be questioned or cross-examined. At the inquiry, anyone involved may use a lawyer or other professional to put their case. The Inspector will make visits to the site, alone, before the inquiry. After the inquiry, the Appellant and the LPA may ask for a visit with the Inspector to discuss any points raised about the site or surroundings.

Costs
The Appellant and the LPA will normally pay their own expenses, whichever procedure is used. However, if there is an inquiry or hearing, the Appellant can ask the LPA to pay some or all of the costs. The LPA may do likewise. The SoS will only agree to this if the party claiming can show that the other side behaved unreasonably and put them to unnecessary expense.

The decision

The Inspector sends the decision to the Appellant with copies to the LPA and anyone else entitled or who asked for a copy. The Inspector sends a report to the SoS with a recommendation as to whether or not the appeal should be allowed. The SoS does not have to accept the Inspector's recommendations. New evidence may put new light on the subject. In these cases, both parties will have a chance to comment before a decision is made and the inquiry may be re-opened.

The High Court

The only way an appeal can be made against the Inspector's decision is on legal grounds in the High Court. This challenge must be made within 6 weeks of the date of the decision. To succeed, it must be proved that the Inspectorate or the SoS have exceeded their powers or that proper procedures were not followed.

Source: *A Guide to Planning Appeals*

Party wall awards

The Party Wall Act 1996 has effect throughout England and Wales and involves the following proposed building work:

1 Work to an existing party wall, such as taking support for a new beam, inserting full-width DPCs, underpinning, raising, rebuilding or reducing the wall.
2 Building a new party wall on or astride a boundary line between two properties.
3 Constructing foundations for a new building within 3 m of a neighbouring building, where the work will go deeper than the neighbouring foundations.
4 Constructing foundations for a new building within 6 m of a neighbouring building where the work will cut a line drawn downwards at 45° from the bottom of the neighbour's foundations.

Notices must be served by the *building owner* to the *adjoining owner* or owners, which may include landlords as well as tenants, at least 2 months before the work starts or 1 month in advance for new work as described in 3 and 4 above. There is no set form for the Notice, but it should include: the owner's name and address; the address of the building (if different); full detailed drawings of the proposed work; and the starting date. It may also include any proposals to safeguard the fabric of the adjoining owner's property. The adjoining owner cannot stop someone exercising their rights given them by the Act, but can influence how and when the work is done. Anyone receiving a notice may give consent within 14 days, or give a counter-notice setting out modifications to the proposals. If the adjoining owner does not reply, a dispute is assumed to have arisen.

The Award
When consent is not received the two owners agree to appoint one surveyor to act for both sides, or two surveyors, one to act for each side. Surveyors appointed must take into account the interests of both owners. The surveyors draw up and supervise the *Award*, which is a statement laying down what work will be undertaken and how and when it will be done. It should include a *Schedule of Condition*, which describes in detail the state of the wall viewed from the adjoining owner's side. The Award will also specify who pays the construction costs and the surveyors' fees – usually the owner who initiates the work. The Award is served on all relevant owners, each of whom is bound by the Award unless appeals are made within 14 days to the county court.

Sources: *A Short Guide to the Party Wall Act 1996*
The Party Wall etc. Act 1996: Explanatory Booklet

Listed buildings

English Heritage has the task of identifying and protecting historic buildings. This is done by recommending buildings of special architectural or historic interest to be included on statutory lists compiled by the Secretary of State, for National Heritage.

Buildings may be listed because of age, rarity, architectural merit, method of construction and occasionally because of an association with a famous person or historic event. Sometimes whole groups of buildings such as a model village or a complete square may be listed.

All buildings largely in their original condition before 1700 are likely to be listed, as are most between 1700 and 1840. Later on the criteria became tighter with time, so that post-1945 only exceptional buildings are listed.

Grades

Listed buildings are graded as follows:

Grade I   buildings of exceptional interest
Grade II*   important buildings of more than special interest
Grade II   buildings of special interest warranting every effort
           to preserve them

Of the 500 000 or so buildings currently listed, nearly 95 per cent are Grade II.

Listing applies to the entire building, including anything fixed to the building or in the grounds before 1 July 1948.

See p. 44 for permissions needed to add, alter or demolish a listed building.

Grade I and II* buildings may be eligible for grants from English Heritage, as may some Grade II buildings in conservation areas.

Residential listed buildings may be VAT zero-rated for approved alterations.

For advice on how to get a building listed or other information, consult the Department of Culture, Media and Sport.

For listed buildings in Scotland, Northern Ireland and Wales, consult Historic Scotland, CADW, and Historic Buildings and Monuments Belfast respectively.

Sources: *Listing Buildings – The Work of English Heritage*
What Listing means – A Guide for Owners and Occupiers

Building Regulations 2000

The approved documents

These documents are published as *practical guidance* to the Building Regulations. i.e. they are not the Building Regulations as such.

The mandatory **Requirement** is highlighted in green near the beginning of each document. The remaining text is for guidance only.

The Building Inspectorate accept that if this guidance is followed then the requirement is satisfied. There is no obligation to comply with these guidelines providing evidence is produced to show that the relevant requirement has been satisfied in some other way.

The purpose of the Building Regulation is to secure reasonable standards of health, safety, energy conservation and the convenience of disabled people.

A separate system of control applies in Scotland and Northern Ireland.

The regulations are published for the Office of the Deputy Prime Minister, available from TSO (Stationery Office Shops).

A	**Structure**	**1992** edition
A1	Loading	amended 2000
A2	Ground movement	
A3 & A4	Disproportionate collapse	
B	**Fire safety**	**2000** edition
B1	Means of warning and escape	amended 2002
B2	Internal spread of fire (linings)	
B3	Internal spread of fire (structure)	
B4	External fire spread	
B5	Access and facilities for the fire service	
C	**Site preparation and resistance to moisture**	**1992** edition
C1	Preparation of site	amended 2000
C2	Dangerous and offensive substances	
C3	Subsoil drainage	
C4	Resistance to weather and ground moisture	
D	**Toxic substances**	**1992** edition
		amended 2000

E   **Resistance to the passage of sound**   **2003** edition

E1   Protection against sound from other parts of the building
building and adjoining buildings

E2   Protection against sound within a dwelling-house etc

E3   Reverberation in the common internal parts of buildings
containing flats or rooms for residential purposes

E4   Acoustic conditions in schools

F   **Ventilation**   **1995** edition

F1   Means of ventilation   amended 2000

F2   Condensation in roofs

G   **Hygiene**   **1992** edition

G1   Sanitary conveniences and washing facilities   amended 2000

G2   Bathrooms

G3   Hot water storage

H   **Drainage and waste disposal**   **2002** edition

H1   Foul water drainage

H2   Waste water treatment and cess pools

H3   Rainwater drainage

H4   Building over sewers

H5   Separate systems of drainage

H6   Solid waste storage

J   **Combustion appliances and fuel storage systems**   **2002** edition

J1   Air supply

J2   Discharge of products of combustion

J3   Protection of building

J4   Provision of information

J5   Protection of liquid fuel storage systems

J6   Protection against pollution

K   **Protection from falling, collision and impact**   **1998** edition
amended 2000

L   **Conservation of fuel and power**   **2002** edition

L1   Conservation of fuel and power in dwellings

L2   Conservation of fuel and power in buildings
other than dwellings

M   **Access and facilities for disabled people**   **1999** edition

M1   Interpretation   amended 2000

M2   Access and use

M3   Sanitary conveniences

M4   Audience or spectator seating

N   **Glazing – safety in relation to impact, opening and cleaning**   **1998** edition
amended 2000

N1   Protection against impact

N2   Manifestations of glazing

N3   Safe opening & closing of windows, skylights & ventilators

N4   Safe access for cleaning windows etc

**Approved document to support regulation 7
Materials and workmanship**   **1999** edition
amended 2000

Construction Design and Management Regulations

In the mid-1990s, fatal accidents in the construction industry were five to six times more frequent than in other areas of manufacture. Also, all construction workers could expect to be temporarily off work at least once in their working life as a result of injury. The Construction Design and Management Regulations (CDM) 1994, effective from 31 March 1995, were drafted to try and improve these statistics. The regulations make *designers* responsible for making buildings 'safely constructible and to provide safety information'.

The purpose of the CDM Regulations can be summarized as follows:

- To ensure Health and Safety (H & S) issues are considered from the beginning of a project and to consider the H & S implications during the life of the structure in order to achieve a safe working environment during construction and beyond.
- To ensure the professionals appointed are competent to comply with the CDM Regs. These include designers, planning supervisors, contractors and sub-contractors.
- To see that an *H & S Plan* is prepared for the construction period and that an *H & S File* is prepared for the completed structure.
- To ensure that adequate resources are allocated to comply with the legislation imposed by the Health and Safety Executive (HSE).

Planning Supervisor

To implement the regulations, a *Planning Supervisor* (PS) must be appointed by the client. This can be anyone competent, and may be a member of the design team, contractors or even the client. Alternatively, architects should develop an H & S team by bringing in outside expertise or use a CDM advice service. The PS must notify the HSE of the project; see that designers do their CDM duty and co-operate on site safety matters; prepare the H & S plan, on time, for the construction work, and prepare an H & S file for the client on completion. They may also, if requested by a client, advise on the appointment of consultants and contractors as to their competence and resources in regard to CDM matters. If architects are to act as Planning Supervisors they must ensure that they receive certified HSE training, as failure to comply with the regulations could lead to criminal prosecution.

When CDM regulations are not applicable

Listed below are situations where the CDM regulations need not apply. However, the designer is still legally obliged to avoid foreseeable risks; give priority to protection for all; and include adequate H & S information in the design.

- Minor works in premises normally inspected by the Local Authority, who will be the *Enforcing Authority*, e.g. storage of retail goods or dangerous substances, exhibition displays of goods for sale, animal accommodation.
- Work carried out for domestic householders, on their own residences, used solely as a private dwelling (i.e. not as an office as well as a home).
- Work which is for 30 days or less duration and involves four persons or less on site and does not involve demolition or dismantling of a structure.

Source: *Managing Construction for Health and Safety CDM Regulations 1994*

Standards – in the construction industry

Efforts are being made to harmonize standards throughout Europe so as to open up the single market for construction products. It is still something of a minefield, as harmonization at the beginning of the twenty-first century is not complete. Listed alphabetically below are the organizations and standards involved, which may help to clarify the current situation.

BBA – British Board of Agrément. This organization assesses and tests new construction products and systems which have not yet received a relevant BS or EN. It issues Agrément Certificates to those  that meet their standards. The Certificate gives an independent opinion of fitness for purpose. Holders are subject to 3-yearly reviews to ensure standards are maintained. The BBA represents the UK in the UEAtc and is designated by the government to lead the issuing of ETAs.

BSI – British Standards Institution. This was the first national standards body in the world. It publishes British Standards (BS) which give recommended minimum standards for materials, products and processes. These are not mandatory, but some are quoted directly in the Building Regulations (see also EN below). All materials and components complying with a particular BS are marked with the BS kitemark together with the relevant BS number. BSI also publishes codes of practice (CP) which give recommendations for good practice in relation to design, manufacture, construction, installation and maintenance, with the main objectives being safety, quality, economy and fitness for purpose. Drafts for Development (DD) are issued when there is insufficient information for a BS or a CP. These are similar to ENVs.

CE mark – Communauté Européenne mark. This mark was introduced by the CPD, and is a symbol applied to products by their manufacturers to indicate their compliance with European member state regulations. It has nothing to do with  quality or safety (unlike the BS kitemark). If the CE mark has a number attached, this signifies that the product has been independently tested.

CEN – Comité Européen de Nationalisation (also known as the European Committee for Standardisation). Its main aims are to harmonize national standards; promote imple-mentation of the ISO; prepare ENs; co-operate with EFTA and other international governmental organizations and CENELEC (the electrotechnical counterpart of CEN). The BSI is a mem-ber of CEN.

CPD – Construction Products Directive. This is a directive produced by the European Commission introducing the CE mark.

EN – Euronorm (also known as European Standard). European Standards are published by the CEN for a wide range of materials. A full EN, known in the UK as a BS EN, is mandatory and overrules any conflicting previous BS, which must be withdrawn. Prospective standards where documenta-tion is still in preparation are published as European pre-standards (ENV). These are normally converted to full ENs after a 3-year experimental period.

EOTA – European Organization for Technical Approvals. Members of this organization issue ETAs. The UK is represent-ed in EOTA by the BBA. EOTA polices organizations nominat-ed by member states to make sure they all apply the same tests and level of expertise when preparing ETAs.

ETA – European Technical Approval. ETAs are issued by members of EOTA. They are available for products whose performance or characteristics fall outside the scope of a European Standard (EN) mandated by the EC, and are based upon assessment methods known a ETAGs (European Technical Approval Guidelines). Both ETAs and ENs enable products to which they refer to be placed in the single European market.

ISO – International Organization for Standardization. This organization prepares International Standards for the whole world. They are prefixed ISO and many are compatible and complement British Standards. In the UK, BSs and ENs that are approved by the ISO are prefixed BS ISO or BS EN ISO.

MOAT – Method of Assessment and Testing. These are the criteria and methods used by the BBA when testing products. Many MOATs have been developed in consultation with the European Agrément organizations under the aegis of the UEAtc.

QA – Quality Assurance. BS EN 9001 lays down procedures for various organizations to conform to a specification and thus acquire QA for a production or a service.

UEAtc – European Union of Agrément technical committee. A technical committee to which all European Agrément institutes belong, including the BBA for the UK. Its principal function is to facilitate trade in construction products between member states, primarily through its Confirmation process, whereby an Agrément Certificate issued by a UEAtc member in one country can be used to obtain a Certificate in another.

Sustainability, energy saving and green issues

A checklist of matters which are considered relevant at the beginning of the twenty-first century.

Sustainability has been described as 'development that meets the needs of the present without compromising the ability of those in the future to meet their own needs'. Living in equilibrium with the environment will become the key issue in constructing buildings. Sustainability combines social, economic and environmental goals; it involves governments, the commercial world, communities and individuals.

Local planning should integrate housing with workplaces and shops to reduce the need for CO_2 (carbon dioxide) emitting transport. Ideally the site should be reasonably level to promote walking and bicycling. Hills might be used for wind farms and, where possible, land set aside for local food production. Facilities should be provided for the collection of materials for recycling.

Transport is responsible for at least 30 per cent of all UK CO_2 emissions. To discourage the use of fossil-fuelled private cars, sites should be close to public transport routes. Walking distances to bus stops should ideally be within 300 m. Electric cars and buses offer the possibility of zero CO_2 emissions if the electricity is supplied from renewable sources. The electric bicycle is at present the most efficient mode of transport, using only 0.01 kWh per passenger kilometre as opposed to 0.39 kWh for a 1.1 litre petrol car. The provision of dry and secure bicycle storage will encourage cycling.

The design of buildings in the UK should maximize solar gain by incorporating thermal mass and by making windows face south or not more than 30° either side of south. Openings on north and north-eastern sides should be kept to a minimum to conserve heat. Guard against heat losses at night from large areas of glazing. The exception to this is south-facing conservatories, which act as a source of solar heated air, which can reduce the demand for back-up space heating. South-facing glazing should ideally be unshaded in winter from 9 am to 3 pm. Therefore nothing should obscure it within an altitude angle of 10°. In summer, solar shading is needed to reduce the demand for mechanical ventilation. Optimize thermal efficiency with the use of good insulation, triple glazing and airtight detailing.

Services, carefully designed, can play a major role in energy conservation. Low energy design can include on-site generation of heat and power with solar collectors, photovoltaic cells and windmills – systems that produce no CO_2 and once installed are cheap to run.

Use radiant heat rather than warm-air systems. Use gas-fuelled condensing boilers for space heating. Where possible, reclaim heat wasted from cookers and refrigerators.

Hot water systems should be designed to avoid long heat-wasting pipe runs.

Domestic controls should include individual thermostatic radiator valves; 7-day programmers with separate settings for space heating and hot water; outside sensors and boiler energy managers (BEMs).

Avoid air conditioning – it is seldom necessary in the UK except for very special atmospheric or conservation needs. Use natural ventilation or passive stack ventilation systems with humidity control intakes and extracts. Alternatively, use a mechanical ventilating system with heat recovery. Avoid excessive air changes, a potential source of heat loss.

In considering lighting, optimize daylight by making sure glazing is regularly cleaned and that as many workstations as possible are positioned near windows. Choose efficient luminaires with low energy or high frequency fluorescent lamps. In large buildings install occupancy sensors to turn off lights when not required.

Provide operating and maintenance manuals for occupants to operate all systems as efficiently as intended. Consider installing monitor systems to maintain and improve efficiency.

Water consumption is rising in the UK and global warming appears to be reducing rainfall, so the need to conserve water is imperative. Careful consumption can also reduce operating costs. Devices to conserve water include leak detectors, control devices, flow regulators and the recycling of rainwater and grey water.

Rainwater collection for recycling or garden watering can range from simple butts to underground tanks with filters and submersible pumps supplying water back to points of use.

Grey water from baths, showers and washbasins (not kitchen wastes, because of grease and food particles) can be collected in sealed storage vessels and pumped to header tanks, treated with disinfectant and recycled back to WC and urinal cisterns. A mains connection to the header tank will still be needed to ensure sufficient water is always available.

Appliances should be chosen with minimum water consumption in mind. WC cisterns can be dual-flush or have low volume flushing. Older cisterns can be filled with volume reducers. Infra-red sensors can be fitted to urinal cisterns. Public washbasins can be fitted with electronic taps, push-top taps or infra-red controlled taps. All taps should have aerating filters. Showers with low flow (max 6 l/min) heads use less water than baths. Washing machines and dishwashers should be fitted with flow and pressure limiter restrictors if fed by mains cold water and also to the hot supply if the water is supplied from a combination heating boiler.

Other water saving strategies include installing water meters, replacing washers and seatings on dripping taps, and repairing faulty ball valves to cisterns.

Landscaping might incorporate green corridors, to encourage birds and animals, through which could pass footpaths and cycle paths along existing hedgerows and waterways. Avoid large areas of mown grass, which have low wildlife value and are labour intensive to maintain.

Shelter belts provide windbreaks and lessen noise, although care must be taken not to obscure south-facing glazing and solar collectors.

Where possible, use grasscrete and gravel for minor roads to discourage motor traffic.

New housing developments need space for allotments, sports fields, playgrounds and landscaped car parks.

The use of water and tree planting can provide buffer zones between housing and industry.

New planting should incorporate as many drought-resistant plants as possible. Typical species are: cypress, corsican pines, juniper, box, myrtle, broom, santolina, cistus, rosemary and other silver-leaved shrubs.

Where watering is necessary, irrigate with trickle hoses monitored by humidity sensors and time clocks. Isolated plants are best watered by controlled-rate drippers, which direct water straight to the plant's roots.

Materials should ideally include those of low *embodied energy*, which is a term used to describe all the energy used in their production and transportation.

Where possible, use local materials to reduce pollution from transport.

Materials should be *non-toxic* and offer minimum emissions of *formaldehyde*, *volatile organic compounds* (VOCs) and *solvent vapours*. Avoid materials that produce static.

TIMBER should be supplied by a Forest Stewardship Council (FSC) accredited source.
See p. 250.

TIMBER TREATMENTS, unless water-based, are a source of VOCs. Pre-treatment of timber as opposed to on-site treatment is preferable, as tighter controls are possible under factory conditions.

MDF should be low or zero-formaldehyde.

PVC is manufactured using toxic chemicals. Disposing of PVC by fire produces dioxins, some of the most toxic chemicals known. It is used in a vast range of building materials, from window frames to piping. Wherever possible, specify some less hazardous material.

FLOORING comes in many renewable forms, which may be preferable to synthetic materials; these include rubber, coir, wool, cork, linoleum (hessian and linseed oil) and recycled tyres. Reclaimed timber or FSC-accredited timber make attractive and durable floor finishes.

PAINTS should be low odour, solvent-free and water based.

WALLPAPERS can be made from recycled packaging or pulp from managed forests. Vinyl papers may contain toxic VOCs and solvent-based inks and preservatives.

Sources: *Building for Energy Efficiency*
Building a Sustainable Future
Lighting for people, energy efficiency and architecture
Tomorrow's World
Water Conservation in Business

Anthropometric data

Standing

Dimensions given are the average for British men and women. They include an allowance for clothing and shoes.

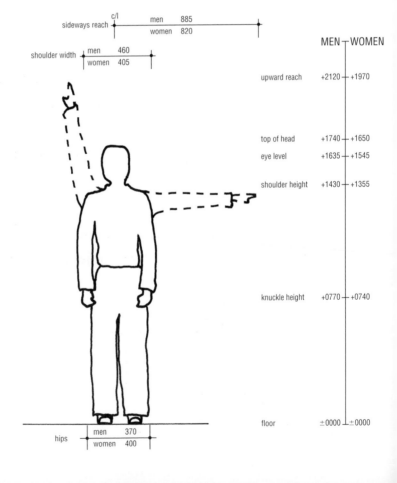

	MEN	WOMEN
sideways reach	c/l men 885	women 820
shoulder width	men 460	women 405
upward reach	+2120	+1970
top of head	+1740	+1650
eye level	+1635	+1545
shoulder height	+1430	+1355
knuckle height	+0770	+0740
floor	±0000	±0000
hips	men 370	women 400

Sitting

Dimensions given are the average for British men and women. They include an allowance for clothing and shoes.

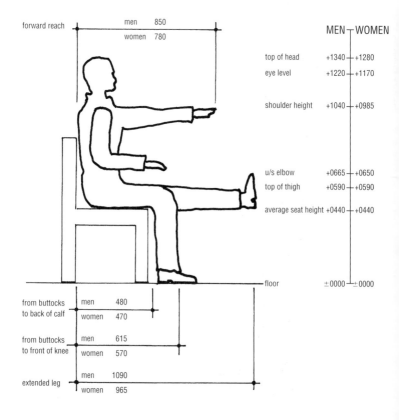

	MEN	WOMEN
top of head	+1340	+1280
eye level	+1220	+1170
shoulder height	+1040	+0985
u/s elbow	+0665	+0650
top of thigh	+0590	+0590
average seat height	+0440	+0440
floor	±0000	±0000

forward reach — men 850 / women 780

from buttocks to back of calf	men 480 / women 470
from buttocks to front of knee	men 615 / women 570
extended leg	men 1090 / women 965

Wheelchairs

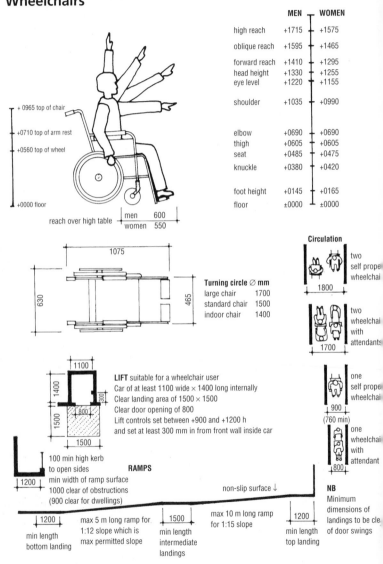

	MEN	WOMEN
high reach	+1715	+1575
oblique reach	+1595	+1465
forward reach	+1410	+1295
head height	+1330	+1255
eye level	+1220	+1155
shoulder	+1035	+0990
elbow	+0690	+0690
thigh	+0605	+0605
seat	+0485	+0475
knuckle	+0380	+0420
foot height	+0145	+0165
floor	±0000	±0000

+ 0965 top of chair
+0710 top of arm rest
+0560 top of wheel
+0000 floor

reach over high table men 600 women 550

1075
630
465

Turning circle ⌀ mm
large chair 1700
standard chair 1500
indoor chair 1400

Circulation

1800 two self propelled wheelchairs

1700 two wheelchairs with attendants

900 (760 min) one self propelled wheelchair

800 one wheelchair with attendant

1100
1400
300
800
1500
1500

LIFT suitable for a wheelchair user
Car of at least 1100 wide × 1400 long internally
Clear landing area of 1500 × 1500
Clear door opening of 800
Lift controls set between +900 and +1200 h
and set at least 300 mm in from front wall inside car

100 min high kerb to open sides
min width of ramp surface
1000 clear of obstructions
(900 clear for dwellings)

RAMPS

non-slip surface ↓

NB
Minimum dimensions of landings to be clear of door swings

1200 min length bottom landing

1200 max 5 m long ramp for 1:12 slope which is max permitted slope

1500 min length intermediate landings

max 10 m long ramp for 1:15 slope

1200 min length top landing

Wheelchair access
Entrance lobbies & corridors – not in dwellings

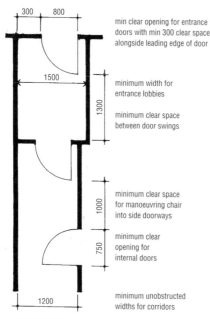

min clear opening for entrance doors with min 300 clear space alongside leading edge of door

minimum width for entrance lobbies

minimum clear space between door swings

minimum clear space for manoeuvring chair into side doorways

minimum clear opening for internal doors

minimum unobstructed widths for corridors

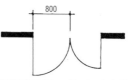

Double doors to have at least one leaf with 800 mm clear opening

NB:
Minimum clear opening for doorways means clear of door thickness, doorstops and any full length pull handle.
In practice this requires a 1000 mm doorset to achieve a minimum 800 clear opening.

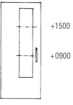

Principal entrance doors, doors in frequent use and doors across circulation routes should have glazed panels at least between heights of +0900 and +1500 but preferably with the u/s at +0450.

Means of Escape
See Approved Document B of the Building Regulations and BS 5588 : Part 8 : 1988

Audience & Spectator Seating
Six wheelchair spaces or 1/100th of spectator seating whichever is greater should be provided.
Each space to be 1400 × 900 with unobstructed view and adjacent to seated companions. The space may be created by readily removing seats for the occasion.

NOTE
No frameless glass doors. No revolving doors unless very large as in airports. Door pulls and lever handles for easy opening. Any door closers to be adjusted to open with minimum force and close slowly.

DWELLINGS
NOTE; Part M of the Building Regulations applies only to NEW DWELLINGS, not to existing dwellings nor extensions to existing dwellings.

ENTRANCE DOORS to have min clear opening 775 mm DOORWAYS in relation to CORRIDORS as table below:

Doorway – clear opening mm	Corridor – minimum width mm
750 or wider	900 when approach head-on
750	1200 when approach not head-on
775	1050 when approach not head-on
800	900 when approach not head-on

A WC must be provided in the entrance storey of a dwelling – or the principal storey if there are no habitable rooms at the entrance level.

This WC compartment must be min. 900 wide with an opening-out door and a clear space 750 deep in front of the pan clear of any wash basin. This WC may be part of a bathroom.

ACCESS to dwellings not steeper than 1:20 or ramps as shown on opposite page with dropped kerbs to any pavements.

ELECTRICAL SWITCHES & SOCKETS
Height of switches, socket outlets, bell pushes, telephone jacks, TV aerial sockets etc to be positioned between +0450 and +1200 above FFL.

Sources:
Approved Document M of the Building Regulations
Metric Handbook
Designing for Accessibility

Furniture and fittings data

Living room

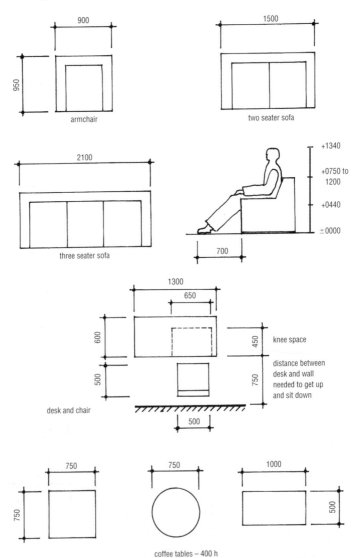

armchair

two seater sofa

three seater sofa

three seater sofa dimensions: 2100; seated figure heights +1340, +0750 to 1200, +0440, ±0000; depth 700

desk and chair: 1300, 650, 600, 500, knee space 450, distance between desk and wall needed to get up and sit down 750, 500

coffee tables – 400 h

Living room – continued

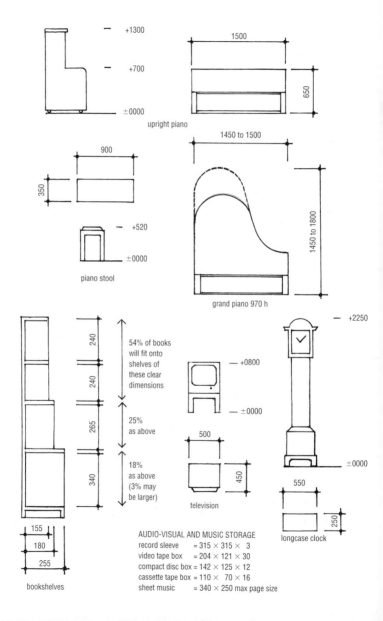

+1300

+700

±0000

1500

650

upright piano

900

350

+520

±0000

piano stool

1450 to 1500

1450 to 1800

grand piano 970 h

240

240

265

340

54% of books
will fit onto
shelves of
these clear
dimensions

25%
as above

18%
as above
(3% may
be larger)

+0800

±0000

500

450

television

+2250

±0000

550

250

longcase clock

155

180

255

bookshelves

AUDIO-VISUAL AND MUSIC STORAGE
record sleeve   = 315 × 315 × 3
video tape box   = 204 × 121 × 30
compact disc box = 142 × 125 × 12
cassette tape box = 110 × 70 × 16
sheet music   = 340 × 250 max page size

Kitchen

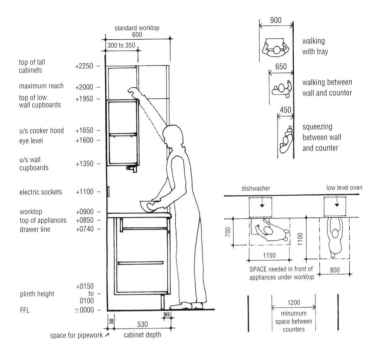

standard worktop
600

300 to 350

top of tall cabinets	+2250
maximum reach	+2000
top of low wall cupboards	+1950
u/s cooker hood	+1650
eye level	+1600
u/s wall cupboards	+1350
electric sockets	+1100
worktop	+0900
top of appliances	+0850
drawer line	+0740
plinth height	+0150 to 0100
FFL	±0000

space for pipework ⤢   cabinet depth

530   65

50

900
walking with tray

650
walking between wall and counter

450
squeezing between wall and counter

dishwasher   low level oven

700   1150   1100

SPACE needed in front of appliances under worktop   800

1200
minumum space between counters

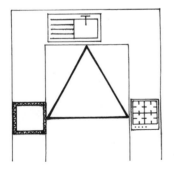

KITCHEN TRIANGLE

To achieve a compact yet workable kitchen the triangle formed by lines linking sink to cooker and refrigerator should total between 3.6 m and 6.6 m long with a maximum of 7.0 m. Avoid circulation through the triangle – particularly between sink and cooker which should not be more than 1.8m apart.

Allow a minimum 400 mm between hob and sink and any tall cupboards for elbow room.

Cooker should not be positioned near door or in front of window.

Keep electric sockets well away from sink area.

Provide lighting over worktops.

Install extractor fan over hob.

CABINETS width dimensions

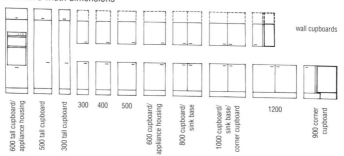

wall cupboards

600 tall cupboard/appliance housing
500 tall cupboard
300 tall cupboard
300   400   500
600 cupboard/appliance housing
800 cupboard/sink base
1000 cupboard/sink base/corner cupboard
1200
900 corner cupboard

APPLIANCES

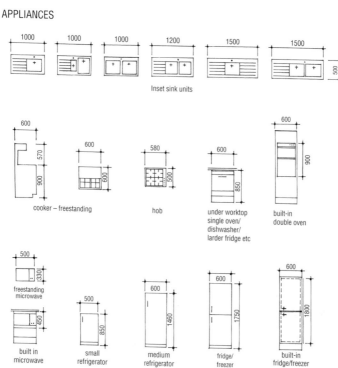

1000   1000   1000   1200   1500   1500

Inset sink units

cooker – freestanding

hob

under worktop single oven/dishwasher/larder fridge etc

built-in double oven

freestanding microwave

built in microwave

small refrigerator

medium refrigerator

fridge/freezer

built-in fridge/freezer

Dining room

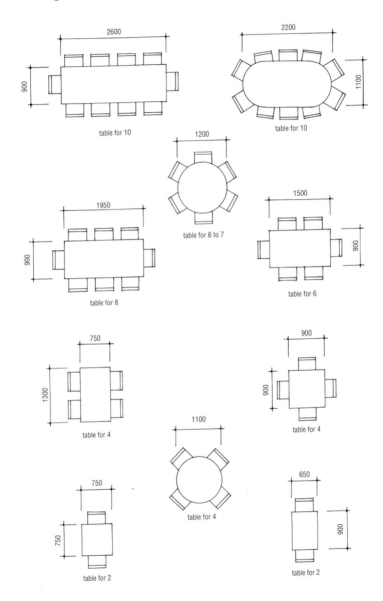

table for 10

table for 10

table for 6 to 7

table for 8

table for 6

table for 4

table for 4

table for 2

table for 4

table for 2

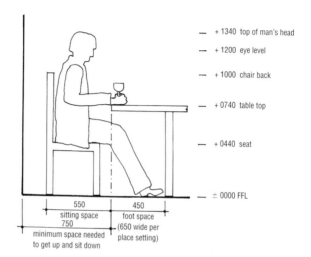

+ 1340 top of man's head

+ 1200 eye level

+ 1000 chair back

+ 0740 table top

+ 0440 seat

± 0000 FFL

550
sitting space
450
foot space
750
minimum space needed
to get up and sit down
(650 wide per
place setting)

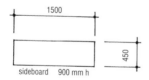

1500

450

sideboard   900 mm h

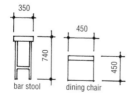

350

740

bar stool

450

450

dining chair

Bedroom

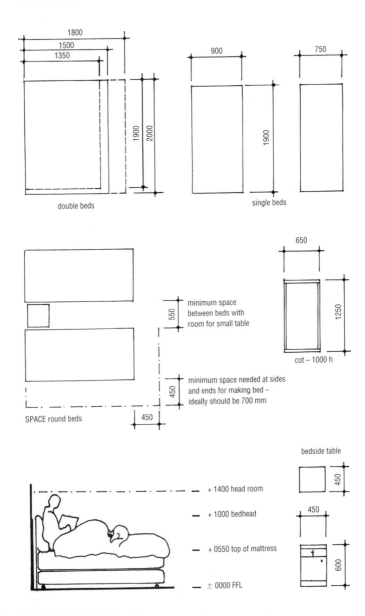

double beds

single beds

minimum space between beds with room for small table

minimum space needed at sides and ends for making bed – ideally should be 700 mm

SPACE round beds

cot – 1000 h

bedside table

+ 1400 head room

+ 1000 bedhead

+ 0550 top of mattress

± 0000 FFL

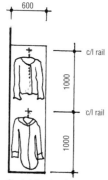

600

1000

c/l rail

1000

c/l rail

Short clothes hanging space

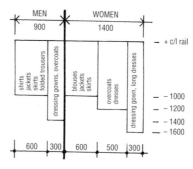

| MEN | | WOMEN | |
| 900 | | 1400 | |

+ c/l rail

shirts jackets skirts folded trousers

dressing gowns, overcoats

blouses jackets skirts

overcoats dresses

dressing gown, long dresses

— – 1000
— – 1200
— – 1400
— – 1600

| 600 | 300 | 600 | 500 | 300 |

HANGING CLOTHES – average space requirements

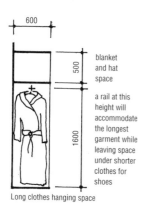

600

500

blanket and hat space

1600

a rail at this height will accommodate the longest garment while leaving space under shorter clothes for shoes

Long clothes hanging space

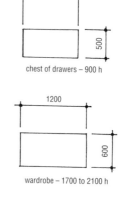

1000

500

chest of drawers – 900 h

1200

600

wardrobe – 1700 to 2100 h

BOOTS and SHOES	size overall per pair
men's Wellington boots	330 × 240 × 430 h
men's walking shoes	330 × 240 × 120 h
women's high heeled shoes	280 × 180 × 150 h
women's flat shoes	280 × 180 × 90 h

Bathroom

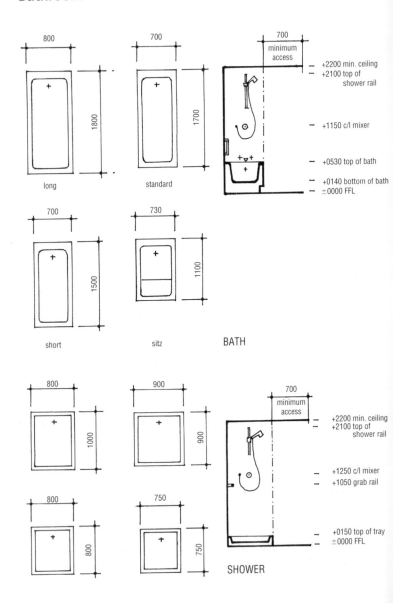

long	800 × 1800
standard	700 × 1700
short	700 × 1500
sitz	730 × 1100

BATH

+2200 min. ceiling
+2100 top of shower rail
+1150 c/l mixer
+0530 top of bath
+0140 bottom of bath
±0000 FFL

700 minimum access

SHOWER

800 × 1000
900 × 900
800 × 800
750 × 750

+2200 min. ceiling
+2100 top of shower rail
+1250 c/l mixer
+1050 grab rail
+0150 top of tray
±0000 FFL

700 minimum access

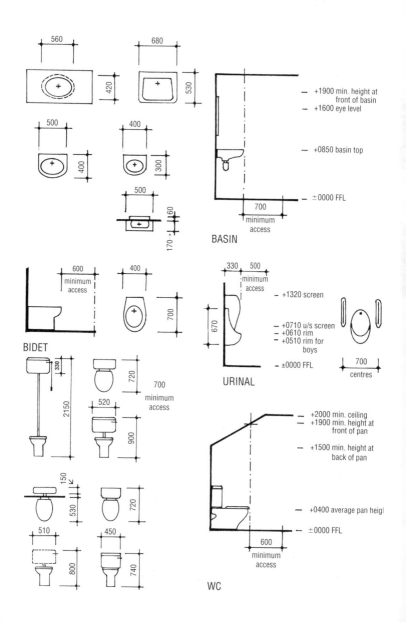

560

680

420

530

500

400

400

300

500

60

170   160

BASIN

+1900 min. height at
front of basin
+1600 eye level

+0850 basin top

±0000 FFL

700
minimum
access

600
minimum
access

400

700

BIDET

330   500
minimum
access

670

+1320 screen

+0710 u/s screen
+0610 rim
+0510 rim for
boys

±0000 FFL

URINAL

700
centres

330

2150

720

520

900

700
minimum
access

150

530

720

510

800

450

740

+2000 min. ceiling
+1900 min. height at
front of pan

+1500 min. height at
back of pan

+0400 average pan heigh

±0000 FFL

600
minimum
access

WC

Miscellaneous data
Laundry

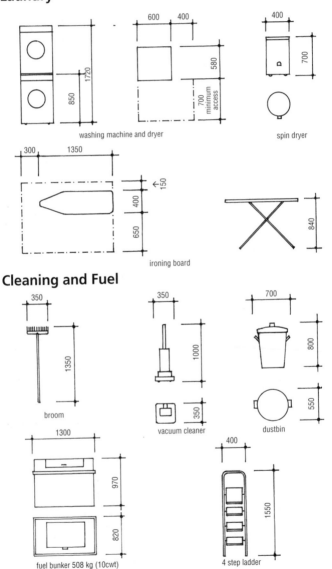

washing machine and dryer

spin dryer

ironing board

Cleaning and Fuel

broom

vacuum cleaner

dustbin

fuel bunker 508 kg (10cwt)

4 step ladder

Hall and shed

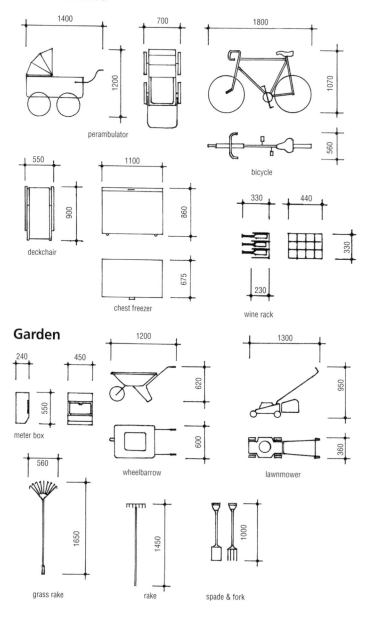

perambulator

bicycle

deckchair

chest freezer

wine rack

Garden

meter box

wheelbarrow

lawnmower

grass rake

rake

spade & fork

Domestic garages

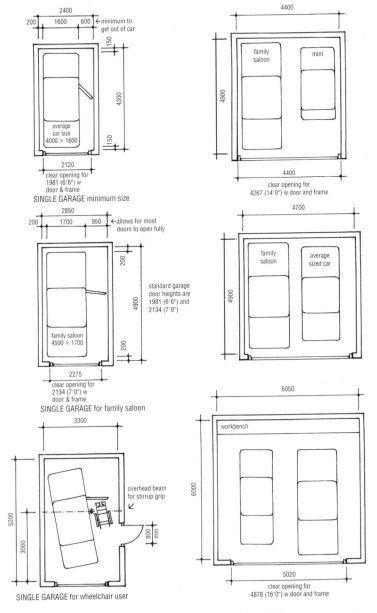

2400
200 | 1600 | 600 ←minimum to get out of car

150

4300

average
car size
4000 × 1600

150

2120
clear opening for
1981 (6'6") w
door & frame
SINGLE GARAGE minimum size

2850
200 | 1700 | 950 ←allows for most doors to open fully

200

4900

family saloon
4500 × 1700

standard garage
door heights are
1981 (6'6") and
2134 (7'0")

200

2275
clear opening for
2134 (7'0") w
door & frame
SINGLE GARAGE for family saloon

3300

overhead beam
for stirrup grip
←

5200

3000

800
min

SINGLE GARAGE for wheelchair user

4400

family
saloon   mini

4900

4400
clear opening for
4267 (14'0") w door and frame

4700

family
saloon   average
sized car

4900

clear opening for

6050

workbench

6000

5020
clear opening for
4878 (16'0") w door and frame

Vehicle sizes and parking bay

VEHICLE	l	w*	h	radius
wheelchair – standard	1075	630	965	1500
bicycle	1800	560	1070	–
motor bicycle	2250	600	800	–
small car (Mini)	3050	1400	1350	4800
average sized car	4000	1600	1350	5250
family saloon	4500	1700	1460	5500
caravan – average touring	4500	2100	2500	–
Rolls Royce	5350	1900	1670	6350
hearse	5900	2000	1900	–
skip lorry	7000	2500*	3350	8700
dustcart – medium capacity	7400	2290*	4000	7000
fire engine – medium size	8000	2290*	4000	7600
pantechnicon	11000	2500*	4230	10 050

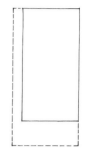

PARKING BAY
The standard parking bay is 2400 × 4800 which will accommodate most European cars.
2800 × 5800 will accommodate American and other large cars.

*widths exclude wing mirrors which may add 600 to 800 mm to the body width

Radii should not necessarily be considered as turning circles. Turning circles depend upon the speed the vehicle is travelling, the hand of the driver (left hand differs from right), and overhang, particularly at front and back of vehicle. Allow 1.2 m clear space both sides of carriageway to accommodate overhang.

Bicycle parking

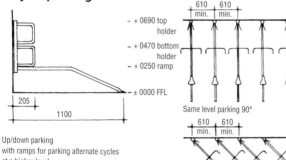

Up/down parking
with ramps for parking alternate cycles at a higher level
90° parking @ minimum 310 mm centres
45° parking @ minimum 450 mm centres

Source: Autopa Ltd

Sanitary provision for public buildings

Summary of *minimum* facilities

There should be separate facilities for men and women.

Generally washbasins should be provided in equal numbers to WCs with one for every five urinals.

In most public buildings, a minimum of two WCs should be provided so that one may act as a reserve if the other is out of order.

At least one WC should be designed for disabled people see pages 62 and 63.

Offices and shops

No. of persons	No. of WCs and basins
Up to 15	1
16–30	2
31–50	3
51–75	4
76–100	5
over 100	1 extra for each additional 25

There is no specific requirement for urinals, but if provided men's facilities may be reduced to:

No. of persons	No. of WCs and basins
Up to 20	1
21–45	2
46–75	3
76–100	4
over 100	1 extra for each additional 25

Factories

WCs	1 per 25 persons
Urinals	No specific requirement
Basins	1 per 20 persons for clean processes
	1 per 10 persons for dirty processes
	1 per 5 persons for injurious processes

Restaurants

	Men		Women	
WCs	Up to 400:	1 per 100	Up to 200:	2 per 100
	Over 400:	1 extra for each additional 250 or part thereof	Over 200:	1 extra for each additional 100 or part thereof
Urinals	1 per 25 persons			
Basins	1 per WC and 1 per 5 urinals		1 per 2 WCs	

Concert halls, theatres and similar buildings for public entertainment

	Men		Women	
WCs	Up to 250:	1	Up to 50:	2
	Over 250:	1 extra for each additional 500 or part thereof	50–100:	3
			Over 100:	1 extra for each additional 40 or part thereof
Urinals	Up to 100:	2		
	Over 100:	1 extra for each additional 80 or part thereof		

Cinemas

	Men		Women	
WCs	Up to 250:	1	Up to 75:	2
	Over 250:	1 extra for each additional 500 or part thereof	76–100:	3
			Over 100:	1 extra for each additional 80 or part thereof
Urinals	Up to 200:	2		
	Over 200:	1 extra for each additional 100 or part thereof		

WC compartments for disabled people

Wheelchair user

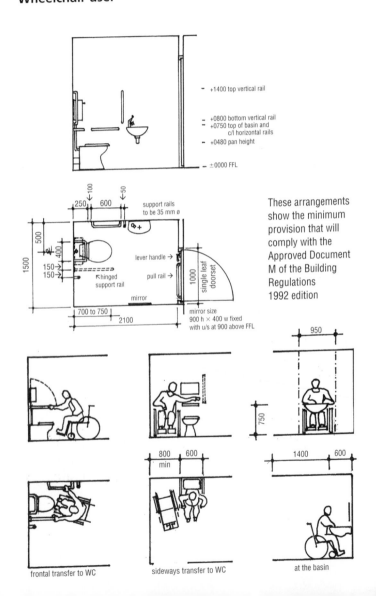

+1400 top vertical rail

+0800 bottom vertical rail
+0750 top of basin and
c/l horizontal rails
+0480 pan height

±0000 FFL

support rails
to be 35 mm ø

lever handle →

pull rail →

single leaf
doorset

↖hinged
support rail

mirror

250 · 600

100

50

500

1500

400

150→
150→

700 to 750

2100

mirror size
900 h × 400 w fixed
with u/s at 900 above FFL

These arrangements
show the minimum
provision that will
comply with the
Approved Document
M of the Building
Regulations
1992 edition

950

750

800
min

600

1400

600

frontal transfer to WC

sideways transfer to WC

at the basin

Ambulant disabled user

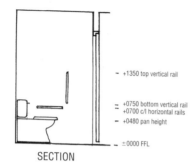

- +1350 top vertical rail

- +0750 bottom vertical rail
- +0700 c/l horizontal rails
- +0480 pan height

- ±0000 FFL

SECTION

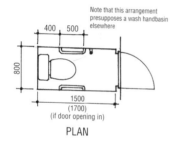

Note that this arrangement presupposes a wash handbasin elsewhere

400 | 500

800

1500
(1700)
(if door opening in)

PLAN

480

wc height

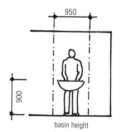

950

900

basin height

Source: Pressalit Ltd

Trees for towns

Name	Ht m 25 yrs	Ht m mature	Loca-tion	Description
Acacia – false *Robinia pseudoacacia*	14	21	S	Open headed, rugged bark, thorny twigs. Ornamental and very drought and pollution tolerant
Ailanthus *Altissima* (tree of heaven)	18	21	S	Fast growing, imposing, with ash-like leaves. Female trees produce spectacular red fruit. Tolerant of industrial pollution
Almond *Prunus dulcis*	7	8	S	Pink or white flowers early spring, before dark green finely-toothed leaves and velvety green fruit
Birch – Himalayan *Betula utilis jaquemontii*	10	18	R	Vivid white bark, very strong upright stem. Forms a striking avenue. Casts only light shade
Catalpa *Bignonioides* (Indian bean)	10	12	P	Wide, domed crown, heart-shaped leaves, white flowers July, in hot weather. Avoid cold/exposed sites. Good specimen tree
Cherry – gean* *Prunus avium* 'Plena'	12	15	S	One of the loveliest cherries, hardy, invariably producing masses of pure white drooping double flowers
Cherry – bird* *Prunus padus* 'Albertii'	7	14	S	Upright form of native 'bird cherry'. Racemes of white flowers in May, ideal for street planting
Chestnut – red *Aesculus x carnea* 'Briottii'	7	12	A	Slow growing, compact form with deep crimson flowers in June. Especially suitable for streets and avenues
Crab apple – *Malus floribunda*	5	9	S	Arching branches with early crimson flowers opening to white. Popular in streets and gardens. Scab and mildew-resistant
Crab apple *Malus tschonoskii*	6	12	S	Strong growing conical habit, good for narrow streets. Flowers tinged pink. Excellent autumn colour
Hawthorn (May) *Crataegus x lavellei*	6	8	S	Dense headed, with long glossy dark green leaves until December. Orange fruit persisting until January
Lime – silver *Tilia tomentosa*	10	18	R	Pyramidal dense habit, with large dark green leaves with white felted undersides. Aphid-free, so no drips – good for car-parking areas
Maidenhair *Ginko biloba*	7	30	P	Slow growing superb specimen tree, pale green, small, fan-shaped leaves turning yellow in autumn. Pollution-tolerant
Maple – field* *Acer campestre* 'Streetwise'	7	10	S	Neat form with dominant central leader and balanced crown. Brilliant autumn colour, very hardy
Maple – silver *Acer saccarinum* 'Laciniatum'	15	25	R	Fast growing with pale green deeply cut leaves turning clear yellow in autumn. Good for wide roadsides. Not for windy sites

Trees for towns (continued)

Name	Ht m 25 yrs	Ht m mature	Loca- tion	Description
Mountain ash* *Sorbus aucuparia*	7	8	S	Strong growing with neat upright habit. Abundant bright orange berries in autumn. Good for street planting in grass verges
Oak – evergreen *Quercus ilex* (Holm oak)	7	28	P	Slow growing, broad-leaved evergreen specimen tree for parks. Good for coastal regions but not for coldest inland areas
Oak – scarlet *Quercus coccinea* 'Splendens'	15	18	P	Superb tree for large parks, with shiny dark green leaves. Spectacular crimson leaf colour in autumn. Requires lime-free soil
Plane – London *Platanus x hispanica*	12	28	S	Large, fast growing with boldly lobed leaves and flaking bark. Good street tree, tolerant of atmospheric pollution
Sycamore *Acer pseudoplatanus*	12	25	R	Fast growing. Wide-headed tree. Good for quick shelter in difficult situations and maritime sites. Tolerant of pollution
Tulip tree *Liriodendron tulipifera*	12	30	A	Fast growing, three-lobed leaves turning butter yellow. Good for avenues. Green/white July flowers on mature trees. Smoke-tolerant
Whitebeam* *Sorbus aria* 'Majestica'	7	12	S	Handsome round head, large bright green leaves with vivid white undersides. Very hardy and smoke-resistant

* = native tree
A = avenue
P = park
R = roadside
S = street

Trees listed above are recommended for various urban situations. Other varieties may be equally suitable, but check that they do not have invasive root runs, surface roots, brittle branches or cannot tolerate pollution.

All the trees listed, except the evergreen oak, are deciduous. Conifers are generally too large for most urban situations, and very few can cope with atmospheric pollution.

Sources: *The Hillier Designer's Guide to Landscape Plants*
Tree Planting Year 1973

Hedges

Name	Leaves	Flowers	Growth	Prune	Site	Description
Beech＊ *Fagus silvatica*	D	–	fast	Aug	W, C	Pale green leaves in spring turning to rich copper, persisting through winter
Berberis *Berberis darwinii*	E	✽	fast	July	Sh	Shiny dark green prickly foliage, orange flowers in May followed by blue berries
Box – common＊ *Buxus sempervirens*	E	–	slow	Aug–Sep	Sh	Bushy shrub with glossy dark green leaves. Use the variety 'Suffruticosa' for dwarf edging
Cotoneaster *Cotoneaster sinosii*	SE	✽	medium	Feb–Aug	Sh	Leathery deep green leaves, small white flowers in June and persistent red berries in autumn
Eleagnus *Eleagnus pungens* 'Maculata'	E	–	fast	April	W, Sh	Leathery leaves with bright gold splash on slightly prickly twigs making dense hedge
Escallonia *Escallonia* 'C. F. Ball'	E	✽	medium	Oct	St, W	Glossy dark green leaves and crimson flowers June–Oct. Good for seaside. Not for cold areas.
Firethorn *Pyracantha* 'Watereri'	SE	✽	fast	May–July	Sh	Dense prickly stems, clusters of small white flowers in June and bright red fruits in autumn
Hawthorn (May)＊ *Crataegus monogyna*	D	✽	fast	July–Mar	W, Wet	Very thorny, white or pink blossom with small red haws in autumn
Holly＊ *Ilex aquifolium*	E	–	slow	Aug	Sh, W	Very dense prickly dark green leaves, bright red berries if both male and female plants adjacent
Hornbeam＊ *Carpinus betulus*	D	–	medium	Aug	Wet, Sh	Similar to beech, retaining coppery leaves in winter. Good for frost pockets and pleaching
Laurel *Prunus laurocerasus*	E	✽	medium	Aug	W, Sh	Large leathery glossy green leaves, long white flower spikes in April if buds not pruned
Photinia *P. x fraserii* 'Red Robin'	E	–	medium	Mar	–	Brilliant red new growth persisting until summer, reverting to dark green in winter
Privet *Ligustrum ovalifolium*	SE	–	fast	as nec.	Sh	Dense hedge with medium-sized green leaves, clusters of creamy white flowers in July
Yew＊ *Taxus baccata*	E	–	slow	Aug	W, C, Sh	Very hardy, dense dark green needles with bright red fruits attractive to birds

＊ = native species; E = evergreen; D = deciduous; SE = semi-evergreen; W = wind resistant;
C = will grow on chalk; Sh = will tolerate shade; St = will tolerate salt-laden winds.

Sources: Buckingham Nurseries Hedging catalogue
The Right Hedge for You

3
Structures

Weights of materials

Material	Description	Quantity of unit	kg/m²	kg/m³
aluminium	cast			2 770
aluminium roofing	longstrip	0.8 mm	3.70	
asphalt roofing	with vapour barrier	20 mm	47.00	
ballast	loose, graded			1 600
bituminous felt roofing	3 layers + vapour barrier		11.10	
blockboard	sheet	18 mm	10.50	
blockwork	high strength	100 mm	220.00	
	aerated	100 mm	64.00	
	lightweight	100 mm	58.00	
	foundation	255 mm	197.00	
brass	cast			8 425
brickwork	blue	115 mm	276.60	2 405
	engineering	115 mm	250.00	2 165
	sand/cement	115 mm	240.00	2 085
	London stock	115 mm	212.00	1 845
	fletton			1 795
calcium silicate board	sheet	6 mm	5.80	
cement				1 440
concrete	reinforced 2% steel			2 400
	plain			2 300
chalk				2 125
chipboard	flooring grade C4	18 mm	13.25	
	furniture grade C1A	18 mm	11.75	
chippings	flat roof finish	1 layer	4.75	
clay	undisturbed			1 925
copper	cast			8 730
copper roofing	longstrip	0.6 mm	5.70	
cork	granulated			80
cork insulation	board	50 mm	6.50	
cork flooring	tiles	3.2 mm	3.00	
felt	roofing underlay		1.30	

Weights of materials – continued

Material	Description	Quantity of unit	kg/m²	kg/m³
glass	clear float	4 mm	10.00	
	clear float	6 mm	15.00	
	clear float	10 mm	25.00	
glass wool	quilt	100 mm	1.02	
gravel	loose			1 600
hardboard	standard	3.2 mm	2.35	
hardboard	medium	6.4 mm	3.70	
hardwood	greenheart			1 040
	oak			720
	iroko, teak			660
	mahogany			530
hardwood flooring	boards	23 mm	16.10	
iron	cast			7 205
lead	cast			11 322
	sheet	code 4	20.40	
	sheet	code 7	35.72	
lime	lump			705
	quick			880
linoleum	sheet	3.2 mm	4.50	
MDF	sheet	18 mm	13.80	
mortar	lime			1 680
partitions	plastered brick	115 + 25 mm	250.00	
	plastered block	100 + 25 mm	190.00	
	p/b & skim on timber studs	100 + 25 mm	120.00	
parquet	flooring	15 mm	7.00	
paving	concrete	50 mm	122.00	
patent glazing	alum.bars @ 600 mm c/c	single	19.00	
	alum.bars @ 600 mm c/c	double	35.00	
perspex	corrugated sheets		4.90	
plaster	lightweight – 2 coat	13 mm	10.20	
	hardwall – 2 coat	13 mm	11.60	
	lath and plaster		29.30	
plasterboard	gyproc wallboard	9.5 mm	9.00	
	plaster skimcoat	3 mm	2.20	
plywood	sheet	6 mm	4.10	
polystyrene	expanded, sheet	50 mm	0.75	
PVC roofing	single ply membrane	2 mm	2.50	

Material	Description	Quantity of unit	kg/m²	kg/m³
quarry tiles	laid in mortar	12.5 mm	32.00	
roofing tiles	clay – plain	100 mm gauge	77.00	
	clay – single pantile	315 mm gauge	42.00	
	concrete – double roman	343 mm gauge	45.00	
	concrete – flat slate	355 mm gauge	51.00	
rubber stud flooring	tiles	4 mm	5.90	
sand	dry			1 600
sarking	felt		1.30	
screed	cement/sand	50 mm	108.00	
shingle	coarse, graded, dry			1 842
shingles	roof, untreated	95 mm gauge	8.09	
	tantalized	"	16.19	
slate	slab	25 mm	70.80	
slate roofing	best	4 mm	31.00	
	medium strong	5 mm	35.00	
	heavies	6 mm	40.00	
snow	fresh			96
	wet, compact			320
softboard	sheet	12.5 mm	14.45	
softwood	pitch pine, yew			670
	spruce			450
	western red cedar			390
softwood flooring	boards	22 mm	12.20	
soil	loose			1 440
	compact			2 080
stainless steel roofing	longstrip	0.4 mm	4.00	
steel	mild			7 848
	sheet	1.3 mm	10.20	
stone	slate			2 840
	marble			2 720
	granite			2 660
	York			2 400
	Bath			2 100

Weights of materials – continued

Material	Description	Quantity of unit	kg/m²	kg/m³
stone chippings				1 760
tarmac		25 mm	53.70	
thatch	including battens	300 mm	41.50	
terrazzo	paving	16 mm	34.20	
timber	*see* hardwood softwood			
vinyl flooring	tiles	2 mm	4.00	
water				1 000
weatherboarding	softwood	19 mm	7.30	
		25 mm	8.55	
woodwool	slabs	50 mm	36.60	
zinc	cast			6 838
zinc roofing	longstrip	0.8 mm	5.70	

Newtons

The unit of force, the *newton*, is derived from the unit of mass through the relationship that force is equal to mass times the gravitational pull of 9.81 metres per second per second (9.81 m/s^2), in the direction of the force,
e.g. 1 kilogram f = 9.81 newtons.
For approximate purposes 100 kgf = 1 kN.

Alternatively one newton is that force which, if applied to a mass of one kilogram, gives that mass an acceleration of one metre per second per second (1 m/s^2) in the direction of the force, so 1 N = 1 kg $\times$ 1 m/s^2.

When calculating the weight of materials for structures, the kilograms must be multiplied by 9.81 to get the equivalent figure in newtons (or 9.81 $\div$ 1000 for kN).

As a general rule, the following expressions are used:

superimposed loads   kN/m^2
mass loads   kg/m^2 or kg/m^3
stress   N/mm^2

1 kN.m = 10^6.Nmm (often written 1 kNm = 10^6 Nmm)

1 N/mm^2 = 10^3 kN/m^2

Imposed loads

Imposed floor loads

Floor type	Distributed load kN/m²	Concentrated load kN
Houses and blocks of flats under four storeys	1.5	1.4
Institutional bedrooms, stairs* in houses less than three storeys	1.5	1.8
Hotels bedrooms, hospital wards	2.0	1.8
College and guest house dining rooms, lounges, billiard rooms	2.0	2.7
Operating theatres, X-ray rooms, utility rooms	2.0	4.5
Offices for general use	2.5	2.7
Garages for vehicles under 2500 kg	2.5	9.0
Classrooms, chapels	3.0	2.7
Hotel kitchens and laundries, laboratories	3.0	4.5
Offices with fixed computing equipment	3.5	4.5
Assembly buildings with fixed seating	4.0	†
Shop floors for retailing	4.0	3.6
Corridors etc, footbridges subject to crowd loads	4.0	4.5
Hotel bars	5.0	†
Assembly buildings without fixed seating, gymnasia, dance halls	5.0	3.6
Office filing and storage, corridors etc subject to wheeled trolleys	5.0	4.5
Factories, workshops and similar buildings	5.0	4.5
Garages, parking and workshops for vehicles exceeding 2500 kg	5.0	9.0
Boiler rooms, plant rooms including weight of machinery	7.5	4.5
Bookstores, warehouses (per metre of storage height)	2.4	7.0
Stationery stores (per metre of storage height)	4.0	9.0

* Stairs in buildings over three storeys – same as floors to which they give access.

† Where no value is given for concentrated load, it is assumed that the distributed load is adequate for design purposes.

Reduction in total distributed imposed floor load

Number of floors including roof carried by member	1	2	3	4	5–10	10+
Percentage reduction in total distributed load on all floors carried by member	0	10	20	30	40	50
Area supported m^2	40	80	120	160	200	240
Percentage reduction in total distributed imposed load*	0	5	10	15	20	25

* Where floor is designed for 5 kN/m^2 or more, these reductions may be taken providing the loading assumed is not less than it would have been if all the floors had been designed for 5 kN/m^2 with no reductions.

Imposed roof loads

Roof type	Comments	Distributed load kN/m²		Concentrated load kN
Flat roofs and sloping roofs up to 10°	Where access is needed in addition to that needed for cleaning and repair	1.5	or	1.8*
Flat roofs and sloping roofs up to 30°	Where no access is needed except for cleaning and repair	0.6	or	0.9*
Roof slopes between 0° and 60° measured on plan	Where no access is needed except for cleaning and repair	0.6	or	0.9*
Roof slopes 60° or more		0		0

* Whichever produces the greater stress.

Where access is needed for cleaning and repair, these loads assume spreader boards will be used during work on fragile roofs.

For buildings in areas of high snowfall, snow loading should be taken into consideration. The superimposed load would normally be increased to 1 kN/m² except for certain highland areas in Scotland where it might be increased to 1.25 kN/m²

Partial safety factors

In design, each of the combinations (a) to (d) below should be considered and that giving the most severe conditions adopted. Where alternative values are shown, select that producing the most severe conditions.

		Loading	Partial safety factor
(a)	design and imposed load	design dead load design imposed load	0.9 or 1.4 1.6
(b)	dead and wind load	design dead load design wind load	0.9 or 1.4 1.4 or 0.015 whichever greater
(c)	dead, imposed and wind load	design dead load design imposed load design wind load	1.2 1.2 1.2 or 0.015 whichever greater
(d)	accidental damage	design dead load design imposed load design wind load	0.095 or 1.05 0.35 or 1.05* 0.35

* Use 1.05 in the case of buildings used predominantly for storage or where imposed load is of a permanent nature.

Source: BS 5628 Part 1 : 1992

Wind loads – simple calculation

BS 6262 : 1982 CP describes a simple method of obtaining wind loads. This can be used for buildings less than 10 metres above ground level and where the design wind speed is less than 52 metres per second (m/s). This method should not be used for cliff-top buildings.

Find the basic wind speed from the map on p. 1. Multiply by a correction in Table 1 to get the design wind speed (m/s). Find the appropriate maximum wind loading from Table 2.

Table 1:   Correction factors for ground roughness and height above ground

Height above ground	Category 1	Category 2	Category 3	Category 4
3 m or less	0.83	0.72	0.64	0.56
5 m	0.88	0.79	0.70	0.60
10 m	1.00	0.93	0.78	0.67

Category 1   Open country with no obstructions. All coastal areas.
Category 2   Open country with scattered wind breaks.
Category 3   Country with many wind breaks, e.g. small towns, city outskirts.
Category 4   Surfaces with large and frequent obstructions, e.g. city centres.

Table 2:   Wind loading – probable maximum

Design wind speed m/s	Wind loading N/m^2	Design wind speed m/s	Wind loading N/m^2
28	670	42	1510
30	770	44	1660
32	880	46	1820
34	990	48	1920
36	1110	50	2150
38	1240	52	2320
40	1370		

Fire resistance

Minimum periods for elements of structure (minutes)

Building type		Basement storey		Ground or upper storeys			
		more than 10 m deep	less than 10 m deep	less than 5 m high	less than 18 m high	less than 30 m high	more than 30 m high
Flats and maisonettes		90	60	30ᵃ	60ᶜ	90ᵇ	120ᵇ
Houses		n/a	30ᵃ	30ᵃ	60ᵍ	n/a	n/a
Institutionalᵈ, residential		90	60	30ᵃ	60	90	120ᵉ
Offices	without sprinklers	90	60	30ᵃ	60	90	X
	with sprinklers	60	60	30ᵃ	30ᵃ	60	120ᵉ
Shops & Commercial	without sprinklers	90	60	60	60	90	X
	with sprinklers	60	60	30ᵃ	60	60	120ᵉ
Assembly & Recreational	without sprinklers	90	60	60	60	90	X
	with sprinklers	60	60	30ᵃ	60	60	120ᵉ
Industrial	without sprinklers	120	90	60	90	120	X
	with sprinklers	90	60	30ᵃ	60	90	120ᵉ
Storage & other non-residential	without sprinklers	120	90	60	90	120	X
	with sprinklerss	90	60	30ᵃ	60	90	120ᵉ
Car parks for light vehicles	open sided park	n/a	n/a	15ᶠ	15ᶠ	15ᶠ	60
	any other park	90	60	30ᵃ	60	90	120ᵉ

X = not permitted

a   Increased to 60 minutes for compartment walls separating buildings.

b   Reduced to 30 minutes for any floor within a maisonette, but not if that floor contributes to the support of the building.

c   As b above and, in the case of existing houses, of no more than three storeys being converted into flats. This may be reduced to 30 minutes providing the means of escape conform to section 2 of requirement B1.

d   Multi-storey hospitals should have a minimum 60 minutes standard.

e   Reduced to 90 minutes for elements not forming part of the structural frame.

f   As a above and increased to 30 minutes for elements protecting the means of escape.

g   30 mins for 3 storey dwellings; 60 mins for compartment walls.

Source: *Building Regulations Approved Document B2003 -*
Table A2.

Bending moments and beam formulae

Bending moments and deflection formulae

Type of beam	Loading diagram	Maximum bending moment	Maximum shear	Maximum deflection d
Freely supported with central load	W, C, L	$\dfrac{WL}{4}$	$\dfrac{WL}{2}$	$dc = \dfrac{WL^3}{48EI}$
Freely supported with distributed load	W = wL, C	$\dfrac{WL}{8}$	$\dfrac{W}{2}$	$dc = \dfrac{5WL^3}{348EI}$
Freely supported with triangular load	W, C	$\dfrac{WL}{6}$	$\dfrac{W}{2}$	$dc = \dfrac{WL^3}{60EI}$
Fixed both ends with central load	C	$\dfrac{WL}{8}$	$\dfrac{W}{2}$	$dc = \dfrac{WL^3}{192EI}$
Fixed both ends with distributed load	W = wL, C	$\dfrac{WL}{12}$	$\dfrac{W}{2}$	$dc = \dfrac{WL^3}{348EI}$
One end fixed, the other end freely supported	A, W = wL, B, x ←	$\dfrac{WL}{8}$	$SA = \dfrac{5W}{8}$ $SB = \dfrac{3W}{8}$	$d = \dfrac{WL^3}{185EI}$ at x = 0.42 L
Cantilever with end load	W, B	WL	W	$dB = \dfrac{WL^3}{3EI}$
Cantilever with distributed load	W = wL, B	$\dfrac{WL}{2}$	W	$dB = \dfrac{WL^3}{8EI}$

W	=	total load	↓ = point load
w	=	kN/m	▦ = distributed load
L	=	length	↑ = free support
E	=	modulus of elasticity	
I	=	moment of inertia	▨ = fixed support
S	=	shear	

Rectangular timber beam formula

1   Obtain the imposed and dead
    loading for the beam.
2   Select a strength class of
    timber to define bending
    stress (f).
3   Choose breadth of beam.
4   Calculate the maximum
    bending moment M in kNm

$$M = \frac{WL}{8}$$

$$M = fZ, \text{ and } Z = \frac{bd^2}{6}$$

$$\therefore \ M = f\frac{bd^2}{6} \text{ or } bd^2 = \frac{6M}{f}$$

hence $d = \sqrt{\dfrac{WL \times 6 \times 10^6}{8 \times b \times f}}$

b = breadth of beam, mm
d = depth of beam, mm
f = flexural stress, N/mm^2
L = clear span, m
M = bending moment, kNm
W = total load, kN
Z = section modulus, mm^3

Safe loads on subsoils

Presumed allowable bearing values under static loading

Subsoil	Type	Bearing kN/m²
Rocks	Strong igneous and gneissic rocks in sound condition	10 000
	Strong limestones and sandstones	4 000
	Schists and slates	3 000
	Strong shales, mudstones and siltstones	2 000
Non-cohesive soils	Dense gravel, dense sand and gravel	> 600
	Medium dense gravel, medium dense sand and gravel	< 200 to 600
	Loose gravel, loose sand and gravel	< 200
	Compact sand	> 300
	Medium dense sand	100 to 200
	Loose sand	< 100
Cohesive soils	Very stiff boulder clays, hard clays	300 to 600
	Stiff clays	150 to 300
	Firm clays	75 to 150
	Soft clays and silts	< 75

Notes:

1 These values are for preliminary design only. Foundations always require site investigation first.
2 No values are given for very soft clays and silts; peat and organic soils; made-up or filled ground as presumably these would be thought unsuitable for any building.
3 Values for **Rocks** assume that foundations are carried down to unweathered rock.
4 Widths of foundations for **Non-cohesive soils** to be not less than one metre.
5 **Cohesive soils** are susceptible to long-term settlement.
6 Generally foundations should not be less than 1.0 to 1.3 m depth to allow for soil swell or shrink, frost and vegetation attack.

Source: BS 8004 : 1986

Timber

Grade stress and moduli of elasticity for various strength classes

Strength Class	Bending parallel to grain N/mm²	Tension parallel to grain N/mm²	Compression parallel to grain N/mm²	Compression* perpendicular to grain N/mm²		Shear parallel to grain N/mm²	Modulus of elasticity mean N/mm²	minimum N/mm²	Density average Kg/m³
C14	4.4	2.5	5.2	2.1	1.6	0.60	6 800	4 600	350
C16	5.3	3.2	6.8	2.2	1.7	0.67	8 800	5 800	370
C18	5.8	3.5	7.1	2.2	1.7	0.67	9 100	6 000	380
C22	6.8	4.1	7.5	2.3	1.7	0.71	9 700	6 500	410
C24	7.5	4.5	7.9	2.4	1.9	0.71	10 800	7 200	420
TR26	10.0	6.0	8.2	2.5	2.0	1.10	11 000	7 400	450
C27	10.0	6.0	8.2	2.5	2.0	1.10	12 300	8 200	450
C30	11.0	6.6	8.6	2.7	2.2	1.20	12 300	8 200	460
C35	12.0	7.2	8.7	2.9	2.4	1.30	13 400	9 000	480
C40	13.0	7.8	8.7	3.0	2.6	1.40	14 500	10 000	500
D30	9.0	5.4	8.1	2.8	2.2	1.40	9 500	6 000	640
D35	11.0	6.6	8.6	3.4	2.6	1.50	10 000	6 500	670
D40	12.5	7.5	12.6	3.9	3.0	2.00	10 800	7 500	700
D50	16.0	9.6	15.2	4.5	3.5	2.20	15 000	12 600	780
D60	18.0	10.8	18.0	5.2	4.0	2.40	18 500	15 600	840
D70	23.0	13.8	23.0	6.0	4.6	2.60	21 000	18 000	1 080

Notes:

C14–C40 are for softwoods

C16 is considered to be sufficient for general use (former classification = SC3)

C24 is a good general quality timber (former classification = SC4)

TR26 is for manufactured softwood trusses

D30–40 are for hardwoods

* Where the specification prohibits wane at bearing areas, use the higher value

Source: BS 5268: Part 2: 1996

Timber floor joists

Maximum clear spans for C16 grade softwood (m)

Dead load (kN/m²)	<0.25		0.25 to 0.50		0.50 to 1.25	
Joist centres (mm)	400	600	400	600	400	600
Joist size (mm)						
97 × 50	2.08	1.67	1.98	1.54	1.74	1.29
122 × 50	2.72	2.37	2.60	2.19	2.33	1.77
147 × 50	3.27	2.86	3.13	2.69	2.81	2.27
170 × 50	3.77	3.29	3.61	3.08	3.21	2.63
195 × 50	4.31	3.73	4.13	3.50	3.65	2.99
220 × 50	4.79	4.17	4.64	3.91	4.07	3.35
97 × 63	2.32	1.92	2.19	1.82	1.93	1.53
122 × 63	2.93	2.57	2.81	2.45	2.53	2.09
147 × 63	3.52	3.08	3.37	2.95	3.04	2.58
170 × 63	4.06	3.56	3.89	3.40	3.50	2.95
195 × 63	4.63	4.07	4.44	3.90	4.01	3.35
220 × 63	5.06	4.58	4.91	4.37	4.51	3.75

Dead loads exclude the self weight of the joist.
The table allows for an imposed load of not more than 1.5 kN/m².
Softwood t & g floorboards should be at least   16 mm finished thickness
for 400–500 c/c,
and   19 mm finished thickness
for 500–600 c/c.

Source: *Building Regulations Approved Document A* - Table A1

Timber ceiling joists

Maximum clear spans for C16 grade softwood (m)

Dead load (kN/m²)	<0.25		0.25 to 0.50	
Joist centres (mm)	400	600	400	600
Joist sizes (mm)				
72 × 38	1.15	1.11	1.11	1.06
97 × 38	1.74	1.67	1.67	1.58
122 × 38	2.37	2.25	2.25	2.11
147 × 38	3.02	2.85	2.85	2.66
170 × 38	3.63	3.41	3.41	3.16
195 × 38	4.30	4.02	4.02	3.72
220 × 38	4.98	4.64	4.64	4.27
72 × 50	1.31	1.27	1.27	1.21
97 × 50	1.97	1.89	1.89	1.78
122 × 50	2.67	2.53	2.53	2.37
147 × 50	3.39	3.19	3.19	2.97
170 × 50	4.06	3.81	3.81	3.53
195 × 50	4.79	4.48	4.48	4.13
220 × 50	5.52	5.14	5.14	4.73

The table allows for an imposed load of not more than 0.25 kN/m².
No account has been taken for other loads such as water tanks.
Minimum bearing for ceiling joists should be 35 mm.

Source: *Building Regulations Approved Document A* - Table 3

Brickwork and blockwork

Slenderness ratio
of load bearing brickwork and blockwork walls

The slenderness ratio involves the thickness and height and the conditions of support to the top and bottom of a wall, pier or column. It is defined as effective height ÷ effective thickness.

Effective height of walls
When the floor or roof spans at right angles to the wall with sufficient bearing and anchorage:
effective height = $3/4$ of actual height between centres of supports
For concrete floors having a bearing on walls, irrespective of the direction of span:
effective height = $3/4$ of actual height
For floors or roof spanning parallel with wall without bearing:
effective height = actual height
For walls with no lateral support at top:
effective height = $1^1/2$ times actual height

Effective thickness of walls
For solid walls:
effective thickness = actual thickness
For cavity walls:
effective thickness = $2/3$ × (thickness of one leaf + thickness of the other)

The slenderness ratio should never exceed 27, except in cases of walls less than 90 mm thick where it should not exceed 20.

Source: BS 5628 : Part 1 : 1992

Brickwork: characteristic strength

Mortar designation	Compressive strength of standard format bricks (N/mm²)								
	5	10	15	20	27.5	35	50	70	100
I	2.5	4.4	6.0	7.4	9.2	11.4	15.0	19.2	24.0
II	2.5	4.2	5.3	6.4	7.9	9.4	12.2	15.1	18.3
III	2.5	4.1	5.0	5.8	7.1	8.5	10.6	13.1	15.5
IV	2.2	3.5	4.4	5.2	6.2	7.3	9.0	10.8	12.6

For mortar designation see p. 195

Blockwork: characteristic strength

Mortar designation	Compressive strength of solid concrete blocks* (N/mm²)							
	2.8	3.5	5	7	10	15	20	35
I	2.8	3.5	5.0	6.8	8.8	12.0	14.8	22.8
II	2.8	3.5	5.0	6.4	8.4	10.6	12.8	18.8
III	2.8	3.5	5.0	6.4	8.2	10.0	11.6	17.0
IV	2.8	3.5	4.4	5.6	7.0	8.8	10.4	14.6

* Blocks having a ratio of height to least horizontal dimension of between 2.0 and 4.0.
For mortar designation, see p. 195

Concrete

BS 5328 contains 15 grades of which nine are listed below. Note that the grade number generally refers to its characteristic strength in N/mm². It is often possible to select one grade of concrete for each purpose, i.e. mass, in situ, reinforced, precast and prestressed. For the simplest reinforced concrete works, two grades are generally sufficient.

Grades of concrete

Lowest appropriate grade	N/mm²	Appropriate use
C 7.5	7.5	blinding concrete
C 10	10.0	filling holes in weak ground
C 15	15.0	general mass concrete
C 20	20.0	reasonable quality reinforced concrete
C 25	25.0 ⎫	
C 30	30.0 ⎬	good quality reinforced concrete
C 40	40.0 ⎭	
C 50	50.0	concrete with post-tensioned tendons
C 60	60.0	concrete with pre-tensioned tendons

Aggregate
For all in situ and reinforced precast or post-tensioned members, 20 mm aggregate will normally suffice unless a special finish is required. Very small cross sections may need 10–14 mm maximum aggregate. Mass concrete will normally contain 40 mm or larger aggregate. However, where only a small quantity of mass concrete is required, it may be easier to use a low grade of reinforced concrete, if required elsewhere, thus avoiding additional mixing and testing.

Ready-mixed concrete
Over 80 per cent of in situ concrete is now supplied ready-mixed. Although most convenient, particularly for the smaller site with restricted space for materials and plant, there are pitfalls to be aware of:

- it can be more expensive than in situ concrete;
- it does not always arrive on time;
- the right mix is not always supplied;
- quality control and cleanliness of equipment may be doubtful.

Exposure conditions of concrete surfaces

Mild   Protected against weather or aggressive conditions.

Moderate   Sheltered from severe rain or freezing while wet; subject to condensation; continuously under water; in contact with non-aggressive soil.

Severe   Exposed to severe rain; alternate wetting and drying or occasional freezing or severe condensation.

Very severe Exposed to sea water spray, de-icing salts (directly or indirectly), corrosive fumes or severe freezing conditions while wet.

Extreme   Exposed to abrasive action, e.g. sea water carrying solids, or flowing water with pH $\leq$ 4.5, or machinery or vehicles.

Reinforcement cover to meet exposure conditions

Exposure conditions	Nominal cover (mm)				
Mild	25	20	20	20	20
Moderate	–	35	30	25	20
Severe	–	–	40	30	25
Very severe	–	–	50	40	30
Extreme	–	–	–	60	50
Maximum free water/cement ratio	0.65	0.60	0.55	0.50	0.45
Minimum cement content kg/m^3	275	300	325	350	400
Lowest grade of concrete	C 30	C 35	C 40	C 45	C 50

Source: BS 5328 : 1980

Concrete mixes for small works

Use	Site mixed (proportions by volume)	Ready-mixed
General Purpose	1 : 2 : 3 cement : sand : 20 mm aggregate OR 1 : 2 : 4 cement : sand : combined aggregates	C 20 medium to high workability 20 mm maximum aggregate
Foundations footings, foundations bases for precast paving	1 : 2½ : 3 cement : sand : 20 mm aggregate OR 1 : 2½ : 5 cement : sand : combined aggregates	C 7.5 high workability 20 mm maximum aggregate
Paving exposed in situ paving and drives (Use ready-mixed if possible)	1 : 1½ : 2½ cement : sand : 20 mm aggregate OR 1 : 1½ : 3½ cement : sand : combined aggregates	special prescribed mix: min. cement content 330 kg/m³; 5% entrained air; target slump 75 mm

Source: British Cement Association

Reinforced concrete lintels – precast, cast on site or cast in situ

Clear span mm	Lintel depth on brick mm	Lintel depth on block mm	No. ms bars	Bar ø mm	Min. bearing on brickwork mm	Min. bearing on blockwork mm
up to 700	150	150	1	12	100	100
700 to 1100	225	200	1	10	100	150
1100 to 1300	225	200	1	12	100	150
1300 to 1600	300	300	1	12	100	150
1600 to 1900	300	300	2	10	150	200
1900 to 2200	300	300	2	12	150	200

Notes:
1   These lintels are suitable for low rise buildings on 115 mm brick or 100 mm block walls.
2   For 225 mm brick or 200 mm block walls, double the number of reinforcing bars.
3   Seek advice for walls thicker than 225 mm or loads exceeding 10 kN/m.

Prestressed concrete lintels – safe loads (kg/m)

Clear span	Lintel sizes w × d (mm)				
	100 × 65	150 × 65	150 × 100	100 × 150	100 × 215
600	1 061	1 499	3 039	5 127	15 995
750	732	1 034	2 100	3 549	11 497
900	533	753	1 533	2 599	8 968
1 050	404		1 166	1 981	
1 200	316	446	914	1 558	5 507
1 350	253		734	1 256	
1 500	206	291	600	1 032	3 670
1 650	171		499	861	
1 800	143	202	420	729	2 614
1 950	121		357	624	
2 100	103	146	307	539	1 951
2 250	89		265	469	
2 400	77	108	231	412	1 508
2 550	67		202	364	
2 700	58	82	178	323	1 197
2 850	48		157	288	
3 000	40	63	140	258	971

150 mm minimum bearings for all lintels

Source: ACP Concrete Ltd

Steelwork

Universal beams – Safe distributed loads (kN) for grade 43 steel

Beam size mm	Mass kg/m	2.0	2.5	3.0	3.5	4.0	4.5	5.0	5.5	6.0	7.0	8.0
		Spans (m) / Deflection co-efficients										
		112.0	71.68	49.78	36.57	28.00	22.12	17.92	14.81	12.44	9.143	7.0
406 × 140	46	**513**	**411**	**342**	**293**	**257**	228	205	187	171	147	128
	39	**414**	**331**	**276**	**236**	**207**	184	165	150	138	118	103
356 × 171	67	**662**	**567**	**472**	405	354	315	283	258	236	202	177
	57	**574**	**473**	**394**	338	296	263	237	215	197	169	148
	51	**519**	**420**	**350**	**300**	263	234	210	191	175	150	131
	45	**453**	**363**	**302**	**259**	227	201	181	165	151	130	113
356 × 127	39	**377**	**302**	**252**	216	189	168	151	137	126	108	94
	33	**311**	**248**	**207**	177	155	138	124	113	104	89	78
305 × 165	54	**479**	**398**	**331**	284	249	221	199	181	166	142	124
	46	**412**	**342**	**285**	**244**	214	190	171	155	143	122	107
	40	**370**	**296**	**247**	**212**	185	165	148	135	123	106	93
305 × 127	48	**404**	323	269	231	202	180	162	147	135	115	101
	42	**351**	280	234	200	175	156	140	127	117	100	88
	37	**311**	249	207	178	156	138	124	113	104	89	78
305 × 102	33	**274**	219	183	156	137	122	110	100	91	78	68
	28	**232**	185	154	132	116	103	93	84	77	66	58
	25	**190**	152	127	109	95	84	76	69	63	54	47
254 × 146	43	**333**	**267**	222	191	167	148	133	121	111	95	83
	37	**286**	**229**	191	164	143	127	115	104	95	82	72
	31	**233**	186	155	133	117	104	93	85	78	67	58
254 × 102	28	203	163	135	116	102	90	81	74	68	58	51
	25	175	140	117	100	88	78	70	64	58	50	37
	22	149	119	99	85	74	66	60	54	50	43	37
203 × 133	30	**184**	147	123	105	92	82	74	67	61	53	
	25	153	122	102	87	77	68	61	56	51		
203 × 102	23	136	109	90.6	77.7	68.0						
178 × 102	19	101	80.8	67.3	57.7	50.5						
152 × 89	16	72.6	58.1	48.4	41.5	36.3						
127 × 76	13	49.6	39.6	33.0	28.3	24.8						

Notes: See p. 113

Steel joists (RSJ) –
Safe distributed loads (kN)
for grade 43 steel

Joist size mm	Mass kg/m	Spans (m)										
		1.50	1.75	2.0	2.25	2.50	2.75	3.0	3.25	3.5	4.0	4.25
		Deflection co-efficients										
		199	146	112	88.5	71.7	59.2	49.8	42.4	36.6	28.0	24.8
254 × 203	82				**518**	**500**	**454**	**416**	**304**	*357*	*312*	*294*
203 × 152	52	**362**	**356**	**311**	**277**	*249*	*226*	*207*	*191*	178	156	146
152 × 127	37	*210*	*180*	*158*	*140*	*126*	115	105	97	90	79	74
127 × 114	29	*136*	*116*	*102*	90	81	74	68	63	58	51	48
127 × 114	27	*131*	*112*	*98*	87	79	71	65	60	56	49	46
102 × 102	23	*84*	72	63	56	51	46	42	39	36	32	30
89 × 89	19	*61*	52	46	41	36	33	30	28	26	23	21
76 × 76	13	37	31	27	24	22	20	18	17	16	14	13

Notes:

Loads printed in **bold** type may cause overloading of the unstiffened web, the capacity of which should be checked.

Loads printed in *italic* type do not cause overloading of the unstiffened web, and do not cause deflection exceeding span / 360.

Loads printed in ordinary type should be checked for deflection.

Source: British Constructional Steelwork Association Ltd

Steel hollow sections

Hot formed structural hollow sections (SHS) are manufactured to BS 4360 : 1990 and BS 4848 Part 2: 1991.

The square and rectangular sections have tight corner radii which have higher geometric properties and therefore a higher load carrying capacity in compression than cold formed sections.

Cold formed hollow sections (CFHS) are manufactured to BS 6363: 1989.

The square and rectangular sections have larger corner radii which give lower geometric properties than hot formed sections of the same size and thickness. Cold formed hollow sections must NOT be substituted in a direct size-for-size basis for hot formed hollow sections without checking the design. Where structural properties are not critical, CFHS provide a cheaper solution.

SHS = structural hollow section
CHS = circular hollow section
RHS = rectangular hollow sections including square sections
CFHS = cold formed hollow section

Structural steel hollow sections
External sizes in mm

Hot formed			Cold formed		
circular	square	rectangular	circular	square	rectangular
21.3	40 × 40	50 × 30	26.9	20 × 20	50 × 25
26.9	50 × 50	60 × 40	33.7	25 × 25	50 × 30
33.7	60 × 60	80 × 40	42.4	30 × 30	60 × 40
42.4	70 × 70	90 × 50	48.3	40 × 40	80 × 40
48.3	80 × 80	100 × 50	60.3	50 × 50	80 × 60
60.3	90 × 90	100 × 60	76.1	60 × 60	90 × 50
76.1	100 × 100	120 × 60	88.9	70 × 70	100 × 40
88.9	120 × 120	120 × 80	114.3	80 × 80	100 × 50
114.3	140 × 140	150 × 100	139.7	90 × 90	100 × 60
139.7	150 × 150	160 × 80	168.3	100 × 100	100 × 80
168.3	160 × 160	200 × 100		120 × 120	120 × 40
193.7	180 × 180	200 × 120		150 × 150	120 × 60
219.1	200 × 200	200 × 150			120 × 80
244.5	250 × 250	250 × 100			150 × 100
273.0	260 × 260	250 × 150			160 × 80
323.9	300 × 300	260 × 140			200 × 100
355.6	350 × 350	300 × 100			
406.4	400 × 400	300 × 200			
457.0		300 × 250			
508.0		350 × 150			
Seamless	*Jumbo*	350 × 250			
hot formed	hot formed	400 × 120			
hollow	square hollow	400 × 150			
sections	sections also	400 × 200			
also	available with	400 × 300			
available	thicker walls	450 × 250			
with thicker	350 to 600 mm	500 × 200			
walls	square	500 × 300			
193 to					
660 mm ø					

Source: Corus: tubes and pipes

Steel lintels for cavity walls
Sizes and safe loads

Code	Size h × w mm	Gauge	Lengths mm	Weight kg/m	Safe load tonnes
CN7	143 × 245	E	750 to 1500	8.3	1.75
		F	1650 to 2100	9.3	2.0
		A	2250 to 2700	9.9	2.0
CN8	219 × 245	B	2700 to 3600	15.8	3.0
		C	3900 to 4575	19.2	3.0
		C	4800	19.2	2.6
CN3	143 × 265	E	750 to 1500	8.6	1.75
		F	1650 to 2100	9.7	1.85
		A	2250 to 2700	10.2	2.0
CN4	219 × 265	B	2700 to 3600	16.1	3.0
		C	3900 to 4575	20.4	3.0
		C	4800	20.4	2.6
CN43	143 × 270	E	750 to 1500	8.8	1.75
		F	1650 to 2100	9.9	2.0
		A	2250 to 2700	10.4	2.0
CN44	219 × 270	B	2700 to 3600	16.5	3.0
		C	3900 to 4575	20.2	3.0
		C	4800	20.2	2.6
CN41	143 × 285	E	750 to 1500	9.2	2.0
CN42	219 × 280	B	2250 to 3300	17.0	3.0
		C	3600 to 4200	20.5	3.0
CN11	143 × 285	E	750 to 1500	9.2	2.0
		F	1650 to 2100	10.4	2.25
		A	2250 to 2700	10.8	2.0
CN12	219 × 285	B	2700 to 3600	16.9	3.0
		C	3900 to 4575	20.5	3.0
		C	4800	20.5	2.6
CN14	219 × 295	A	750 to 2700	13.1	3.0
		B	2850 to 3600	16.5	3.0
		C	3900 to 4575	20.0	3.0
		C	4800	20.0	2.6
CN57	143 × 310	E	750 to 1500	9.5	1.75
		F	1650 to 2100	10.6	1.85
		A	2250 to 2700	11.1	1.95
CN58	219 × 310	B	2700 x 3600	18.0	3.0
		C	3900 x 4575	21.8	3.0
		C	4800	21.8	2.6

Safe loads are safe working loads at maximum length.
All figures based on a minimum end bearing of 150 mm.
Standard lengths available in 150 mm increments up to 3000 mm length and 300 mm increments thereafter.

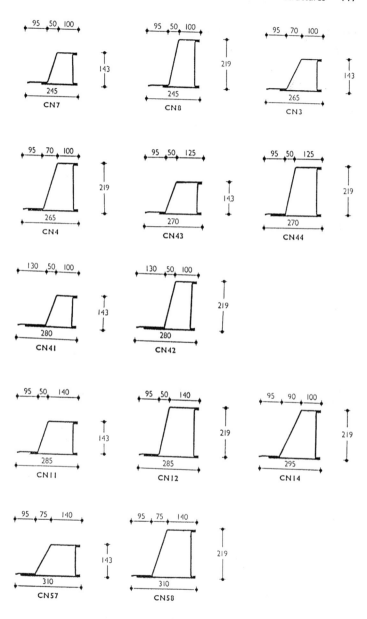

Steel lintels for cavity walls – continued

Construction
Steel lintels, as detailed on pages 92 and 93, are called *combined* lintels. They are made up of three pieces of metal, not all of which are the same gauge. The gauge code letters represent combinations which range from the lightest, E, averaging 1.6 mm, through F, A, B, C to D the heaviest, averaging 3.0 mm.

Heavy duty lintels are also available in thicker gauges.

Lintels are made from galvanised steel with polyester powder corrosion resisting coating.

Bases of lintels are slotted for plaster key.

Slabs of insulation are fitted inside profiles.

Other profiles
Open back lintels – useful where the inner skin is fair faced.

Rebated combined lintels – for window/door frames set back in reveals.

Lintels for closed eaves – for windows tight under sloping roofs.

Lintels for walls with masonry outer skin and timber frame inside.

Lintels for masonry outer skin where inner skin is carried by concrete lintel.

Lintels for internal partitions and load bearing walls.

Special profiles for various styles of arches and cantilevered masonry corners.

Stainless steel
All the above lintels are available in stainless steel at approximately $2\frac{1}{2}$ to 3 times the cost.

Source: Caradon Catnic Ltd

4
Services

Drainage

Foul drains
recommended minimum gradients

Peak flow l/s	Pipe size mm	Minimum gradient	Maximum capacity l/s
< 1	75	1 : 40	4.1
< 1	100	1 : 40	9.2
> 1	75	1 : 80	2.8
> 1	100	1 : 80 *	6.3
> 1	150	1 : 150 †	15.0

* Minimum of 1 WC   † Minimum of 5 WCs

Land drains
in normal soils – minimum gradients

Pipe Ø	Gradient	Pipe Ø	Gradient
50	1 : 500	150	1 : 2160
75	1 : 860	175	1 : 2680
100	1 : 1260	200	1 : 3200
125	1 : 1680	225	1 : 3720

Traps
minimum sizes and seal depths

Appliance	Ø trap mm	Seal depth mm		Ø trap mm	Seal depth mm
washbasin	32	75	waste disposer	40	75
bidet	32	75	urinal	40	75
bath*	40	50	sink	40	75
shower*	40	50	washing machine*	40	75
syphonic WC	75	50	dishwasher*	40	75

*Where these fittings discharge directly into a gully the seal depth may be reduced to a minimum of 38 mm.

Source: *Building Regulations – Approved Document H*

Inspection chamber covers
Typical dimensions

Covers are manufactured in steel plate, galvanised steel and cast iron – overall sizes for cast iron will be larger. Covers may have single or double seals; plain or recessed tops, and be multiple leaf or continuous for ducting. Alternative features include chambered keyholes, handlift recesses and locking screws.

Most covers are available in the load classes shown below.

Typical clear opening mm	Overall frame mm
300 × 300	370 × 370
450 × 450	520 × 520
600 × 450	670 × 520
600 × 600	670 × 670
750 × 600	820 × 670
750 × 750	820 × 820
900 × 600	970 × 670
900 × 900	970 × 970
1000 × 1000	1070 × 1070

Load classes for inspection chamber covers

Class	Wheel load (slow moving traffic)	Typical application
A	5 kN	Pedestrian, cycle tracks
AA	15 kN	Private drives, car parking areas
AAA	25 kN	Restricted access roads
B	50 kN	Commercial delivery, refuse collection
C	65 kN	All roads but positioned within 0.5 m of kerb
D	108 kN	All roads restricted only by wheel loading

Sources: Caradon Jones Ltd, Glynwed Brickhouse

Single stack drainage system

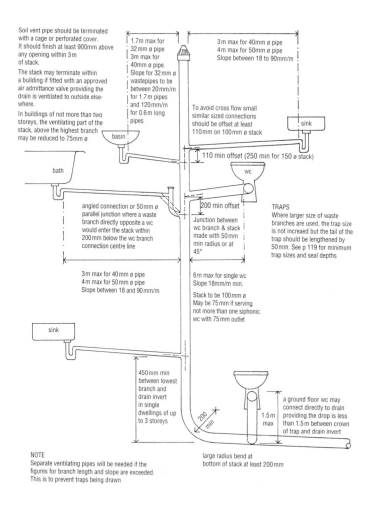

Soil vent pipe should be terminated with a cage or perforated cover. It should finish at least 900mm above any opening within 3m of stack.

The stack may terminate within a building if fitted with an approved air admittance valve providing the drain is ventilated to outside elsewhere.

In buildings of not more than two storeys, the ventilating part of the stack, above the highest branch may be reduced to 75mm ø

1.7m max for 32mm ø pipe 3m max for 40mm ø pipe. Slope for 32mm ø wastepipes to be between 20mm/m for 1.7m pipes and 120mm/m for 0.6m long pipes

3m max for 40mm ø pipe 4m max for 50mm ø pipe Slope between 18 to 90mm/m

To avoid cross flow small similar sized connections should be offset at least 110mm on 100mm ø stack

basin

sink

110 min offset (250 min for 150 ø stack)

bath

wc

200 min offset

TRAPS
Where larger size of waste branches are used, the trap size is not increaed but the tail of the trap should be lengthened by 50mm. See p 119 for minimum trap sizes and seal depths

angled connection or 50mm ø parallel junction where a waste branch directly opposite a wc would enter the stack within 200mm below the wc branch connection centre line

Junction between wc branch & stack made with 50mm min radius or at 45°

3m max for 40mm ø pipe 4m max for 50mm ø pipe Slope between 18 and 90mm/m

6m max for single wc Slope 18mm/m min.

Stack to be 100mm ø May be 75mm if serving not more than one siphonic wc with 75mm outlet

sink

450mm min between lowest branch and drain invert in single dwellings of up to 3 storeys

200 min

1.5 m max

a ground floor wc may connect directly to drain providing the drop is less than 1.5m between crown of trap and drain invert

NOTE
Separate ventilating pipes will be needed if the figures for branch length and slope are exceeded. This is to prevent traps being drawn

large radius bend at bottom of stack at least 200mm

Source: *Building Regulations – Approved document H*

Rainwater disposal

Calculation of gutter and downpipe sizes

In the UK, the maximum rainfall intensity is generally taken as 75 mm per hour or 0.0208 litres per second (l/s). Note that this does not necessarily mean only high rainfall areas such as West Wales and Scotland but, in surprisingly odd pockets like Norfolk and Oxford, heavy downpours can exceed this figure.

To calculate the size of rainwater goods it is necessary to determine the *effective roof area* which, in the case of pitched roofs, is as follows:

Effective
roof area $= (H \div 2 + W) \times L = m^2$
Where H = vertical rise between
eaves and ridge
W = plan width of slope
L = length of roof

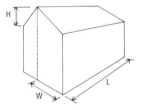

To determine the maximum flow
multiply the effective area by 0.0208.

Typical maximum flow capacities

		Outlet at one end of roof				Outlet at centre of roof			
Gutter mm	Downpipe mm	Level gutter		Gutter to fall		Level gutter		Gutter to fall	
		m²	l/s	m²	l/s	m²	l/s	m²	l/s
75 half round	51 Ø	15	0.33	19	0.40	25	0.54	30	0.64
110 half round	69 Ø	46	0.96	61	1.27	92	1.91	122	2.54
116 square	62 sq	53	1.10	72	1.50	113	2.36	149	3.11

Refer to manufacturers' catalogues for actual flow capacities, as profiles of gutters can vary.

Rule of thumb
100–112 mm gutter with 68 mm Ø down pipe placed at centre of gutter will drain 110 m² effective roof area; placed at end of gutter will drain 55 m² effective roof area. Gutter will drain more if laid to slight (1 : 60) fall.

Water Supply Regulations

The Water Supply (Water Fittings) Regulations 1999 supersede the Water Supply Byelaws. Their aim is to prevent: waste, misuse, undue consumption, contamination or false measurement of water supplied by a *Water Undertaker*(WU). The regulations should be read in conjunction with the WRAS Guide, which includes detailed information of sizes, flow rates, valves etc. Below is a VERY BROAD and BRIEF interpretation of the regulations.

Application of the regulations

The regulations apply only to fittings supplied with water by a WU. They do not apply to water fittings for non-domestic or non-food production purposes providing the water is metered; the supply is for less than 1 month (3 months with written consent) and no water can return through a meter to a mains pipe. They do not apply to fittings installed before 1 July 99.

Notification

Water undertakers must be notified of the following:
Erecting any building, except a pond or swimming pool of less than 10,000 litres capacity
Altering any water system in non-residential premises
Changing the use of a property
Installing :

- A bath with a capacity greater than 330 litres
- A bidet with ascending spray or flexible hose
- A single shower unit with multi-head arrangement
- A pump or booster drawing more than 12 litres/min
- A water softener with a waste or needing water for regeneration or cleaning
- A reduced pressure zone valve or any mechanical device which presents serious health risks
- A garden watering system other than hand-held hose
- External pipes higher than 730mm or lower than 1350mm
- An automatically filled pond or swimming pool with a capacity of more than 10,000 litres

Contractor's certificate

Contractors approved by the WU must issue certificates to clients stating that the work complies with the regulations. For items of *Notification* (see above) copies of these certificates must be sent to the WU. Contravention of the regulations may incur a fine not exceeding £1,000 (in 2000 AD).

Fluid categories

Water is described in five fluid categories ranging from 'wholesome' water supplied by a WU to water representing serious health hazards. These categories are used, amongst other things, to define which type of *backflow prevention* (see below) is required.

Contamination and corrosion

Water for domestic use or food purposes must not be contaminated by materials such as lead and bitumen. Water fittings must not be installed in contaminated environments such as sewers and cesspits.

Quality and testing

Water fittings should comply with British Standards or European equivalent and must withstand an operating pressure of not less than 1.5 times the maximum operating pressure. All water systems must be tested, flushed and, if necessary, disinfected before use.

Location

Water fittings must not be installed in cavity walls; embedded in walls or solid floors; or below suspended or solid ground floors unless encased in an accessible duct. External pipes, underground must not be joined by adhesives nor laid less than 750mm deep or more than 1350mm deep unless written consent is obtained.

Protection against freezing

All water fittings outside buildings or located within buildings but outside the thermal envelope should be insulated against freezing. In very cold conditions, in unheated premises, water should be drained down before the onset of freezing or alternative devices installed to activate heating systems.

Backflow protection

Except where expanded water from hot water systems is permitted to flow backwards, water installations must have adequate devices for preventing backflow as follows :

- To prevent backflow between separate premises
- Connection of grey or rainwater to a 'wholesome' water pipe
- Bidets with flexible hoses, spray handsets, under-rim water inlets or ascending sprays
- WC cisterns with pressure flushing valves
- WCs adapted as bidets
- Baths with submerged inlets (eg Jacuzzis)
- Non-domestic washing machines and dishwashers
- Sprinkler systems, fire hose reels and fire hydrants
- Garden hoses and watering systems

Cold water services

Every dwelling, including those in multi-story dwellings should have separate *stop valves* for mains entry pipes inside each premises.

Drain taps must be provided to completely drain water from all pipes within a building.

All domestic premises must have at least one tap for *drinking water* supplied directly from the mains.

Cold water cisterns

Cold water cisterns for dwellings are no longer mandatory providing there is adequate *water flow rate* and *mains pressure in the street*. Check this with the WU before designing new installation.

Cisterns must be fitted with *float valves* and *servicing valves*. *Overflow/warning* pipes, with vermin and insect-proof screens must be fitted to discharge conspicuously to outside. Where cisterns are joined together, care must be taken to avoid one cistern overflowing into another and that water is fully circulated between cisterns and not short-circuited. Cisterns should be *insulated* and be fitted with light and insect-proof *lids*. 330mm minimum unobstructed space must be provided above the cistern for inspection and maintenance.

Hot water services

Temperature control devices and *relief valves* must be fitted to unvented water heaters. *Expansion valves* must be fitted to unvented hot water systems larger than 5 litres. Primary circuit vent pipes should not discharge over domestic cisterns nor to a secondary system. Secondary circuit vent pipes should not discharge over feed and expansion cisterns connected to a primary circuit. Ideally, hot water should be stored at 60°C and discharged at 50°C (43°C for shower mixers). Long lengths of hot water pipes should be *insulated* to conserve energy.

Garden water supplies

Double check valves (DCVs) must be fitted to hose union taps in new houses. Hose union taps in existing houses should be replaced with hose union taps which incorporate DCVs. Watering systems must be fitted with DCVs as well as *pipe interrupters with atmosphere vent and moving element* at the hose connecting point or a minimum of 300mm above the highest point of delivering outlet.

Pools and fountains filled with water supplied by a WU must have an *impervious lining*.

WCs and Urinals

Single flush cisterns to WCs should not exceed 6 litres capacity.

Manual *pressure flushing* valves to WC cisterns must receive at least 1.2 litres/second flow at the appliance. WC cisterns installed before July 99 must be replaced with the same size cistern. Existing single flush cisterns may not be replaced by dual-flush cisterns.

Automatic *urinal flushing cisterns* should not exceed 10 litres capacity for a single urinal and 7.5 litres/hour per bowl, stall or 700mm width of slab.

Urinal pressure valves should deliver no more than 1.5 litres per flush.

Sources: The Water Supply (Water Fittings) Regulations 1999
The WRAS Water Regulations Guide

Water storage
Plastic cold water cisterns
Rectangular

litres	galls	size l × w × h mm	weight kg*
18	4	442 × 296 × 305	0.9
68	15	630 × 448 × 420	3.2
91	20	665 × 490 × 510	4.2
114	25	700 × 540 × 532	5.0
182	40	940 × 610 × 590	7.3
227	50	1155 × 635 × 600	9.0

Circular

litres	galls	size Ø @ top × h mm	weight kg*
114	25	695 × 510	3.5
182	40	795 × 590	4.4
227	50	860 × 620	4.8
273	60	940 × 620	5.8
455	100	1060 × 750	10.4
591	130	1060 × 920	14.5

* Empty weight – one litre of water weighs one kilogram so full weight of cistern equals litre capacity in kilograms plus empty weight.

Source: Titan Plastech

Water hardness

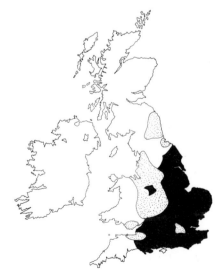

- ☐ soft to moderately soft
- ▨ hard to moderately soft
- ■ hard to very hard

Hot water usage

Typical average consumption – litres

bath	60 per bath
shower	13 per 5 minutes
handwashing	2 per person
hairdressing	10 per shampoo
cleaning	10 per dwelling per day
kitchen sink	5 per meal
dishwasher	20 per cycle
washing machine	55 per cycle

Hot water storage

Typical storage requirements @ 65 °C – litres per person

house or flat	30
office	5
factory	5
day school	5
boarding school	25
hospital	30
sports centre	35
luxury hotel	45

Domestic indirect copper hot water cylinders

BS Ref	diameter* mm	height* mm	heating surface m²	litres	gallons
0	380	1680	0.35	96	21.1
1	430	980	0.27	72	15.8
2	480	980	0.35	96	21.1
3	480	1130	0.42	114	25.1
4	530	755	0.31	84	18.5
5	530	830	0.35	95	20.9
6	530	905	0.40	106	23.3
7	530	980	0.44	117	25.7
8	530	1130	0.52	140	30.8
9	530	1280	0.61	162	35.6
10	580	1280	0.75	190	41.8
11	580	1580	0.87	245	53.9
12	680	1280	1.10	280	61.6
13	680	1580	1.40	360	79.2
14	680	1880	1.70	440	96.8

* Sizes include 40 mm sprayed on insulation

Building Regulations require hot water cylinders to have factory applied insulation designed to restrict heat losses to 1 watt per litre or less.

In soft water areas, copper cylinders should be specified with an aluminium protector rod which is fixed inside the dome by the manufacturers. This encourages the formation of a protective film on the copper and will lengthen the life of the cylinder which may otherwise be subject to pitting.

Source: Range Cylinders Ltd

U-values

To understand the use of U-values it is necessary to distinguish between the thermal measurement expressions below:

Thermal conductivity (k-value)
The heat (W) transmitted through unit area (m^2) of a material of unit thickness (m) for unit temperature difference (K) between inside and outside environments, expressed as **W/mK** (or W/m °C).

Thermal resistivity (r-value)
The reciprocal of thermal conductivity, i.e. **mK/W** (or m °C/W). It measures how well a material resists the flow of heat by conduction.

Thermal resistance (R-value)
This means how well a *particular thickness* of material resists the passage of heat by conduction, calculated from the r-value in units of **m^2K/W** (or m^2 °C/W).

Thermal transmittance (U-value)
The reciprocal of thermal resistance, i.e. **W/m^2K** (or W/m^2 °C). This measures the amount of heat transmitted per unit area of the fabric per unit temperature difference between inside and outside environments.

U-value calculation formula:

$$U = \frac{1}{R_{SI} + R_{SO} + R_A + R_1 + R_2 + R_3 \ldots}$$

where R_{SI} = thermal resistance of internal surface
R_{SO} = thermal resistance of external surface
R_A = thermal resistance of air spaces within construction
R_1, R_2, R_3 etc.= thermal resistance of successive components

$$R = \frac{1}{k\text{-value}} \times \frac{\text{thickness of material mm}}{1000}$$

R-values

Surface resistance R-values normal exposure		m²K/W
	Rsɪ inside surface	Rsᴏ outside surface
roof/ceiling	0.10	0.04
wall	0.12	0.06
floor	0.14	0.04

Air space R-values 25 mm exposure	m²K/W Rᴀ
in cavity wall	0.18
loft space under sarking	0.18
between metal cladding & lining	0.16
in cold flat roof	0.16
loft space under metal cladding	0.14
between roofing tiles & felt	0.12
behind tile hanging	0.12

K-values

Thermal conductivity of typical building materials

Material		kg/m³	W/mK	Material		kg/m³	W/mK
asphalt	19 mm	1700	0.50	phenolic foam	board	30	0.020
blocks	lightweight	1200	0.38	plaster	gypsum	1280	0.46
	med. weight	1400	0.51		sand/cement	1570	0.53
	heavyweight	2300	1.63		vermiculite	640	0.19
bricks	exposed	1700	0.84	plasterboard	gypsum	950	0.16
	protected	1700	0.62	polystyrene	expanded	25	0.035
calcium silicate	board	875	0.17	polyurethane	board	30	0.025
chipboard		800	0.15	rendering	external	1300	0.50
concrete	aerated slab	500	0.16	roofing tiles	clay	1900	0.85
	lightweight	1200	0.38		concrete	2100	1.10
	dense	2100	1.40	screed		1200	0.41
felt/bitumen	3 layers	960	0.50	stone	reconstructed	1750	1.30
fibreboard		300	0.06		sandstone	2000	1.30
fibreglass	quilt	25	0.04		limestone	2180	1.50
glass	sheet	2500	1.05		granite	2600	2.30
hardboard	standard	900	0.13	stone chippings		1800	0.96
mineral wool	quilt	12	0.04	timber	softwood	650	0.14
	slab	25	0.035	vermiculite	loose	100	0.65
mortar	normal	1750	0.80	woodwool	slabs	600	0.11

Conservation of fuel and power

The *requirement* of Building Regulation part L is that reasonable provision shall be made to limit heat loss through the building fabric, hot water and hot air systems. In the case of non residential buildings, provision must be made to limit solar overheating and to provide energy efficient light systems.

To show compliance it is necessary to produce **SAP** (Standard Assessment Procedure) energy ratings for buildings which can be done in three ways:

an *elemental* method; a *target U-value* method and a *carbon index* method.

The elemental method is suitable for small works and where it is desired to minimise calculations. The requirement will be met if the U-values of the elements do not exceed those listed below <u>and</u>, in the case of dwellings, providing the area of windows, doors and roof lights does not exceed 25% of the total floor area.

In addition, the efficiency of the boiler in a dwelling must equal or exceed the **SEDBUK** (Seasonal Efficiency of a Domestic Boiler in the UK) ratings set out below. Note that the elemental method cannot be used for buildings with direct electric heating.

Standard U-values for construction elements

Exposed element	W/m²K
Pitched roof (between 11° - 70°) with insulation between rafters	0.20
Pitched roof with insulation between joists	0.16
Flat roof (0° - 10°) or roof with integral insulation	0.25
Walls, including basement walls	0.35
Floors, including ground floors and basement floors	0.25
Metal framed windows, roof windows, rooflights (area weighted average for the whole building)	2.20
Wooden or PVC framed windows, roof windows, rooflights, doors (area weighted average for the whole building	2.00
Vehicle access and similar large doors	0.70

Type of boiler	minimum SEDBUK % rating
mains natural gas	78
LPG	80
Oil (combination boiler only)	82
Oil	85

Summary of U-values:
Elemental method of calculation

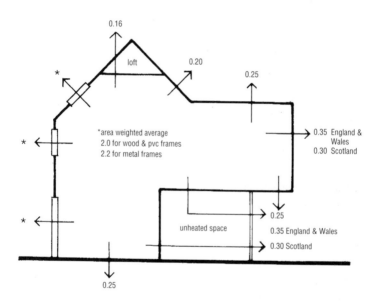

Source : Building Regulations Approved Documents L1 & L2

Heat losses

As a rough guide, building heat losses will be between 20 to 50 W/m^3.

For normal conditions and temperatures 30 W/m^3 is average. Higher figures for tall, single storey buildings or large areas of glazing, lower figures for well insulated buildings with minimal exposure, e.g. a building with 400 m^3 of heated space may require between 8 kW and 20 kW depending on conditions.

Recommended indoor temperatures	**°C**
Warehousing; factory – heavy work	13
General stores	15
Factory – light work; circulation space	16
Bedroom; classroom; shop; church	18
Assembly hall; hospital ward	18
Offices; factory – sedentary work	19
Dining room; canteen; museum; art gallery	20
Laboratory; library; law court	20
Living room; bed-sitting room;	21
Sports changing room; operating theatre	21
Bathroom; swimming pool changing room	22
Hotel bedroom	22
Indoor swimming pool	26

Source: *Series A Design data CIBSE*

Heat loss calculation

The heat loss from a room is the addition of all the individual *surface heat losses* of the doors, windows, walls, floor and ceilings, plus any *ventilation loss*.

Surface heat loss from any of these elements is calculated as:

element area m² × (inside °C − outside °C) ×
U-value of fabric = watts lost

For inside temperatures see list of *Recommended Indoor Temperatures* on p. 116. For outside temperature −1°C is the figure normally used in the UK.

Ventilation loss is the heat lost through cracks and gaps in doors and windows.

With an average level of draughtproofing the following air changes per hour are assumed:

living rooms, bed-sitting rooms = 1
bedrooms   = ¹/₂
kitchens and bathrooms   = 2
halls and stairways   = 1¹/₂
rooms with chimneys **add**   = +1

Ventilation loss is then calculated as:

no. air changes/hour × room volume m³ ×
(inside °C − outside °C) × 0.33 = watts lost

When assessing the size of a radiator for a room it is usual to add between 10 per cent and 15 per cent to allow for imprecision of heat loss calculations and for faster warm-up times.

Source: *The Which? Book of Plumbing and Central Heating*

Central heating and hot water systems

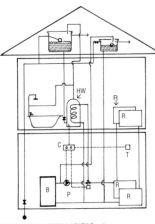

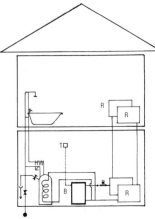

CONVENTIONAL CENTRAL HEATING and HOT WATER INSTALLATION

This system uses storage cisterns, usually located in the roof space to provide pressure for the hot water storage system, which consists of an indirect cylinder being fed from the boiler. Cold water may also be distributed around the house from the main storage cistern.

● = service main   ⬤ = pump   B = boiler   C = controls
◄► = stopcock   ✖ = motorised valve   R = radiator   T = thermostat

INDIRECT UNVENTED STORAGE SYSTEM with SEALED PRIMARY

This system stores hot water at mains pressure and provides space heating and water heating by means of a separate primary circuit. The hot water cylinder may be located anywhere.

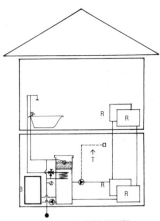

UNVENTED SYSTEM with INSTANTANEOUS COMBINATION BOILER

This system is most suitable for small houses and flats where space is at a premium. As there is no hot water storage cylinder, the flow of hot water will be somewhat reduced but this is usually only noticed when running a bath or simultaneously using several taps.

PRIMARY HEAT STORE with DIRECT VENTED PRIMARY

Here the hot water is stored at low pressure in a tank which is fed by a small feed tank over it. Mains water is fed into a high capacity coil where it is heated at mains pressure and blended with cold to stabilise the temperature. The system may be heated by a boiler or an immersion heater. With a boiler the recovery time is very fast. The flow rate is slightly less than an unvented storage system.

Source: Ideal Standard Ltd

Radiators typical sizes and outputs

Panel radiators – steel

Heights: 300, 450, 600, 700 mm
Lengths: 400 to 3000 in 100 mm increments

Type	Thickness	Approx Output*
Single panel without convector	47 mm	1500 W/m^2
Single panel with convector	47 mm	2200 W/m^2
Double panel with convector	77 mm	3300 W/m^2
Double panel with double convector	100 mm	4100 W/m^2

* m^2 measured on elevation

Multicolumn radiators – steel

Heights: 185, 260, 300, 350, 400, 450, 500, 550, 600, 750, 900, 1000, 1100, 1200, 1500, 1800, 2000, 2200, 2500, 2,800, 3000 mm

Type	Thickness	Approx Output*
Two columns wide	62 mm	2150 W/m^2
Three columns wide	100 mm	3000 W/m^2
Four columns wide	136 mm	3700 W/m^2
Five columns wide	173 mm	4600 W/m^2
Six columns wide	210 mm	5400 W/m^2

* m^2 measured on elevation

Sources: Caradon Stelrad
Zehnder Ltd

Ventilation

Means of ventilation

Required by the Building Regulations for rooms without full mechanical ventilation

	Rapid ventilation (e.g. opening window)	Background ventilation	Minimum fan extract rates or PSV*
Domestic buildings			
Habitable room	1/20th floor area	8000 mm^2	no requirement
Kitchen	opening window (unsized) **or** fan with 15 mins overrun timer	4000 mm^2	30 l/s (108 m^3/h) adjacent to hob **or** 60 l/s (216 m^3/h) elsewhere **or** PSV
Utility Room	opening window (unsized) **or** fan with 15 mins overrun timer	4000 mm^2	30 l/s (108 m^3/h) **or** PSV
Bathroom (with or without WC)	opening window (unsized) **or** fan with 15 mins overrun timer	4000 mm^2	15 l/s (54 m^3/h) **or** PSV
Sanitary accommodation (separate from bathroom)	1/20th floor area **or** fan @ 6 l/s (21.6 m^3/h)	4000 mm^2	no requirement (but see rapid ventilation)
Non-domestic buildings			
Occupiable room	1/20th floor area	<10 m^2 = 4000 mm^2 >10 m^2 = 4000 mm^2 + 400 mm^2 per m^2 of extra floor area	no requirement

	Rapid ventilation (e.g. opening window)	Background ventilation	Minimum fan extract rates or PSV*
Non-domestic buildings continued			
Kitchen (domestic type i.e. not a commercial kitchen)	opening window (unsized)	4000 mm²	30 l/s (108 m³/h) adjacent to hob **or** 60 l/s (216 m³/h) elsewhere
Bathrooms (including shower rooms)	opening window (unsized)	4000 mm² per bath/ shower	15 l/s (54 m³/h) per bath/shower
Sanitary accommodation (and/or washing facilities)	1/20th floor area **or** fan @ 6 l/s (21.6 m³/h) per WC **or** 3 air changes/h	4000 mm² per WC	no requirement (but see rapid ventilation)
Common spaces (where large numbers of people gather)	1/50th floor area **or** fan 1 l/s (3.6 m³/h) per m²	no requirement	no requirement (but see rapid ventilation)
Rest rooms (where smoking permitted)	1/20th floor area	< 10m² = 4000 mm² > 10 m² = 4000 mm² + 400 mm² per m² of extra floor area	16 l/s (57.6 m³/h) per person

* PSV = passive stack ventilation
See notes overleaf

Means of ventilation
Notes to tables on pages 138 and 139

Rapid ventilation openings should have some part at least 1.75 m above floor level. Methods of **background ventilation** are typically adjustable trickle ventilators or airbricks with hit-and-miss louvres located at least 1.75 m above floor level.

PSV means passive stack ventilation operated manually and/or automatically by sensor or controller in accordance with BRE Information Paper 13/94 or a BBA Certificate.

An **open flued appliance** may be considered to provide ventilation if it has a free flue area of at least 125 mm diameter and is permanently open, i.e. no damper.

However if an open flued appliance is within the same room as an extract fan this may cause spillage of flue gases so:

Where a **gas appliance** and a fan are located in a kitchen the *maximum* extract rate should be 20 l/s (72 m³/h).

An extract fan should *not* be provided in the same room as a **solid fuel appliance**.

Kitchens, utility rooms, bathrooms and WCs which do not have openable windows should be provided with an *air inlet*, e.g. a 10 mm gap under the door.

Kitchen extract ventilation 'adjacent to hob' means within 300 mm of centreline of hob and should be either a cooker hood or a fan with a humidistat.

Utility rooms which are accessible only from outside the building need not conform with the ventilation requirements of the Building Regulations.

Adjacent rooms may be considered as one room if there is a permanent opening(s) of at least 1/20th of the combined floor areas, in the dividing wall.

Where a non-habitable space such as a **conservatory** adjoins a habitable room, the habitable room may be ventilated with opening(s) of at least 1/20th of the combined floor areas in both the dividing wall and the wall to the outside, both openings to have at least 8000 mm^2 background ventilation. The opening(s) to the dividing wall may be closable.

Source: *Building Regulations Approved Document F1 1998*

Extractor fans

Sizing of fans
The size of a fan should take into account the size of the room and not necessarily be the minimum required by the Building Regulations.

It therefore makes sense to calculate the size of fan needed by using the desired number of air changes per hour and relating them to the room size.

Suggested air changes per hour for typical situations

Domestic		Non-domestic	
Living rooms	3–6	Cafés and restaurants	10–12
Bedrooms	2–4	Cinemas and theatres	6–10
Bathrooms	6–8	Dance halls	12-15
WCs	6–8	Factories and workshops	6–10
Kitchens	10–15	Commercial kitchens	20–30
Utility rooms	10–15	Offices	4–6
Halls and passages	3–5	Public toilets	6–8

To calculate the extract performance needed for a fan, multiply the volume of a room (m^3) by the number of air changes per hour required (ACH):

e.g. Domestic kitchen 4 m × 5 m × 2.5 m = 50 m^3
air changes required = 12
50 × 12 = **600 m^3/h**

one m^3/h = 0.777 l/s
one l/s = 3.6 m^3/h

Siting of fans

- Site fans as far away as practicable from the main source of air replacement which is usually the room door.
- Site fans where there is reasonable access for cleaning and maintenance.
- Fans in bathrooms must be sited out of reach of a person using a fixed bath or shower and must be kept well away from all sources of spray.
- Insulate ducts passing through unheated roof spaces to minimize condensation.
- Slope horizontal ducts slightly away from fan.
- Vertical ducts, and ducts in roof spaces, should be fitted with a condensate trap with a small drainpipe to outside.
- See pp. 138–140 for Building Regulation requirements and siting of extractor fans.

Types of fans

Axial fans are designed to move air over short distances, as through walls or windows.

Centrifugal fans are designed to move air over long distances and perform well against resistance built up over long lengths of ducts.

Sources: Vent-Axia Ltd and Xpelair Ltd

Electrical installation

Electricity

Electricity is sold by the *unit*.
One unit is consumed at the rate of one kilowatt for one hour (kWh)

Comparative costs of domestic appliances

Appliance	Time per unit
3 kW radiant heater	20 minutes
2 kW convector heater	30 minutes
iron	2 hours
vacuum cleaner	2 hours
colour TV	6 hours
100 watt lamp	10 hours
60 watt lamp	16 hours
refrigerator	24 hours

Typical usage of larger appliances		kWh
chest freezer	per week	$1^1/_2$
dishwasher	one full load	$2^1/_2$
cooker	per week for family of four	23
hot water cylinder	per week for family of four	85

Fuses – rating for 230 volt AC appliances

Rating	Colour	Appliance wattage
2 amp	black	250 to 450
3 amp	red	460 to 750
5 amp	black	760 to 1250
13 amp	brown	1260 to 3000

To find the correct amp rating of a socket for an appliance, divide the watts of the appliance by the volts
i.e. watts ÷ 230 = amps.

Electrical installation graphic symbols

SUPPLY and DISTRIBUTION

electricity meter	
transformer	
distribution board	
isolator	
terminal to earth	
fuse	
circuit breaker	
lightning protection	

cable / conduit on diagrams _____

cable / conduit on plans _ _ _ _ _ _

POWER

socket outlet	
switched socket outlet	
twin socket outlet	
socket outlet with pilot lamp	
connection unit	
switched connection unit	
connection unit with cable outlet	
connection unit with pilot lamp	
connection unit, four gang	
shaver socket	
cooker control unit with two pole switch	

COMMUNICATIONS SOCKETS

FM radio	FM
television	TV
private service television	PTV
closed circuit television	CCTV
telephone	T
telex	TX
modem	M
fax	F

SWITCHES

one pole switch	
one pole switch, two gang	
two, three, four pole switches	
two way switch	
intermediate switch	
switch with pilot lamp	
pull cord switch	
switch, time operated	
switch, period operated	
switch, temperature operated	
dimmer switch	
push button switch	
push switch, illuminated	
push on/push off switch	

LUMINAIRES

luminaire	
enclosed luminaire	
reflector	
spotlight open, enclosed	
flood open, enclosed	
linear open, enclosed	
emergency/safety open, enclos	
emergency/safety self containe	
linear emergency/safety open, enclosed	
luminaire on wall open, enclos(	
luminaire on pole open, enclos(	
luminaire on suspension cable	
luminaire with built-in pull cord	

Source: BS 1192: Part 3: 1987

Electric circuits in the home

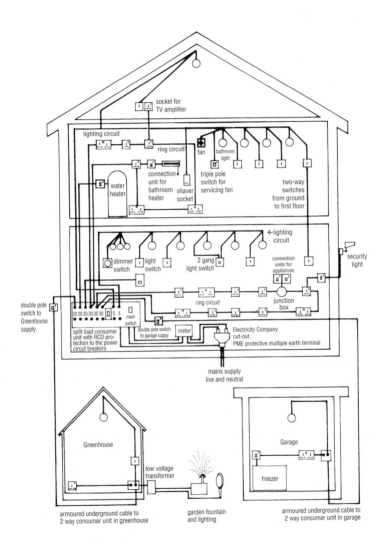

Lighting

Lighting glossary

candela (cd)   The SI unit of *luminous intensity* which is either light flux per solid angle – explained as quantities, or lumen per steradian – defined in terms of units.

CIE   Commission Internationale de l'Eclairage, who devised the *Colour Rendering Index*.

colour rendering   The ability of a light source to render colours naturally without distorting the hues seen under a full radiator (similar to daylight) in which all the wavelengths of the visible spectrum are present.

Colour Rendering Index (CRI)   An index based on eight standard test colours where the unit is *Ra*. Ra100 is the maximum value. Ra85 and above is considered appropriate for everyday comfort. The index can also be arranged in values of 1 to 4 according to DIN 3035.

colour temperature   The absolute temperature of a black radiator (reference light source) which emits the same colour irradiation as a given light source measured in degrees Kelvin (K).

Correlated Colour Temperature (CCT)   The colour appearance determined from its colour temperature given in degrees Kelvin. The lower the figure the warmer the light. Less than 3300 K is warm (red); 3300–5300 K intermediate and more than 5300 K cold (blue). The human eye cannot differentiate between individual spectral colours of a light source, it can only perceive a mixture of colours.

crown silvered lamp   A GLS lamp with part of the bowl silvered to project light backwards to avoid glare. Normally used with parabolic reflectors to give a narrow beam forwards.

dichroic mirror lamp   A small lamp with a built-in spiral, often faceted mirror reflector. This may be specifically made with honeycomb facets for medium–wide distribution and trapezoid facets for narrow beams. The mirror is made to reflect only certain colours of light and transmit heat radiation so as to produce a cool beam of light. The facets help to reduce striations in the beam, producing softer focusing with blurred edges to the beam.

discharge lamp   A light source from an electrical discharge passing through a glass containing vapour or gas.

efficacy   The ratio of initial lumens divided by lamp watts (lm/W). Typical efficacy for a GLS lamp is 8–18 rising to 100–180 for a low pressure sodium lamp.

elliptical (E)   The shape of some discharge lamps.

flood (F)   A lamp designed with a wide beam.

fluorescent tube   A discharge tubular lamp, generally fitted with argon and low pressure mercury vapour. It has a phosphor coating on the inside giving off light (fluorescing) when excited by an electric arc through the vapour.

GLS   General Lighting Service: standard *tungsten filament* pear shaped lamps.

halogen lamp   An incandescent lamp filled with low pressure vapour of iodine or bromine. Sometimes referred to as *tungsten-halogen*.

HID   High Intensity Discharge lamps, i.e. *metal-halide, mercury* and *sodium* lamps.

HP   High Pressure, descriptive of some *mercury* and *sodium* lamps.

ILCOS   *International Lamp Coding System* produced by the International Electrotechnical Commission in 1993.

illuminance   The amount of light falling on a surface. The unit is *lux* which is one lumen per square metre (lm/m^2).

incandescent lamp   A tungsten filament enclosed in a glass envelope either under vacuum or filled with inert gas so that it can be electrically heated without burning out. Incandescent means luminous or glowing with heat; as a result can be an inefficient light source emphasizing reds, yellows and greens while subduing blues.

initial lumens   The light output of a lamp measured after one hour for incandescent lamps and 100 hours for fluorescent and discharge lamps. Lumens quoted in manufacturers' catalogues are 'initial' lumens.

IS   Internally Silvered. Used to describe the internal lining of a reflector lamp.

LIF   Lighting Industry Federation (UK).

Light-Loss Factor (LLF)   The loss in light output from a luminaire due to dirt on the lamp or fitting. Now more normally referred to as *maintenance factor*.

Light Output Ratio (LOR)   The ratio of the total light emitted by a luminaire to the total output of the lamp(s) it contains – which is always less than unity.

lumen (lm)   The unit of *luminous flux* used to measure the amount of light given off by a light source.

lumen maintenance   The speed of decline of the initial amount of light.

luminaire   A light fitting.

luminance   The brightness of a surface in a given direction, measured in *candelas* per square metre (cd/m^2).

luminous flux   The flow of light energy from a source, or reflected from a surface, standardized for the human eye and measured in *lumens*. It is used to calculate *illuminance*.

luminous intensity   The amount of energy in a cone of light from a source. Units expressed in *candelas* (lumen/steradian).

lux   The unit of *illuminance* measured in lumens per square metre (lm/m^2). Bright sunlight is 100 000 lux; full moon is 1 lux.

maintained illuminance   The minimum light level over an area immediately prior to cleaning/re-lamping.

maintenance factor   The proportion of initial light output from an installation after some specified time.

mercury lamps   *Discharge lamps* filled with mercury vapour with moderate *colour rendering*, emphasizing yellows and blues which shift towards violet while subduing reds.

metal halide lamps   High pressure mercury discharge lamps with additives which can vary the light appearance from warm to cool.

opal   Describes an internal white silica coating to a lamp which diffuses the light and conceals the filament more positively than *pearl*.

PAR   Parabolic Aluminised Reflector (lamp). The number following PAR is the number of eighths of an inch of the lamp diameter, e.g. PAR38 = $4^3/4"\varnothing$.

pearl   The acid etched internal finish to a lamp to mask and diffuse the glare from the filament. Less positive than *opal* or *satin*.

Rated Average Life (RAL)   The time by which 50 per cent of lamps installed can be expected to have failed.

reflector lamp (R)   A lamp with an *internally silvered* lining.

satin   A lamp finish similar to *opal*.

sodium lamp (SON)   A highly efficient lamp with a warm yellow light, used mainly for street and flood lighting. It has poor colour rendering, with the low pressure (SOX) types making all colours except yellow appear brown or black.

spot (S)   A lamp producing a narrow beam of light as opposed to the medium/wide beam of a *flood*.

switchstart   A fluorescent lamp circuit incorporating a starter switch.

tri-phosphor lamp   A *fluorescent* lamp with good colour rendering.

tungsten-filament lamp   An *incandescent* lamp.

tungsten-halogen lamp   A *halogen* lamp.

Lighting: levels and colours

Comparative light levels	lux
Bright sunlight	100 000
Worktop near window	3 000
Precision task lighting	1 000*
Drawing boards	750*
Kitchen preparation areas	500*
General reading	300*
Entrance halls	150*
Corridors, storage	100*
Full moon on clear night	1

*Recommended minimum light levels

Colour temperatures	K
Blue sky	10 000
Uniform overcast sky	7 000
Average natural daylight	6 500
HP mercury cool white lamp	4 000
Fluorescent warm white lamp	3 000
Halogen filament lamp	3 000
GLS tungsten filament	2 700
HP sodium lamp	2 050

CIE Colour Rendering Index

Ra		Group
100	Where accurate colour matching is required, e.g. printing inspection	1A
90	Where good colour rendering is required, e.g. shops	1B
80	Where moderate colour rendering is acceptable	2
60	Where colour rendering is of little significance but marked distortion unacceptable	3
40	Where colour rendering is of no importance	4
20		

Lamps

Listed on the following pages is a survey of the main types of lamps available.

Excluded are the many variations of certain types and those which may be used for more specialized situations such as infra-red, UV stop, horticultural, black light etc. Also excluded are the high output low sodium lights used mainly for road lighting. The list is therefore not comprehensive and manufacturers' catalogues should be consulted for more information.

Lumens quoted are for *Initial lumens* (see Glossary). The lowest values have been given, which are for pearl or opal versions of a lamp or the 'warmer' colour temperature fluorescent tubes.

Sources: G.E. Lighting Ltd, Osram Ltd, Philips Lighting Ltd, Concord Sylvania

Lamp bases

B22d   B22d–3   B15d   P40s   P28s   BA20d

E40s   E27s   E14s   E12

GX38q   PG22   BHP30s   GX9.5   G17q G17t   G38   G6.35

R7s

G4   GY7–9   GY16   G22   GY9.5   EMEP   GX5.3   GZ4

Incandescent lamps

ILCOS code	Description	Watts	Size l × Ø	Lumens	Peak cd	Colour K	Life h
IAA	**GLS** standard bulb, pearl and clear	25	103 × 60	225	–	2 700	1 000
		40	103 × 60	410	–	2 700	1 000
		60	103 × 60	700	–	2 700	1 000
		75	103 × 60	930	–	2 700	1 000
		100	103 × 60	1 350	–	2 700	1 000
		150	129 × 68	2 100	–	2 700	1 000
		200	160 × 80	3 000	–	2 700	1 000
		300	110 × 88	4 550	–	2 700	1 000
		500	110 × 88	8 200	–	2 700	1 000
IAA	**GLS Rough Service** RS, shock resistant and dustproof	40	103 × 60	240	–	2 700	1 000
		60	103 × 60	485	–	2 700	1 000
		100	103 × 60	850	–	2 700	1 000
I	**GLS mushroom** pearl, smaller than standard GLS	40	88 × 50	385	–	2 700	1 000
		60	88 × 50	660	–	2 700	1 000
		100	94 × 60	1 250	–	2 700	1 000
I	**GLS double life** some also rated 3 000 hours	40	103 × 60	370	–	2 700	2 000
		60	103 × 60	630	–	2 700	2 000
		100	103 × 60	1 200	–	2 700	2 000
		150	129 × 68	1 900	–	2 700	2 000
IAA	**GLS colour** red, blue, green, yellow, orange & pink	15	103 × 60	–	–	2 700	1 000
		25	103 × 60	–	–	2 700	1 000
		40	103 × 60	–	–	2 700	1 000
		60	103 × 60	–	–	2 700	1 000
IBP	**Golf Ball** small round, clear and opal	25	75 × 45	185	–	2 700	1 000
		40	75 × 45	350	–	2 700	1 000
		60	75 × 45	580	–	2 700	1 000
IAG	**Globe** large round, clear & opal	40	138 × 95	260	–	2 700	1 500
		60	138 × 95	470	–	2 700	1 500
		100	138 × 95	1 020	–	2 700	1 500
IBB	**Candle** clear, opal, plain & twisted	25	97 × 35	185	-	2 700	1 000
		40	97 × 35	350	-	2 700	1 000
		60	97 × 35	580	-	2 700	1 000

Incandescent lamps – continued

ILCOS code	Description	Watts	Size l × Ø		Lumens	Peak cd	Colour K	Life h
IRA	**Crown silvered** clear lamp with silvered bowl to avoid glare	60	104 ×	60	485	–	2 700	1 000
		100	128 ×	68	970	–	2 700	1 000
IBS	**Pygmy** clear, compact, also coloured, RS, heat resistant	15	57 ×	28	105	–	2 700	1 000
		25	63 ×	28	175	–	2 700	1 000
IBT	**Striplight** two lengths, clear & opal	30	221 ×	25	190	–	2 700	1 000
		30	284 ×	25	190	–	2 700	1 000
		60	221 ×	25	420	–	2 700	1 000
		60	284 ×	25	420	–	2 700	1 000
IRR	**Reflector** pearl crown with integrated aluminium reflector, variants include coloured R,B,G, A & horticultural	25	85 ×	50	–	180	2 700	1 000
		40	85 ×	50	–	400	2 700	1 000
		60	103 ×	64	–	750	2 700	1 000
		75	115 ×	80	–	1 000	2 700	1 000
		100	115 ×	80	–	1 400	2 700	1 000
		150	180 × 125		–	2 500	2 700	1 000
IRR	**Infra-red Reflector** heater lamp with clear or red front	150	180 × 125		–	–	2 700	6 000
		250	180 × 125		–	–	2 700	6 000
		275	180 × 125		–	–	2 700	6 000
IPAR	**PAR 38** with parabolic reflector, also coloured R, B, G, Y, A	15° 60	136 × 124		–	2 600	2 700	2 000
		30° 60	136 × 124		–	1 100	2 700	2 000
		15° 80	136 × 124		~/	4 000	2 700	2 000
		30° 80	136 × 124		–	1 750	2 700	2 000
		15° 120	136 × 124		–	7 000	2 700	2 000
		30° 120	136 × 124		–	3 000	2 700	2 000
IPAR	**PAR 56** narrow spot medium flood wide flood	300	127 × 178		–	70 000	2 700	2 000
		300	127 × 178		–	30 000	2 700	2 000
		300	127 × 178		–	10 000	2 700	2 000

Incandescent lamps

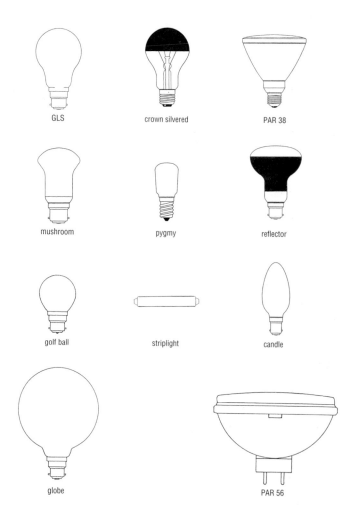

GLS

crown silvered

PAR 38

mushroom

pygmy

reflector

golf ball

striplight

candle

globe

PAR 56

Halogen: low voltage

ILCOS code	Description		Watts	Size l × Ø		Lumens	Peak cd	Colour K	Life h
HRG	**35 mm Ø**	7°	12	41 ×	35	–	6 400	2 900	2 000
	Dichroic 12 V	10°	20	41 ×	35	–	5 500	2 900	3 500
	open and	30°	20	41 ×	35	–	600	2 900	3 500
	closed	8°	35	41 ×	35	–	9 000	2 900	3 500
	versions	30°	35	41 ×	35	–	1 300	2 900	3 500
HRG	**50 mm Ø**	36°	20	49 ×	51	–	500	3 050	3 500
	Dichroic 12 V	18°	35	49 ×	51	–	3 600	3 050	3 500
	open and	38°	35	49 ×	51	–	970	3 050	3 500
	closed	10°	50	49 ×	51	–	12 000	3 050	3 500
	versions	38°	50	49 ×	51	–	1 550	3 050	3 500
HMG	**100 mm Ø**	3°	35	65 × 100		–	53 000	3 000	3 500
	Metal	4°	50	65 × 100		–	55 000	3 000	3 500
	Reflector	21°	50	65 × 100		–	3 300	3 000	3 500
	12 V	18°	75	65 × 100		–	6 750	3 000	3 500
HSG	**Capsule –**		10	33 ×	9	140	–	3 000	3 000
	single ended		20	33 ×	9	350	–	3 000	3 000
	12 V		35	33 ×	9	650	–	3 000	3 000
			50	44 ×	12	1 000	–	3 000	3 000
			75	44 ×	12	1 600	–	3 000	3 000
			100	44 ×	12	2 300	–	3 000	3 000

Halogen lamps

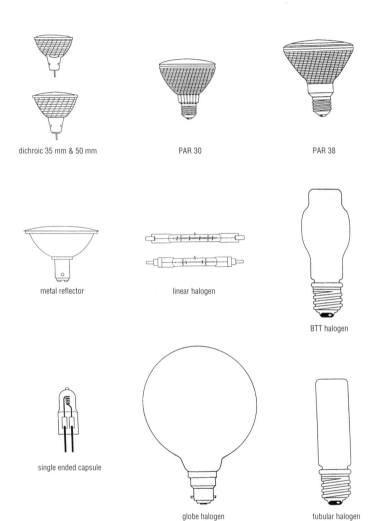

dichroic 35 mm & 50 mm   PAR 30   PAR 38

metal reflector   linear halogen

BTT halogen

single ended capsule

globe halogen   tubular halogen

Halogen: mains voltage

ILCOS code	Description		Watts	Size l × Ø		Lumens	Peak cd	Colour K	Life h
HEGPAR PAR 30		10°	75	91 ×	97	–	6 900	2 900	2 500
	halogen	30°	75	91 ×	97	–	2 200	2 900	2 500
	reflector	10°	100	91 ×	97	–	10 000	2 900	2 500
		30°	100	91 ×	97	–	3 500	2 900	2 500
HEPAR PAR 38		11°	75	136 ×	124	–	10 500	3 050	3 000
	halogen	30°	75	136 ×	124	–	2 800	3 050	3 000
	infra red	11°	100	136 ×	124	–	15 500	3 050	3 000
	reflector	30°	100	136 ×	124	–	4 200	3 050	3 000
HDF	**Linear-halogen**		200	79 ×	10	3100	–	2 900	2 000
	double ended		300	118 ×	8	4800	–	2 900	2 000
	also 100,150,250		500	118 ×	10	9500	–	2 900	2 000
	& 1500 watts and		750	190 ×	10	15000	–	3 000	2 000
	225,375 & 1000		1 000	190 ×	10	21000	–	3 000	2 000
	watt infra-red		2 000	331 ×	10	44000	–	3 000	2 000
	coated								
HDF	**Globe-halogen**		60	139 × 95		700	–	2 900	2 000
	white and clear		100	139 × 95		1 300	–	2 900	2 000
			150	139 × 95		2 000	–	2 900	2 000
HEGBT BTT-halogen			60	115 × 47		700	–	2 900	2 000
	clear & opal		100	115 × 47		1 100	–	2 900	2 000
	replacements for		150	115 × 47		1 450	–	2 900	2 000
	GLS lamps								
HEGT Tubular halogen			75	109 × 33		1 000	–	2 900	2 000
	single ended		100	109 × 33		1 450	–	2 900	2 000
	opal and clear		500	215 × 46		9 500	–	2 900	2 000
	clear		1000	280 × 46		21 000	–	3 000	2 000
	clear								

Compact fluorescent

ILCOS code	Description	Watts	Size l × Ø	Lumens	Colour K	Life h
FSD	**Single U tube** 2 & 4 pin	5	105 × 28	250	2 700 to	10 000
		7	135 × 28	400	4 000	10 000
		9	165 × 28	600	depending on	10 000
		11	233 × 28	900	type of lamp	10 000
		18	225 × 38	1 200		10 000
		24	320 × 38	1 800		10 000
		36	415 × 38	2 900		10 000
FSQ	**Double U tube** 2 & 4 pin	10	110 × 28	600	2 700 to	10 000
		13	138 × 28	900	4 000	10 000
		18	152 × 28	1 200		10 000
		26	170 × 28	1 800		10 000
FSM	**Triple U tube** in triangular arrangement	18	114 × 49	1 200	2 700 to	10 000
		26	131 × 49	1 800	4 000	10 000
		32	153 × 49	2 400		10 000
FBT	**Double U tube** with E27 & B22 caps*	7	125 × 45	460	2 700 to	10 000
		11	125 × 45	600	6 000	10 000
		15	152 × 45	900		10 000
		20	165 × 45	1 200		10 000
FSS	**2D** 2 and 4 pin	10	140 × 140	650	2 700 to	10 000
		16	140 × 140	1 050	6 000	10 000
		21	140 × 140	1 350		10 000
		28	205 × 205	2 050		10 000
		38	205 × 205	2 850		10 000
F	**Globe**-compact fluorescent	15	175 × 110	720	2 700	10 000
		20	200 × 125	960		10 000
F	**Self-ballasted**	9	151 × 73	450	2 700 to	8 000
		13	161 × 73	650	4 000	8 000
		18	171 × 73	900		8 000
		25	181 × 73	1 200		8 000

* as direct replacement for GLS lamps without need for adaptor

Fluorescent lamps and tubes

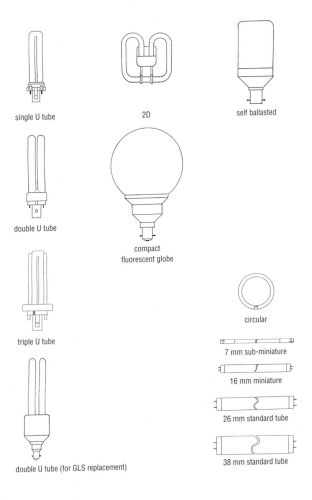

single U tube

2D

self ballasted

double U tube

compact
fluorescent globe

triple U tube

circular

7 mm sub-miniature

16 mm miniature

26 mm standard tube

38 mm standard tube

double U tube (for GLS replacement)

Fluorescent tubes

ILCOS code	Description	Watts	Size l × Ø	Lumens	Colour K	Life h
FD	**7 mm Ø** **sub-miniature**	6	219 × 7	310	3 000 to 4 000	8 000
		8	320 × 7	600		8 000
		11	422 × 7	680		8 000
		13	523 × 7	860		8 000
FD	**16 mm Ø** **miniature**	4	136 × 16	115	2 950 to 6 500	5 000
		6	212 × 16	240		5 000
		8	288 × 16	340		5 000
		13	517 × 16	750		5 000
FD	**26 mm Ø** **tri-phosphor**	15	438 × 26	1 050	2 700 to 6 300	15 000
		18	590 × 26	1 450		15 000
		30	895 × 26	2 500		15 000
		36	1 200 × 26	3 350		15 000
		58	1 500 × 26	5 400		15 000
		70	1 778 × 26	6 550		15 000
FD	**38 mm Ø**	20	590 × 38	1 050	2 950 to 6 500	9 000
		40	1 200 × 38	2 500		9 000
		65	1 500 × 38	4 200		9 000
		75	1 800 × 38	6 400		9 000
		85	1 800 × 38	6 400		9 000
		100	2 400 × 38	8 450		9 000
		125	2 400 × 38	9 300		9 000
FC	**Circular**	22	216 × 29	1 000	3 000	12 000
		32	311 × 32	1 700	3 000	12 000
		40	413 × 32	2 400	3 000	12 000
		60	413 × 32	3 650	3 000	12 000

Lamp comparison

	GLS incandescent lamp		FBT double U compact fluorescent lamp		
	Lumens	**Watts**	**Watts**	**Lumens**	
	410	40	7	460	
	700	60	11	600	
	930	75	15	900	
	1350	100	20	1200	

High-intensity discharge lamps

ILCOS code	Description	Watts	Size l × Ø	Lumens	Colour K	Life h
	Metal halide					
MC	**Compact elliptical** metal halide	75	138 × 54	5 000	3 200	15 000
ME	low wattage	100	138 × 54	8 000	3 200	15 000
	clear and coated	150	138 × 54	12 000	3 200	15 000
MD	**Double ended** metal halide clear	70	120 × 21	6 000	3 200	6 000
		150	137 × 24	13 000	3 200	6 000
		250	162 × 26	20 000	3 200	6 000
MT	**Single ended** metal halide clear	75	84 × 25	5 200	3 000	6 000
		150	84 × 25	12 000	3 000	6 000
	Mercury vapour					
QE	**Standard Elliptical** mercury coated	50	130 × 56	1 800	4 000	20 000
		80	166 × 71	3 800	4 000	20 000
		125	178 × 76	6 300	4 000	20 000
		250	227 × 91	13 000	4 000	20 000
QR	**Mercury Reflector**	80	168 × 125	3 000	4 000	24 000
		125	168 × 125	5 000	4 000	24 000
		160	168 × 125	2 500	4 000	24 000
	Sodium vapour					
ST	**Tubular** HP sodium (SON) clear	50	156 × 39	4 000	2 200	24 000
		70	156 × 39	6 500	2 200	24 000
		100	211 × 48	9 500	2 200	24 000
		150	211 × 48	17 000	2 200	24 000
		250	260 × 48	32 000	2 200	24 000
SE	**Elliptical** HP sodium (SON) coated	50	165 × 72	3 600	2 050	24 000
		70	165 × 72	6 000	2 050	24 000
		100	186 × 76	9 500	2 050	24 000
		150	227 × 91	15 500	2 200	24 000
		250	227 × 91	31 500	2 200	24 000
STH	**Tubular** HP sodium (white SON) clear	50	150 × 32	2 300	2 500	5 000
		100	150 × 32	4 800	2 500	5 000

High-intensity discharge lamps

single ended metal halide

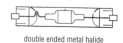

double ended metal halide

mercury elliptical

mercury reflector

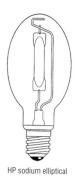

HP sodium elliptical

HP sodium tubular

Sound

Noise levels

The level of hearing is expressed in decibels from 0 dB, the threshold of hearing, to 140 dB, the threshold of pain.

Ears respond to sound frequencies or pitch from around 20 Hz bass to 20 kHz treble. Most people are more sensitive to high rather than low frequencies, but old age reduces the perception of higher frequencies.

Recommended maximum dBA*

- Hospital and general wards   55
- Small consulting rooms   50
- Large offices   45–50
- Private offices   40–45
- Living rooms   40–45
- Small classrooms   40
- Large lecture rooms   35
- Bedrooms   30–40
- Music studios   30

* **dBA** are decibels weighted to simulate the response of our ears as opposed to plain **dB** which do not depend directly on human reaction.

Source: BS 8233 : 1987

Sound levels

	dB range
	140
• Threshold of pain	
	130
• Pneumatic drill	
	120
• Loud car horn @ 1 m	
	110
• Pop group @ 20 m	
	100
• Inside tube train	
	90
• Inside bus	
	80
• Average kerbside traffic	
	70
• Conversational speech	
	60
• Typical office	
	50
• Family living room	
	40
• Library	
	30
• Bedroom at night	
	20
• Broadcasting studio	
	10
• Threshold of hearing	
	0

Source: Pilkington United Kingdom Ltd

Sound transmission loss of some typical building elements

Material	dB
One layer 9.5 mm plasterboard	25
Cupboards used as partitions	25–35
6 mm single glazing	29
75 mm timber studs with 12.5 mm plasterboard both sides	36
115 mm brickwork plastered one side	43
75 mm clinker concrete block plastered both sides	44
6 mm double glazing with 100 mm air gap	44
100 mm timber studs with 12.5 mm plasterboard both sides & quilt in cavity	46
115 mm brickwork plastered both sides	47
230 mm brickwork plastered one side	48
230 mm brickwork plastered both sides	55

5
Building Elements

Stairs

Building Regulations requirements

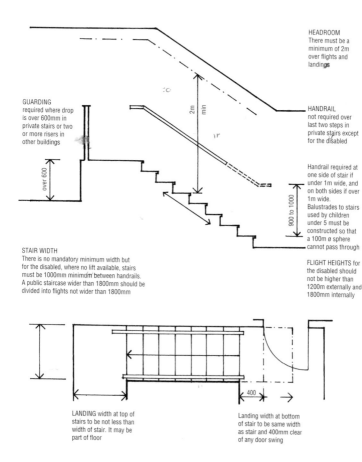

HEADROOM
There must be a
minimum of 2m
over flights and
landings

2m min

GUARDING
required where drop
is over 600mm in
private stairs or two
or more risers in
other buildings

over 600

HANDRAIL
not required over
last two steps in
private stairs except
for the disabled

Handrail required at
one side of stair if
under 1m wide, and
on both sides if over
1m wide.
Balustrades to stairs
used by children
under 5 must be
constructed so that
a 100m ø sphere
cannot pass through

900 to 1000

STAIR WIDTH
There is no mandatory minimum width but
for the disabled, where no lift available, stairs
must be 1000mm minimum between handrails.
A public staircase wider than 1800mm should be
divided into flights not wider than 1800mm

FLIGHT HEIGHTS for
the disabled should
not be higher than
1200m externally and
1800mm internally

LANDING width at top of
stairs to be not less than
width of stair. It may be
part of floor

400

Landing width at bottom
of stair to be same width
as stair and 400mm clear
of any door swing

Building Regulations requirements – continued

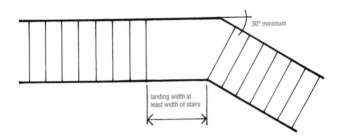

30° minimum

landing width at
least width of stairs

LONG FLIGHTS
Stairs with more than 36 risers in consecutive flights should make at least one change of direction of not
less than 30°. No more than 16 risers in any flight of stairs serving areas used as a shop or for assembly.

TAPERED TREADS measurement of going

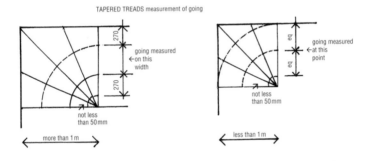

270

going measured
←on this
width

270

not less
than 50 mm

more than 1 m

going
going measured
←at this
point
going

not less
than 50 mm

less than 1 m

ALTERNATING TREADS
may be permitted for
loft conversions where
there is no room for a
proper staircase. They
may only access one
room and must have
handrails both sides
and non-slip surface
to treads.

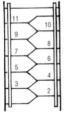

11
10
9
8
7
6
5
4
3
2

LOFT CONVERSIONS
Headroom may be
reduced if height at
centre of stair is at
least 1900 mm and not
less than 1800 mm at
side of stair

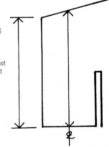

₵

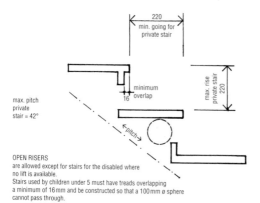

OPEN RISERS
are allowed except for stairs for the disabled where
no lift is available.
Stairs used by children under 5 must have treads overlapping
a minimum of 16 mm and be constructed so that a 100 mm ø sphere
cannot pass through.

SOURCES:
Building Regulations Approved Documents
K   Stairs, ramps and guards
M   Access for disabled people
B   Fire safety
N   Glazing (for glass balustrades)
BS 6180: 1982 for strength of balustrades
Spiral and helical stairs should be in
accordance with BS 5395: Part 2: 1984

RISE and GOING	max. rise	min. going
Private stair	220	220
External stair for the disabled	150	280
Internal stair for the disabled	170	250
Institutional & Assembly stair	180	280
Assembly building < 100 m²	180	250
Other stair	190	250

normal ratio: twice the rise plus going
(2R + G) should be between 550 mm and 700 mm

Gradients

%	Slope	Application
5%	1:20	maximum uphill gradient preferred by cyclists maximum outdoor slope for pedestrians
6.5%	1:15.4	maximum downhill gradient preferred by cyclists
6.7%	1:15	maximum wheelchair ramp for a maximum length of 10 m
8.3%	1:12	maximum wheelchair ramp for a maximum length of 5 m
8.5%	1:11.8	maximum indoor slope for pedestrians
10%	1:10	maximum ramp for lorry loading bays and most car parking garages
12%	1:8.3	any road steeper than this will be impassable in snow without snow tyres or chains maximum for dropped pavement kerbs of less than 1 m long
15%	1:6.7	absolute maximum for multi-storey car parks

Fireplaces

Building Regulation requirements
Fireplace recesses

minimum dimensions of solid non-combustible material

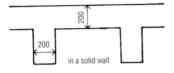

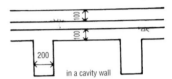

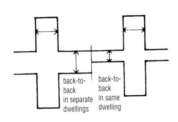

back-to-back in separate dwellings   back-to-back in same dwelling

PREFABRICATED FIREPLACE CHAMBERS
may be used if made of insulating concrete
with the following minimum dimensions:

base	50
side walls	75
rear walls	100
top slab, lintel or throat gather	100

Constructional hearths

minimum dimensions

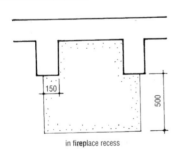

in fireplace recess

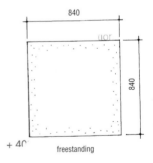

freestanding

CONSTRUCTIONAL HEARTHS are required for an open
fire, a gas flue where the flame is less than 225mm
above floor finish, a solid fuel or oil burning appliance
where the temperature of the floor may exceed 100°C. If
below this temperature then appliance may sit on a non-
combustible board or tiles – both at least 12mm thick.

Hearths must be at least 125mm thick of
solid non-combustible material which
may include the thickness of any non-
combustible decorative surface.

Superimposed hearths –

Minimum dimensions from the face of an appliance

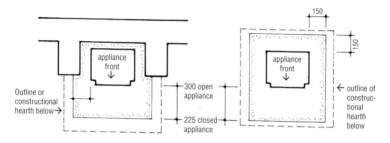

Outline or constructional hearth below→

appliance front ↓

300 open appliance

225 closed appliance

150

150

appliance front ↓

← outline of constructional hearth below

Superimposed hearths are optional. They must be made of solid non-combustible material and be placed over a constructional hearth as shown on P. 170. An appliance must be located on a hearth (whether a constructional or superimposed hearth) with the minimum dimensions as shown in the drawings above. The edge of this area of hearth must be clearly marked such as by a change of level.

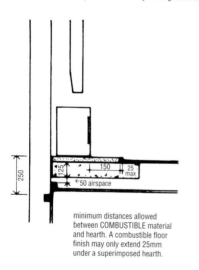

250   125   150   25 max

←50 airspace

minimum distances allowed between COMBUSTIBLE material and hearth. A combustible floor finish may only extend 25mm under a superimposed hearth.

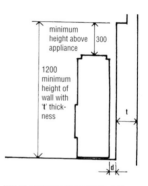

minimum height above appliance   300

1200 minimum height of wall with 't' thickness

t

d

WALLS ADJACENT TO HEARTHS which are not part of a fireplace recess must have the following thickness and be of solid non-combustible material:

	t
HEARTH abutting a wall where **d** is 0–50	200
where **d** is 51–300	75
HEARTH not abutting a wall where hearth edge < 150	75

SOURCE:
This is a summary of some of the requirements from
The Buildings Regulation Approved Document J edition 2002

Chimneys and Flues

Building Regulations requirements

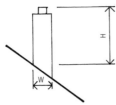

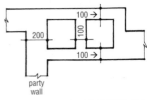

HEIGHT OF CHIMNEY (H) which includes
terminal should not exceed 4½ times the smallest
width dimension (W) (Bld. Regs. doc A)

MINIMUM WALL THICKNESSES of brick
and block chimneys excluding any liner
100 mm between one flue and another
100 mm between flue and outside air
100 mm between flue and another part of
the same building
200 mm between flue and another
compartment or building

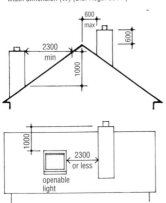

Pitched roofs

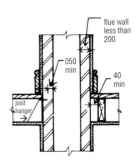

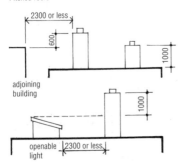

Flat roofs with a pitch of less than 10°

CHIMNEY FLUE OUTLETS minimum height above roof

COMBUSTIBLE MATERIAL should be
separated from masonry chimneys by
at least 200mm from flue OR 40mm
from the outer face of the chimney
unless it is a floorboard, skirting, dado,
picture rail, mantelshelf or architrave.
Metal fixings in contact with
combustible materials should be at
least 50mm away from flue.

These requirements are summarized
from The Building Regulations
Approved Document J 2002 edition

Flues in chimneys should be vertical where possible. Maximum permitted offset is 45° to the vertical. Provision must be made to sweep flues. For sizes of flues – see Table 2.2 in the Building Regs.

FLUE OFFSETS

FLUE PIPES should be used only to connect an appliance to a chimney. They should not pass through a roof space, internal wall or floor except to pass directly into a masonry chimney. Horizontal connections to the back of an appliance should not be longer than 150mm. Flue pipes should have the same diameter or cross sectional area as that of the appliance outlet.

Flue pipes may be made of:
Cast iron to BS 41
Mild steel at least 3mm thick
Stainless steel at least 1mm thick
Vitreous enamelled steel to BS 6999

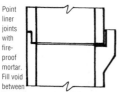

Point liner joints with fire-proof mortar. Fill void between liner and masonry stack with weak mortar or insulating concrete.

Liner sockets should be positioned uppermost to prevent condensation leaking into stack.

Brick and block chimneys should be lined unless made of refractory material.

FLUE LINERS

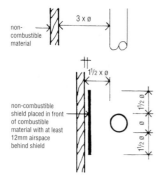

non-combustible material   3 x ø

1¹/₂ x ø

non-combustible shield placed in front of combustible material with at least 12mm airspace behind shield

¹/₂ ø   ø   ¹/₂ ø

UNINSULATED FLUEPIPE — minimum distances away from combustible material

BALANCED FLUES (room sealed) are mandatory for gas appliances fitted in bathrooms, shower rooms and gas fires or heaters of more than 14 kW (gross) in bedrooms. For positioning of balanced flues, see the numerous dimensional limitations as shown in diagram 3.4 of the Building Regs.

Flueless instantaneous gas water heaters should not be installed in rooms less than 5m³.

FACTORY-MADE insulated chimneys should conform to BS 4543 and be fitted to BS 7566.

SOURCE:
These requirements are summarized from The Building Regulations Approved Document J 2002 edition.

Doors

Standard doors are still manufactured primarily in imperial sizes. The manufacturers claim that this is because of demands by the building trade. There is also a need for replacement doors in older properties and the apparently odd size 2'8" × 6'8" is still produced for this reason. There is more demand for metric sizes for large scale building projects but the choice is still limited. Unless a large quantity of doors is ordered, standard sized doors are still significantly cheaper than specials.

Because of the need to accommodate wheelchair users, wider doors are now more in demand. An 800 mm clear opening is considered the absolute minimum for a wheelchair user. Sixty mm should be deducted from the actual door width to arrive at the clear opening size. This dimension takes into account the thickness of the door and hinges standing open at one side and the rebate or stop on the other side.

Typical sizes of single leaf standard doors (metric)

	926 × 2040	826 × 2040	807 × 2000	726 × 2040	626 × 2040	526 × 2040	Thickness (mm)
Exterior							
Solid panelled			*				44
Glazed panelled			*				44
Flush		*	*				44
Steel faced			*				44
Framed and ledged			*				44
Ledged and braced			*				36
Interior							
Solid panelled				*			35
Glazed panelled		*	*	*			40
Flush	*	*		*	*	*	40
Moulded panelled	*	*		*	*	*	35 and 40
Fire							
1/2 hour	*	*	*	*	*	*	44
1 hour		*		*			54

Typical sizes of single leaf standard doors (imperial)

	836 × 1981 2'9" × 6'6"	813 × 2032 2'8" × 6'8"	762 × 1981 2'6" × 6'6"	686 × 1981 2'3" × 6'6"	610 × 1981 2'0" × 6'6"	Thickness (mm)
Exterior						
solid panelled	*	*	*			44
glazed panelled	*	*	*			44
flush	*	*	*	*	*	44
steel faced	*		*			44
framed and ledged	*	*	*	*	*	44
ledged and braced	*	*	*	*	*	36
Interior						
solid panelled	*		*	*	*	35 & 40
glazed panelled	*	*	*	*	*	35 & 40
flush	*	*	*	*	*	35 & 40
moulded panelled	*	*	*	*	*	35 & 40
Fire						
½ hour	*	*	*	*	*	44
1 hour	*	*	*	*		54

Other types of doors

Fire doors

Fire doors are available in most standard sizes in flush doors, and some are also available in internal moulded panelled doors. Half-hour and one-hour fire doors are only rated FD 30(S) and FD 60(S) when used with appropriate door frames which are fitted with intumescent strip (combined with smoke seal). The intumescent strips and smoke seals may also be fitted to the top and long edges of the fire door.

French doors

Two-leaf glazed doors, opening out, are manufactured in hardwood and softwood in the following typical sizes:

Metric   : 1106 wide × 1994 mm high; 1200, 1500 and
             1800 wide × 2100 mm high
Imperial: 1168 wide × 1981 mm high (3'10" × 6'6") and
             914 wide × 1981 mm high (3'0" × 6'6").

Sliding glazed doors

Often called *patio* doors, these are available in hardwood, softwood, uPVC and aluminium in hardwood frames in the following metric nominal opening sizes typically:

2 leaf : 1200, 1500, 1800, 2100,
　　　　　2400 wide × 2100 mm high　　　　OX and XO

3 leaf : 2400 to 4000 wide in
　　　　　200 mm increments × 2100 mm high　　OXO

4 leaf : 3400 to 5000 wide in
　　　　　200 mm increments × 2100 mm high　　OXXO

Opening configurations are often labelled:

O = fixed panel and X = sliding panel when viewed from outside.

Some manufacturers offer all panels sliding.

Garage doors

Garage doors are manufactured in hardwood, softwood, plywood, steel and GRP. The following typical sizes exclude the frame which is recommended to be a minimum of ex 75 mm timber.

	w mm	h mm	
Single :	1981 × 1981		(6'6" × 6'6")
	1981 × 2134		(6'6" × 7'0")
	2134 × 1981		(7'0" × 6'6")
	2134 × 2134		(7'0" × 7'0")
	2286 × 1981		(7'6" × 6'6")
	2286 × 2134		(7'6" × 7'0")
	2438 × 1981		(8'0" × 6'6")
	2438 × 2134		(8'0" × 7'0")
Double :	4267 × 1981		(14'0" × 6'6")
	4267 × 2134		(14'0" × 7'0")

other double doors
available in widths
up to 4878 (16'0")

Louvre doors

Hardwood open louvre doors suitable for cabinet and wardrobe doors.

28mm thick and still made in imperial sizes:

Widths (mm) :	305 (1'0")	530 (1'9")
	380 (1'3")	610 (2'0")
	457 (1'6")	
	also in 1981 (6'6") heights only	
	686 (2'3")	762 (2'6")

Heights (mm) :	457 (1'6")	1524 (5'0")
	610 (2'0")	1676 (5'6")
	762 (2'6")	1829 (6'0")
	915 (3'0")	1981 (6'6")
	1219 (4'0")	

Bi-fold doors

Narrow full height doors, hinged in pairs, suitable for wardrobes. Supplied complete with sliding/folding gear. Typically moulded panelled doors but other larger sizes available with mirrored finishes.

Sizes per pair :	610 mm (2'0") × 1981 (6'6")
(mm)	762 mm (2'6") × 1981 (6'6")
	914 mm (3'0") × 1981 (6'6")

Sources: JELD-WEN UK, Premdor

Door handing

The traditional way of describing the configuration of a door is by the 'hand' – see **1**. There is also the ISO coding method **2** which describes a door's action as clockwise or anticlockwise. Despite its name it is not international and not widely used. Different components for a door sometimes conflict as, for instance, a door which requires a right hand rebated mortice lock may need a left hand overhead door closer. When in doubt, the specifier should draw a diagram.

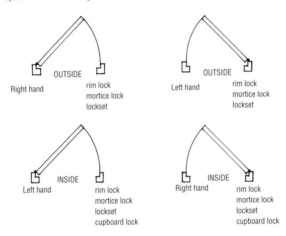

Right hand	OUTSIDE	Left hand	OUTSIDE
	rim lock mortice lock lockset		rim lock mortice lock lockset

Left hand	INSIDE	Right hand	INSIDE
	rim lock mortice lock lockset cupboard lock		rim lock mortice lock lockset cupboard lock

1 Handing method

   The definition of an OUTSIDE FACE of a door is:

   the external side of a door in an external wall;

   the corridor side of a room door;

   the side of a communicating door on which the hinge knuckles are not seen when the door is closed;

   the space between them in the case of twin doors;

   the room side of a cupboard, wardrobe or closet.

opening face 0
closing face 1

clockwise closing 5

opening face 0
closing face 1

anticlockwise closing 6

2   ISO coding method

	CODE		
clockwise closing	= 5	e.g. 5.0 =	clockwise closing / opening face
anticlockwise closing	= 6	5.1 =	clockwise closing / closing face
opening face	= 0	6.0 =	anticlockwise closing / opening face
closing face	= 1	6.1 =	anticlockwise closing / closing face

Direction of CLOSING and DOOR FACE are given to identify the door configuration as examples above.

Traditional wooden doors definitions and typical sections

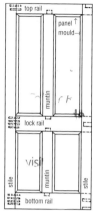

The rails are fixed to the full height styles with haunched tenons & wedged.

Muntins are tenoned to rails

Dowels, as shown on LHS, can also be used for a stronger joint which withstands well uneven shrinkage.

All frame sections are grooved at least 9 mm to house the panels.

Stiles are normally ex 100 × 50 or 125 × 50

Bottom & lock rails are deeper, typically ex 200 × 50

Panels should be min 6 mm ply for internal doors and min 9 mm ply for external doors

Four panelled door

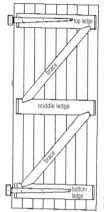

Door made up of ex 150 × 32 ledges and ex 100 × 32 braces with ex 25 mm t+g 'V' jointed boarding not more than ex 125 mm wide.

Ledges are screwed to the boards and the boards are nailed to the ledges.

Door hung with steel Tee hinges or with stronger wrought iron strap hinges and fastened with a suffolk latch.

Ledged & braced boarded door

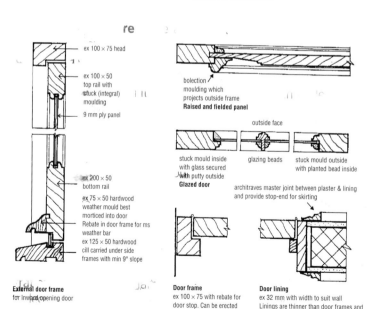

ex 100 × 75 head

ex 100 × 50 top rail with stuck (integral) moulding

9 mm ply panel

ex 200 × 50 bottom rail

ex 75 × 50 hardwood weather mould best morticed into door
Rebate in door frame for ms weather bar
ex 125 × 50 hardwood cill carried under side frames with min 9° slope

External door frame
for inward opening door

bolection moulding which projects outside frame
Raised and fielded panel

outside face

stuck mould inside with glass secured with putty outside | glazing beads | stuck mould outside with planted bead inside
Glazed door

Door frame
ex 100 × 75 with rebate for door stop. Can be erected before walls or built into opening

architraves master joint between plaster & lining and provide stop-end for skirting

Door lining
ex 32 mm with width to suit wall
Linings are thinner than door frames and for internal doors only. They have planted stops and are fitted to finished opening

Windows

Standard windows

Standard windows listed below are manufactured in soft-wood, hardwood and in PVC in a wide range of sizes and types and are the most commonly available. The sizes are approximate.

Side hung casements
This is by far the most common type of standard window. They are available as single sashes or in twos, threes and fours. There are numerous combinations of fully-opening side hung sashes, one or more fixed lights and smaller top hung vents, with or without glazing bars. Side hung sashes can be fitted with concealed friction stays fixed over the top and under the bottom of sashes, in lieu of conventional hinges, for easier cleaning from inside.

Widths : 630, 915, 1200, 1770 and 2340 mm.
Heights : 750, 900, 1050, 1200 and 1350 mm.

Bay windows
Square, splayed at 45°, semi-circular and shallow curved bay windows are available using combinations of fixed lights, side and top hung casements and double hung sashes to suit structural opening widths of approximately 1200 to 3500 mm with projections as little as 130 mm for shallow curved bays and up to 1000 mm for semi-circular bays.

Top hung casements
Top hung sashes generally without glazing bars.

Widths : 630, 915 and 1200 mm singles;
             1770 mm single with fixed side light.
Heights : 450, 600, 750, 900, 1050 and 1200 mm.

Standard windows – continued

Also vertical configurations with central horizontal transom and top hung opening sash to top half mimicking traditional double hung sashes.

Widths : 480, 630, 915, 1200 mm singles;
1700 and 2340 mm doubles.
Heights : 750, 900, 1050, 1200, 1350, 1500 and 1650 mm.

Fixed lights
A range of fixed light windows sometimes referred to as 'direct glazed'.

Widths   : 300, 485, 630 and 1200 mm.
Heights   : 450, 600, 750, 900, 1050, 1200 and 1350 mm.
Circular   : 600 mm Ø 'Bullseye'.
Semi-circular : 630, 915 and 1200 mm Ø fanlights with or
without two 60° glazing bars.

Double hung sashes
Softwood double hung sashes with spiral balances, some fitted with a tilting mechanism allowing for easier cleaning from the inside. With and without glazing bars.

Widths : 410, 630, 860, 1080 mm singles;
1700 and 1860 mm combinations.
Heights : 1050, 1350 and 1650mm.

Tilt and turn windows
Softwood windows with complex hinge mechanism allowing partial projection for ventilation and complete reversal for cleaning. Available also as a side hung escape window.

Widths : 450, 600, 900, 1200, 1350, 1500 and 1800 mm.
Heights : 600, 900, 1050, 1200, 1350, 1500 and 1600 mm.

Sources: JELD-WEN UK, Premdor

Standard windows – typical specification

Glazing
Most windows have rebates suitable for single glazing or double glazing units up to a thickness of 20 mm. Double glazed units are available if required with a choice of plain, obscured, annealed or toughened glass.

Protection
The Building Regulations require that all glazing below 800 mm above floor level in windows and below 1500 mm above floor level in doors and sidelights, and sidelights which are within 300 mm of a door, should be fitted with safety glass. See pp. 240–1. Small panes should have a maximum width of 250 mm and an area not exceeding 0.5 m^2 and should be glazed with glass a min-imum 6 mm thick. See diagrams on p. 190.

Weather stripping
Weather stripping is usually provided as standard to all opening lights.

Finishes
Timber windows are normally supplied primed for painting or with a base coat for staining. Options may include complete painting or staining.

Ventilation
Most windows are now fitted with ventilators in the head-frame providing either 4000 mm^2 in the narrower windows or 8000 mm^2 controllable secure ventilation to suit current Building Regulations in the wider windows.

Fittings
Fasteners, peg stays, hinges etc. all supplied with the windows in gold effect, lacquered brass, brown or white finishes.

Swept heads
Elliptical curves for the tops of panes available factory fitted or supplied loose.

Traditional wooden windows, definitions and typical sections

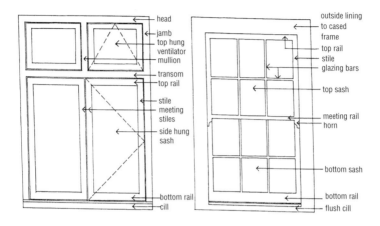

Casement window

Double hung window

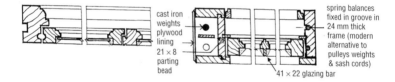

cast iron weights
plywood lining
21 × 8 parting bead

41 × 22 glazing bar

spring balances fixed in groove in 24 mm thick frame (modern alternative to pulleys weights & sash cords)

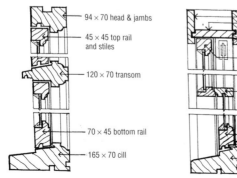

94 × 70 head & jambs

45 × 45 top rail and stiles

120 × 70 transom

70 × 45 bottom rail

165 × 70 cill

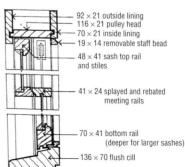

92 × 21 outside lining
116 × 21 pulley head
70 × 21 inside lining
19 × 14 removable staff bead

48 × 41 sash top rail and stiles

41 × 24 splayed and rebated meeting rails

70 × 41 bottom rail (deeper for larger sashes)

136 × 70 flush cill

Roof windows

Horizontally-pivoted roof windows

Designed for roof pitches between 15° and 90°. Pine or polyurethane frames, double glazed with a choice of glass: clear, obscured, toughened, laminated and Low-E coated. Glass cavities can be gas filled to achieve U-values of 1.9 down to 1.5 W/m^2K:

Standard sizes, overall frame w × h mm

550 × 780*					1340 × 980
550 × 980*+	660 × 980	780 × 980*+			
	660 × 1180*	780 × 1180*	940 × 1180	1140 × 1180*+	
		780 × 1400*	940 × 1400	1140 × 1400	1340 × 1400
		780 × 1600	940 × 1600*	1140 × 1600	1340 × 1600
		780 × 1800			

* = ex stock
+ = can be combined with tilted insulated kerb for flat roofs

Finishes :   externally – grey aluminium as standard, other metals available.
internally – lacquered or white painted timber frames; polyurethane frames finished white.

Fittings :   Control bar at head operates window and ventilation flap; friction hinges; barrel bolt for locking in two positions; security bolts.

Flashings :   Available to suit most roofing materials.
If required they can enable windows to be fitted side-by-side or one-above-the-other and in groups.

Accessories : External awning blinds; roller shutters.
Internal insect screens; interior linings.
Roller, black-out, pleated or venetian blinds.
Cord, rod and electronic controls for operating sashes, blinds etc
Break-glass points.
Smoke ventilation system to automatically open window in the event of fire.
Pre-installed electric system to operate high level skylights via an infra-red remote control.

Top hung roof windows

Designed for low roof pitches where a pivoted window might interfere with headroom. Suitable for pitches between 15° and 55° (and up to 77° with special springs). Can be rotated 180° for cleaning. Some versions are available for an escape/access door. Sizes similar to pivoted windows.

Additional fixed light windows

These may be fitted directly above or below a roof window, within the same plane, to extend the view and increase daylight.

Balcony system

A top hung roof window opens out horizontally and is combined with a bottom hung lower sash fixed in the same plane. The lower sash opens out to a vertical position and railings automatically unfold to close the sides and create a small balcony.

Roof terrace system

This system combines a top hung roof window with a vertical side hung opening out sash fixed below with no intermediate transome, allowing access to a balcony or terrace.

Additional vertical windows

Where floor level is below the eaves and more light and view is required, bottom hung or tilt-and-turn windows may be fixed in the vertical plane directly below roof windows fixed in the sloping roof above.

Conservation Area roof windows

Horizontal pivot windows with a central vertical glazing bar, recessed installation and black aluminium external finish suitable for Listed Buildings and Conservation Areas.

Sizes:	550 × 980*	660 × 1180	780 × 1400

* A version of this window is available as a side hung escape/access roof window.

Source : Velux Company Ltd

Rooflights

Individual rooflights are typically square, rectangular or round on plan and come as flat glass sheets, domes or pyramids. Plastic rooflights to be suitable for any space except a protected stairway must be rated TP(a) rigid.

Typical sizes nominal clear roof openings

Square	:	600, 900, 1200, 1500, 1800 mm.
Rectangular	:	600 × 900, 600 × 1200, 900 × 1200, 1200 × 1500, 1200 × 1800 mm.
Round	:	600, 750, 900, 1050, 1200, 1350, 1500, 1800 mm Ø.

Materials

Wired glass	:	Polished or cast glass, single or double glazed Fire rating : Class 0
Polycarbonate	:	Clear, opal and tinted. Almost unbreakable, good light transmission, single, double or triple skins Fire rating : TP(a) Class 1 Average U-values : single skin 5.3 W/m^2K double skin 2.8 W/m^2K triple skin 1.9 W/m^2K
PVC	:	Clear, opal and tinted. Cheaper than polycarbonate but will discolour in time. Single and double skins Fire rating : TP(a) Class 1 U-values : single skin 5.05 W/m^2K double skin 3.04 W/m^2K

Curbs

Curbs are generally supplied with rooflights, but they may also be fitted directly to builder's timber or concrete curbs. Curbs typically have 30° sloping sides, are made of aluminium or GRP and stand up 150–300mm above roof deck.

They may be uninsulated, insulated or topped with various forms of ventilators, normally fixed or adjustable louvres, hand or electrically operated.

Access hatch : Hinged rooflight, manually or electrically operated, typically 900 mm sq.

Smoke vent : Hinged rooflight linked by electron magnets to smoke/heat detecting systems.

Optional extras : Bird and insect mesh for vents in curbs. Burglar bars – hinged grille fixed to curb or in-situ upstand.

Sources: Cox Building Products, Duplus Domes Ltd, Ubbink (UK) Ltd

Patent glazing A system of puttyless glazing normally used for roofs but can also be used for curtain walling. The glazing bars, usually aluminium, can be several metres long and are normally spaced at 600 mm centres. The bars have concealed channels to drain the moisture out at the eaves of the roof or the bottom of the wall glazing. Can be single or double glazed with sealed units.

Leaded lights Windows made up of small panes of glass, either regular or patterned as in stained glass, which are set in lead cames – 'H' section glazing bars.

Security fittings

Security against intruders is becoming ever more sophisticated with new electronic technology. However, it is important to ensure the physical protection of buildings and particularly to have a secure perimeter.

External doors

External doors must be sufficiently strong and properly installed to resist shoulder charges and kicking. Doorframes should have minimum 18-mm rebates and be firmly fixed to openings at 600 mm centres. Doors should have a minimum thickness of 44 mm with stiles at least 119 mm wide to accommodate locks. Panels should not be less than 9 mm thick. Flush doors should be of solid core construction. Meeting styles of double doors should be rebated.

Door ironmongery

Front doors should be fitted with a *high security cylinder lock* for use when the building is occupied, with an additional five- or seven-lever *mortice deadlock* to BS 3621. Back and side doors should be fitted with a similar deadlock with two *security bolts* at the top and bottom. Deadlocks should have *boxed striking plates* to prevent jemmy attack and *hardened steel rollers* to resist hacksawing. Doors should be hung on three (1½ pairs) metal broad *butt hinges.* Outward opening doors should have *hinge bolts* to prevent doors being levered open on the hinge side. Position *letter plates* at least 400 mm from any lock. Fit *door viewers* and *door chains* to any door likely to be opened to strangers. Chains should be fixed with 30 mm long screws to prevent being forced open. Entrance doors should be lit so that callers can be seen at night. Burglars are wary of breaking glass, so glass doors are not necessarily vulnerable providing the glass is fixed from the inside. However, sliding glass doors are particularly vulnerable. The main mortice lock bolt should be supplemented by a pair of key-operated locking bolts fixed at the top and bottom. *Anti-lift devices* should be fitted in the gap between the door panel and frame to prevent the outer door being lifted off the runners.

Windows

Rear windows are most at risk, as are windows accessible from balconies or flat roofs. Sliding windows should be designed so that it is impossible to remove sashes or glass from the outside. External hinge pins and pivots should be secured by burring over. Avoid rooflights which have domes fixed with clips that can be broken from outside. Where escape from fire is not required, fix *metal bars* or *grilles* below rooflights.

Window ironmongery

All ground floor, basement and any upper floor vulnerable windows should be fitted with two *security bolts* to each casement sash and to the meeting rails of double-hung sashes. Upper floor sashes should have at least one security bolt. For greater safety choose locks with a *differ key* rather than those with a common key, which experienced intruders will own.

Other physical devices

Collapsible grilles, *sliding shutters* and, where appropriate, *blast and bullet-proof screens* and *ram stop bollards*.

Safes for domestic use can be as small as 'two brick' *wall safes* or *floor safes* let into floors. Larger floor safes weigh from 370 kg to 2300 kg and must be anchored to floors. Locks may be key, combination or electronic.

Electronic devices include the following:

- Access control – voice/video, keypad, card reading entry, phone systems
- Intruder detection – intruder alarms, CCTV surveillance, security lighting
- Fire protection – smoke and heat detection, fire alarms, 'break glass' switches, automatic linking to fire stations.

Sources: *A Guide to the Security of Homes*
Home Security and Safety
Banham Patent Locks Ltd
Chubb Physical Security Products

Protection for glazing in doors and windows Based on Building Regulations Approved Document N

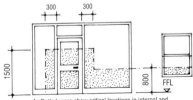

1. Dotted areas show critical locations in internal and external glazing in doors, side panels, screens and windows.

There are certain areas of glazing which can prove hazardous, particularly to children.

1. shows the extent of these areas which should be glazed with safety glass or safety plastic to BS 6206 : 1981.

2. Alternatively glass in these areas should be in small panes **OR**

3. If glazed with standard annealed glass these areas should be protected inside and out with a permanent screen

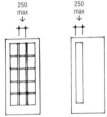

2. If annealed glass is used, it should be in small panes not larger than 0.5 m² with a maximum width of 250 mm. The glass should be at least 6 mm thick.

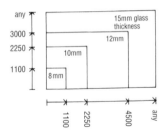

4. Annealed glass thickness/ dimension limits. Some annealed glass is considered suitable for use in public buildings for showrooms, offices etc. and will conform providing it does not exceed the thickness/dimension limitations shown above.

3. If annealed glass is used for low level glazing then it must be protected inside and out with permanent screens. These should be at least 800 mm high, unclimbable, ie not horizontal rails and designed so as to prevent a 75 mm ø sphere touching the glazing.

Large areas of glass in non-domestic buildings should 'manifest' themselves with a line of pattern, logo etc. at 1500 mm above FFL, unless the presence of the glass is made obvious by the use of mullions, transoms, wide frames, large handles or something similar.

6
Materials

Brickwork and Blockwork

Brick sizes

The work (actual) size of the standard brick is

$$215 \times 102.5 \times 65 \text{ mm}$$

For the co-ordinating size, which includes the width of one mortar joint, add 10 mm, i.e.

$$225 \times 112.5 \times 75 \text{ mm}$$

Metric modular sizes:

$$190 \times 90 \times 65 \text{ mm}$$

Other less available brick sizes:

$$215 \times 102.5 \times 50 \text{ mm}$$
$$215 \times 102.5 \times 73 \text{ mm}$$
$$215 \times 102.5 \times 80 \text{ mm}$$

Weights of bricks

	kg/m^3
Blue	2405
Engineering	2165
Sand cement	2085
Fire brick	1890
London stock	1845
Sand lime	1845
Flettons	1795
Red facings	1765
Diatomaceous	480

Bricks – continued

Compressive strengths and percentage water absorption

Brick	N/mm²	water absorption % by mass
Engineering Class A	> 70	< 4.5
Engineering Class B	> 50	< 7.0
Flettons	14 – 25	15 – 25
London stocks	3 – 18	20 – 40
Hand moulded facings	7 – 60	10 – 30

Frost resistance and soluble-salt content of bricks

Designation	Frost resistance	Soluble-salt content
FL	frost resistant	low salt content
FN	frost resistant	normal salt content
ML	moderate frost resistance	low salt content
MN	moderate frost resistance	normal salt content
OL	not frost resistant	low salt content
ON	not frost resistant	normal salt content

Spacing of wall ties

65 – 90 mm leaf thickness   = 450 horizontally / 450 mm vertically
over 90 mm leaf thickness   = 900 horizontally / 450 mm vertically

Cavity wall ties

Flat fishtailed tie
with V' drip

Vertical twist
fishtail tie with
insulation clip

Butterfly tie with
insulation clip

Twin triangle tie
with insulation clip
in position

'Safety' heavy duty
SS strip tie with
vertical twist

'Safety' medium &
light duty SS wire tie

Cavity Wall ties are made in galvanized steel or (better) stainless steel.
Lengths are from 150–300 mm depending on wall and cavity thickness.
Wire diameters from 2.5–4.5 mm
Traditional fish tailed ties are now largely superseded because of their
sharp edges by SS 'safety' ties as less wire is used in their manufacture.
Most ties may be fitted with clips to retain insulation. Condensation
drips from central twists and kinks.

Source: Avon Manufacturing Ltd

Block sizes

The standard block face dimensions are:
440 × 215 mm and 440 × 140 mm, with thicknesses of
75, 90, 100, 140, 150, 190, 200 and 215 mm.

Typical foundation blocks:
440 × 215 mm and 440 × 140 mm, with thicknesses of
224, 275, 305 and 355 mm.

Compressive strength:
Blocks range from 2.8 to 7.0 N/mm² depending on composition.
4.0 N/mm² is average.

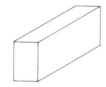

SOLID
440 × 140 × 215 h (most used size)
Load bearing and good for external
fair-faced work

HOLLOW
Voids open at both ends
Can be used for vertical
reinforcement

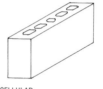

CELLULAR
Voids closed at one end
Voids normally laid uppermost
Lighter and therefore easier to lay
Slightly cheaper than solid blocks

QUOIN
440 × 215 × 215 h
Many other specials available
eg: cavity closers, cills

SOUND ABSORBING
Slots in one face connect to voids filled
with mineral wool
Unplastered & fair faced. Useful for
sports halls, sound studios etc

CONCRETE BLOCKS are generally
available in four main grades:

Architectural:	'The Best'; precision made and consistent in colour for fair faced work
Fair faced:	Good quality for unplastered or painted walls
Paint quality:	Suitable for a direct paint finish
Standard:	Cheapest and suitable for plastering and rendering

Concrete paving slabs

Type	Nominal size (mm)	Thickness	Number/m²
A	600 × 450	50 + 63	3.70
B	600 × 600	50 + 63	2.77
C	600 × 750	50 + 63	2.22
D	600 × 900	50 + 63	1.85

Brickwork bonds

ENGLISH BOND
A strong bond which is easy to lay but is somewhat monotonous in appearance.

FLEMISH BOND
This bond with its even, readily understood pattern is generally considered more attractive than English bond.

ENGLISH GARDEN WALL BOND
This bond reduces the numbers of headers making it easier to build both faces of the wall as fair faced.

FLEMISH GARDEN WALL BOND
This requires a fairly large area of wall for the pattern to be appreciated. Careful laying is needed to keep the perpends true, especially if the headers are a different colour from the stretchers.

BOND STRENGTH
In any bond, it is important that the perpends (vertical joints) should not be less than one quarter of the brick length from those in the adjacent course.

STRETCHER BOND
Sometimes called 'running' bond, this is the bond for half brick walls.

Mortar mixes for brickwork and blockwork

Grade desig-nation	Cement : lime : sand	Masonry cement: sand	Cement : sand with plasticiser	Compressive strengths N/mm^2	
				preliminary	site
I	1 : $^1/_4$: 3	–	–	16.0	11.0
II	1 : $^1/_2$: 4 to 4$^1/_2$	1 : 2$^1/_2$ to 3$^1/_2$	1 : 3 to 4	6.5	4.5
III	1 : 1 : 5 to 6	1 : 4 to 5	1 : 5 to 6	3.6	2.5
IV	1 : 2 : 8 to 9	1 : 5$^1/_2$ to 6$^1/_2$	1 : 7 to 8	1.5	1.0

Notes:
1   Mortar designation I is strongest, IV is weakest.
2   The weaker the mix the more it can accommodate movement.
3   Where sand volume varies, use the larger quantity for well graded sands and the smaller quantity for coarse or uniformly fine sands.
4   Grade I and II for high strength bricks and blocks in walls subject to high loading or walls subject to high exposure such as retaining walls, below DPC, parapets, copings and free standing walls.
5   Grade III and IV for walls between DPC and eaves not subject to severe exposure.

Joints

Flush
Maximum bearing area
Useful for coarse textured bricks

Bucket handle
Better looking than flush and almost as strong and weather resistant

Struck or weathered
Gives a shadow line to joint. If correctly made is strong and weather resistant

Recessed
This can allow rain to penetrate and should be confined to frost resistant bricks.

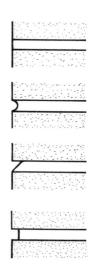

Special bricks

BULLNOSE

single bull-
nose

bullnose internal
return
on flat

cownose

double
bullnose

bullnose external
return
on edge

cownose
stop

single
bullnose
stop

bullnose external
return
on flat

Bullnose, angle, cant and
plinth brick dimensions are
based on the standard brick
215 × 115 × 65 mm

double
bullnose
stop

bullnose
mitre

bullnose
header on
flat

bullnose double
header
on flat

bullnose
stretcher
on flat

bullnose double
stretcher
on flat

ARCH

tapered
header

bullnose internal
return
on end

stop end
to
double
bullnose

tapered
stretcher

bullnose internal
return
on edge

double bullnose
external
return
on edge

Arch bricks are available with
four different tapers to suit
diameters at approximately
900 to 2700 mm.

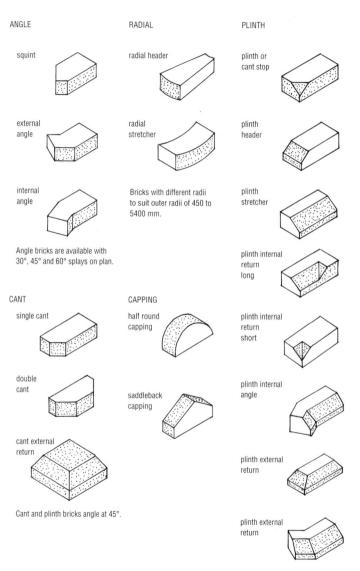

ANGLE

squint

external angle

internal angle

Angle bricks are available with 30°, 45° and 60° splays on plan.

RADIAL

radial header

radial stretcher

Bricks with different radii to suit outer radii of 450 to 5400 mm.

PLINTH

plinth or cant stop

plinth header

plinth stretcher

plinth internal return long

plinth internal return short

plinth internal angle

plinth external return

plinth external return

CANT

single cant

double cant

cant external return

Cant and plinth bricks angle at 45°.

CAPPING

half round capping

saddleback capping

Dotted shading indicates faced surfaces as standard.

Source: Ibstock Building Products Ltd

Brick paving patterns

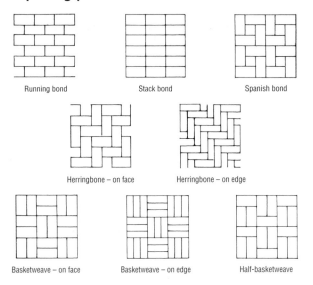

Running bond

Stack bond

Spanish bond

Herringbone – on face

Herringbone – on edge

Basketweave – on face

Basketweave – on edge

Half-basketweave

Clayware – definitions

earthenware Pottery made from brick earth; softer than stoneware. Exposed surfaces are often glazed.

firebrick Bricks made from any clay which is difficult to fuse and generally has a high quartz content. Used for fire backs and boiler liners for temperatures up to 1600°C.

stoneware Highly *vitrified clayware* used for sanitary fittings and drainpipes.

vitreous china A strong high-grade ceramic ware made from white clays and finely ground minerals. All exposed surfaces are coated with an impervious non-crazing vitreous glaze. Used for sanitary ware, it is easy to clean but brittle compared with *glazed stoneware*.

vitrified clayware Clay which is hard-burnt to about 1100°C and therefore vitrified throughout. It has low water absorption, and can be used unglazed for floor tiles, drainpipes etc. Can be fair cut with an angle grinder.

Concrete – some types and treatments

aerated concrete A lightweight concrete with no coarse aggregates, made of cement, lime, sand and chemical admixtures which cause bubbles to make a cellular consistency. It has low strength but good insulation properties. It is easily cut and nailable. There are many grades, some unsuitable below ground. Water absorption will impair its thermal performance.

bush hammering Tooling concrete or stone with a compressed air hammer to remove 1 to 6 mm of the outer skin to reveal a surface texture that improves its appearance.

granolithic finish A thin topping of cement, granite chippings and sand laid over a concrete slab, preferably as a monolithic screed to provide a good wearing surface. Can be made non-slip by sprinkling carborundum powder over the surface before final trowelling.

glass-reinforced concrete (GRC) Precast concrete, reinforced with glass fibre to make thin panels with improved strength and impact resistance.

polymer-impregnated concrete Concrete made with a polymer to improve the strength by filling all the voids normally left in conventional concrete. Water absorption is thus reduced and the concrete has greater dimensional stability.

refractory concrete Concrete made with high alumina cement and refractory aggregate, such as broken firebrick, to withstand very high temperatures.

Stonework

Building stone comes from three rock types:
- **Igneous** rocks formed from cooled molten rock, e.g. granite
- **Metamorphic** rocks formed from the re-crystallization of previous rocks after heat and pressure, e.g. slate and marble
- **Sedimentary** rocks formed from ancient sediments deposited on sea or river beds and then compacted or naturally cemented, e.g. limestone or sandstone.

Typical building stones

Stone	County	Colour	Dry weight kg/m^3	Compressive strength kN/m^2
Granites				
Cornish	Cornwall	silvery grey	2 610	113 685
Peterhead	Grampian	bright red	2 803	129 558
Rubislaw	Grampian	bluish-grey	2 500	138 352
Sandstones				
Bramley Fell	W Yorks.	grey to buff	2 178	42 900
Darley Dale	Derbys.	light grey	2 322	55 448
Forest of Dean	Glos.	grey to blue	2 435	67 522
Kerridge	Derbys.	buff	2 450	62 205
Runcorn red	Cheshire	red & mottled	2 082	27 242
Limestones				
Ancaster	Lincs.	cream to brown	2 515	23 380
Bath	Wilts.	lt. brown to cream	2 082	24 024
Clipsham	Leics.	pale cream to buff	2 322	29 172
Mansfield	Notts.	creamy yellow	2 242	49 550
Portland	Dorset	lt. brown to white	2 210	30 780

Mortar mixes for stonework

Typical mix				Application
cement :	lime :	sand	1 : 3 : 12	most building stones
	lime :	sand	2 : 5	most building stones
cement :	lime :	sand	1 : 2 : 9	exposed details
cement :	lime :	sand	1 : 1 : 6	most sandstones
cement :		sand	1 : 3	only for dense granite
PFA* :	lime :	sand	1 : 1 : 4	less durable stones in sheltered environment

*Pulverised fuel ash

Joints	mm thickness
internal marble cladding	1.5
external cladding	2 to 3
slate cladding	3
large slabs	4.5
polished granites	4.5
fine ashlar	6 maximum
rubble walls	12 to 18

Sources: *Building Construction* – W. McKay,
         Stone in Building – Stone Federation GB

Damp-proof courses (DPCs)

DPCs provide an impermeable barrier to the passage of moisture from below, from above or horizontally. They can be flexible, semi-rigid or rigid. Rigid DPCs are only suitable for rising damp. Soft metal DPCs are expensive but safest for intricate situations. Cavity trays are needed above elements that bridge cavities to direct water to outside. DPCs should be bedded *both* sides in mortar. Seal DPCs to floor membranes. Upper and vertical DPCs should always lap over lower or horizontal ones. DPCs must not project into cavities where they may collect mortar and bridge the cavity.

Type	Material	Minimum thickness mm	Joint	Application	Remarks
Flexible polymer based	polyethylene	0.46	100 mm min lap and sealed	H at base of walls, under cills, vertical jambs	appropriates lateral movement; tough, easy to seal, expensive, can be punctured
	bitumen polymer	1.5	100 mm min lap and sealed	H at base of walls, stepped; CT; V at jambs	
Flexible bitumen based	bitumen/hessian base	3.8	100 mm min lap and sealed	H at base of walls, under copings, cills; CT, V at jambs	hessian may decay, but OK if bitumen not disturbed. If cold, warm DPC before use, may extrude under high loads or temperatures
	bitumen/hessian base/lead	4.4	100 mm min lap and sealed	H at base of walls, under copings, cills; CT, V at jambs	lead lamination gives extra tensile strength
Semi-rigid	mastic asphalt	12.0	none	H under copings	grit should be added for key, liable to expand
	lead	1.8	100 mm min, welted against damp from above	H under copings, chimney stacks	corrodes in contact with mortar, protect by coating both sides with bitumen
	copper	0.25	100 mm min, welted against damp from above	H under copings, chimney stacks	good against corrosion, difficult to work, may stain masonry green
Rigid	slate	two courses 4.0	laid to break joint	H at base of free-standing and retaining walls	very durable, bed in 1 : 3 sand cement
	brick to BS 3921	two courses 150	laid to break joint	H at base of free-standing and retaining walls	good for freestanding walls

H = horizontal; V = vertical; CT = cavity tray.

Damp-proof membranes (DPMs)

DPMs are sheet or liquid membranes designed to resist damp caused by capillary action. They do not have to perform as well as tanking membranes, which must resist water pressure.

DPMs may be positioned under site slabs providing the hardcore is smoothed with 25 mm minimum rolled sand or preferably 25 mm smooth blinding concrete. This position is more vulnerable to damage than placing them over smooth finished site slabs. In this position the membrane can prevent satisfactory bonding between slab and screed, so a thick screed is needed, ideally at least 63 mm.

DPMs must be carried up to lap or join DPCs in walls. Brush-applied membranes are better than sheets in this respect.

Care must be taken not to penetrate membranes when laying. Any pipe ducts must be in position before screeds are poured, as any subsequent chasing could well damage the DPM.

Type	Description
Low density polyethylene film (LDPE)	Min 0.3 mm thick. Cheapest DPM, protects against methane and radon gas. No good against any water pressure. Joints must be rigorously taped. Easy to penetrate on site
Cold-applied bitumen solutions; coal tar; pitch/rubber or bitumen rubber emulsions	Ideally three coats. Must be carefully applied to avoid thin patches and pinholes
Hot applied pitch or bitumen	Ideally three coats. Must be carefully applied to avoid thin patches and pinholes
LDPE plus bitumen sheet	Not as easily displaced as LPDE film and easier to overlap. Small perforations less likely, as will 'self heal'
High density polyethyene (HDPE) with bitumen to both faces	High performance PE core is coated both sides with bitumen, with upper surface bonded to this PE film. Underside has film which is released before laying
Epoxy resin	Two-coat system for newly laid concrete slabs which have not fully dried out. Second coat scattered with fine sand. Suitable for moisture-sensitive flooring, e.g. PVC, cork, lino, wood
Mastic asphalt	12–16 mm thick, not often used under screeds but more often as a combined DPM/floor finish 20–25 mm thick and layed on a glass fibre isolating membrane
Ethylene propylene di-monomer (EPDM)	1.2 and 1.4 mm synthetic rubber sheet (Pirelli), strong and not affected by chemicals, exposure to ozone, UV light, continuous wet, freeze–thaw cycles, microbe attack. Used for foundations, dams, reservoirs etc.

Sources: *Specification 94*
Ruberoid Building Products Ltd

Dampness in buildings

Typical causes

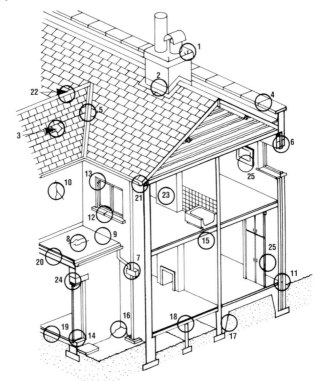

WATER PENETRATION
1 Defective haunching to chimney top
2 Defective chimney flashing
3 Slipped or cracked slates
4 Lack of DPC under parapet coping
5 Defective flashing to valley gutter
6 Lack of cavity tray over window head
7 Cracked RWP and blocked hopper
8 Cracked asphalt to flat roof
9 No asphalt upstand at junction of flat roof to wall
10 Cracked rendering
11 Mortar droppings on cavity ties transmitting water to inner skin
12 Cracked window sill
13 Defective paint and putty to window frame
14 Lack of door threshold letting in driving rain
15 Damp patch on wall from defective sealant round bath edge above

RISING DAMP
16 Earth bridging damp proof course
17 No vertical tanking to earth retaining wall
18 No DPC under timber joists on sleeper walll
19 Faulty DPM under floor

CONDENSATION
20 No vapour barrier in flat roof causing interstitial condensation
21 Blocked eaves ventilation to roof space
22 Lack of ridge ventilator to ventilate roof space
23 Lack of air brick to blocked up flue
24 Cold spot condensation showing inside solid concrete lintel
25 Damp low down on external walls in unventilated cupboards and behind pictures

Source: *Dampness in Buildings*

Plaster and render

External rendering

Rendering mortars are essentially the same as those for laying masonry, but should be made with clean washed plastering sand. See p. 195 for the four mix grades and the table below for what to use where.

Where possible, use the same mix for undercoats as for finishing coats, otherwise the undercoat should be stronger than the finishing coat.

Strong backgrounds, such as concrete or engineering brick, may need an initial keying coat or spatterdash such as 1:1½ or 1:3 cement:sand thrown on and not trowelled.

For severe exposures, two undercoats are preferable.

On metal lathing, two undercoats are invariably needed.

Rendering mixes for different backgrounds and exposures

Use	Background	Severe	Moderate	Sheltered
First and subsequent undercoats	dense, strong	II	II	II
	moderately strong, porous	III	III	III
	moderately weak, porous	III	IV	IV
	metal lathing	I / II	I / II	I / II
Final coats	dense, strong	III	III	III
	moderately strong, porous	III	IV	IV
	moderately weak, porous	III	IV	IV
	metal lathing	III	III	III

Plaster and render glossary

aggregate Sand particles or crushed stone that form the bulk of a mortar or render.

binder A component that hardens to bind aggregates together; normally lime and Portland cement.

browning Undercoat plaster made from *gypsum* and *sand*. It replaced lime and sand 'coarse stuff'. Now generally superseded by pre-mixed *lightweight plasters*.

cement Usually Portland cement, so called because it resembles Portland stone when set. It is a mixture of chalk and clay burnt in a kiln. When mixed with water it hardens in a process known as hydration.

dash External rendering thrown onto a wall by hand or applicator.

dry dash Coarse aggregate thrown onto a wet *render* coat, giving an exposed aggregate finish.

dry hydrated lime Ordinary (non-hydraulic) lime produced as a dry powder by adding just enough water to slake the quicklime (adding more water produces *lime putty*).

gypsum A solid white mined mineral, the main constituent of which is calcium sulphate, used as a *binder* in gypsum plaster.

gypsum plaster Plaster made of gypsum with lightweight aggregates and a *retarder*. It is unsuitable for external work or wet areas. It is used as a smooth finishing coat.

hemihydrate plaster A plaster made by gently heating gypsum to drive off most of its chemically combined water to become half-hydrated. In its pure form it is Plaster of Paris, but with the addition of *retarders* such as keratin it becomes the basic material for all gypsum plaster, and is known as *retarded hemihydrate plaster.*

hydrated lime *Quicklime* slaked with water.

hydraulic lime Lime that can set in the absence of air under water. It is made by burning lime with up to 22 per cent clay.

Keene's cement Hard burnt anhydrous (water-free) gypsum mixed with alum to form a plaster, which can be trowelled to a smooth, intensely hard finish.

lightweight plaster Plaster with lightweight aggregates

such as expanded perlite combined with *retarded hemihydrate plaster*. It has low shrinkage and is thermally insulating.

lime Chalk or limestone burnt in a kiln to 825°C or more.

lime putty *Hydrated lime* soaked to give it plasticity. Used for lime plasters, renders, mortars, grouts and limewash.

mortar A mixture of sand, cement and water, used primarily for bedding and pointing brickwork, laying floor tiles, and as undercoats to plaster and final coats of external walls.

non-hydraulic lime High calcium lime made by slaking relatively pure limestone. Mortars and renders made from this lime set slowly and are relatively soft, but accommodate normal building movement well and have high levels of vapour permeability and porosity.

pebble dash A dry dash finish in which clean washed pebbles are pushed into wet render and left exposed.

plaster Usually gypsum plaster for interiors, or cement render for exterior work.

pozzolana A natural volcanic silica dust originally from Pozzuoli, Italy. When mixed with lime it sets hard, even under water, making Roman cement. The term pozzolanic additive now includes other aggregates, such as pulverized fuel ash (PFA) and brick dust, which have similar hydraulic properties.

rendering *Mortar* undercoats and finishing coats for external walls and to receive tiling in wet areas.

retarder Added to cement, plaster or mortar to slow down the initial rate of setting by inhibiting hydration.

quicklime *Lime* before it has been slaked. It reacts strongly with water to produce *hydrated lime.*

spatter dash Cement and sand in a very wet mix, sometimes with a binding agent, flicked on in small blobs with an applicator. Used to create a key for backgrounds with poor suction.

stucco Smooth rendering, originally lime and sand but now cement lime mortar. Often with decorative mouldings shaped to imitate rusticated masonry or column embellishments.

tyrolean finish A spattered textured render achieved by being thrown against a wall with a hand-operated applicator.

Sources: *The Penguin Dictionary of Building*
Illustrated Dictionary of Building

Pre-mixed plasters

Pre-mixed plasters are made from gypsum, which is a natural mineral deposit – calcium sulphate dihydrate. They should conform to BS 1191 Part 2 : 1973 *Specification for gypsum building plasters*.

Pre-mixed plasters should not be used in continuously damp or humid places, nor should they be used where the temperature exceeds 43°C. Gypsum plasters are unsuitable for external work because gypsum is partially soluble in water.

British Gypsum have two brand names, 'Carlite' and 'Thistle', which they keep for historical rather than functional significance:

Carlite Browning	An undercoat plaster for solid backgrounds of moderate suction with an adequate mechanical key.
Carlite HSB Browning	An undercoat plaster for solid backgrounds of high suction with an adequate mechanical key.
Carlite Bonding Coat	An undercoat plaster for low suction backgrounds such as plasterboard, concrete or other surfaces treated with a PVAC agent.
Carlite Finish	A final coat plaster for all three Carlite undercoat plasters.
Thistle Hardwall	An undercoat plaster with high impact resistance and quicker-drying surface. May be applied by hand or machine.
Thistle Multi-Finish	A final coat plaster for a wide range of backgrounds.
Thistle Board Finish	A final coat plaster for plasterboard.

Thistle Dri-Coat

A cement-based undercoat plaster for old walls, where plaster has been removed and a chemical DPC inserted.

Thistle Renovating

An undercoat plaster containing perlite and additives to promote early surface drying when applied to structures containing residual moisture.

Thistle Renovating Finish

Final coat plaster for use with Thistle Renovating plaster. Contains a fungicide and should be applied as soon as the undercoat is set.

Thistle Universal One Coat

One coat plaster suitable for most backgrounds with a smooth white finish. May be applied by hand or machine.

Source: British Gypsum Ltd

Pre-mixed plasters
Selection guide and coat thickness in mm

Background	Carlite				Thistle						Univ. One-Coat
	Browning	HSB Browning	Bonding Coat	Finish	Hardwall	Multi-Finish	Board Finish	Dri-Coat	Renovating	Renovating Finish	
Plasterboard			8+	2		2	2				5
Dry lining foil-backed & thermal laminate boards						2	2				
Brick walls	11 or	11+		2	11+	2			11+	2	13
Dense concrete blocks			11+	2	11+	2			11+	2	13
Lightweight concrete blocks	11 or	11+		2	11+	2			11+	2	13
Normal ballast concrete *			8+	2	8+	2					10
Expanded metal lathing			11+	2	11+	2					13
Stone & brick walls injected with a DPC							2 or 2	11+			

* Concrete which is exceptionally smooth will require a PVAC agent. Very level surfaces may be plastered with a single 2 mm coat of Thistle Multi-Finish or Board Finish.

Source: British Gypsum Ltd

Metals

Metals commonly used in the construction industry

Name	Symbol	Atomic number*	Description
Aluminium	Al	13	Lightweight, fairly strong metal normally used as an alloy for castings, sheet or extrusions
Brass	–	–	An alloy containing zinc and more than 50% copper. Easily formed, strong and corrosion resistant
Bronze	–	–	An alloy of copper and tin, sometimes combined with other elements. Hard and corrosion-resistant
Copper	Cu	29	A durable, malleable metal, easy to form but hardens quickly when worked and needs annealing. Good electrical and thermal conductivity
Iron	Fe	26	A heavy metal, the fourth most abundant element on the earth's crust. Almost always alloyed with other elements
Lead	Pb	82	The heaviest of the heavy metals, dull blue grey, easily fusible, soft, malleable and very durable
Stainless steel	–	–	An alloy of steel and up to 20% chromium and 10% nickel. Corrosion-resistant but more difficult to fashion than carbon steel
Steel	–	–	An alloy of iron and a small, carefully controlled proportion of carbon, normally less than 1%
Tin	Sn	50	A metal nearly approaching silver in whiteness and lustre, highly malleable and taking a high polish. Used to form alloys such as bronze, pewter etc.
Titanium	Ti	22	Relatively light, strong transitional metal found in beach sands. As strong as steel but 45% lighter, and twice as strong as aluminium but 60% heavier
Zinc	Zn	30	A hard, brittle, bluish white metal, malleable and ductile between 95° and 120°C obtained from various ores. Corrodes 25 times more slowly than steel

*A ratio of the average mass of atoms in a given sample to one-twelfth the mass of a carbon 12 atom.

Bi-metal compatibility

Contact between dissimilar metals should be avoided where possible.

Where contact cannot be avoided and moisture may be present, metals should be separated as shown in the table below.

	Stainless steel	Mild steel	Copper/bronze	Cast iron	Aluminium
Stainless steel	✔	✗	✓	✗	✗
Mild steel	✗	✔	✗	✓	✗
Copper/bronze	✓	✗	✔	✗	✗
Cast iron	✗	✓	✗	✔	✗
Aluminium	✗	✗	✗	✗	✔

✔ = may be in contact; ✓ = may be in contact in dry conditions; ✗ = should not be used in contact.

Metals – some commonly used industrial techniques

aluminium extrusions Aluminium sections made by pushing aluminium through a series of dies until the required intricate shapes are obtained.

brazing A simple, inexpensive way of joining two pieces of hot metal with a film of copper-zinc alloy, a hard solder also referred to as the filler. Brazed steel joints are less strong than welded joints.

cast iron An alloy of iron and carbon containing more than 1.7 per cent carbon (normally 2.4–4 per cent). Components are made by casting from remelted pig (ingot) iron with cast iron and steel scrap. It has low melting point and flows well, and is useful for more intricate shapes than steel or wrought iron.

forging (smithing) The act of hammering metal into shape when it is red-hot, traditionally on an anvil. Formerly referred to iron, but now includes steel, light alloys and non-ferrous metals worked with power hammers, drop stamps and hydraulic forging machines.

shot blasting Cleaning metal surfaces by projecting steel shot with a jet of compressed air. Used as a preparation for painting or metal coating.

sweating Uniting metal parts by holding them together while molten solder flows between them, as in a capillary joint, which is a spigot and socket joint in metal tubing.

tempering Reducing the brittleness of steel by heating and slow cooling (annealing).

welding Joining pieces of metal made plastic or liquid by heat and/or pressure. A filler metal whose melting temperature is the same as that of the metal to be jointed may also be used. Arc welding fuses metals together with an electric arc, often with a consumable metal electrode.

wrought iron Iron with a very low carbon content (0.02–0.03 per cent). It is very malleable and cannot be hardened by tempering. It is soft, rusts less than steel but is more expensive, so it has largely been replaced by mild steel. Used for chains, hooks, bars and decorative ironwork.

Metal finishes

anodizing A protective durable film of oxide formed by dipping an aluminium alloy object into a bath of chromic or sulphuric acid through which an electric current is passed. The film may be coloured with dyes.

chromium plating The electrolytic deposition of chromium onto other metals to produce a very hard, bright finish. When applied to iron or steel, chromium adheres best if a layer of nickel or copper is first deposited.

galvanizing A coating for steel which is quite durable and gives good protection against corrosion in moderate conditions. Components are hot dipped in molten zinc or coated with zinc electrolytically.

powder coating Polyester, polyurethane, acrylic and epoxy plastics sprayed and heat-cured onto metals such as aluminium or galvanized steel for a 50–100-micron thick film. Finished components can also be hot dipped in polyethylene or nylon for a 200–300-micron thick film.

sherardizing A protective coating of zinc on small items such as nuts and bolts, which are rolled for 10 hours in a drum containing sand and zinc dust heated to 380°C. The coating is thin but the zinc diffuses into the steel to form a zinc alloy. It does not peel off, distorts less and is more durable than galvanizing.

stove enamelling Drying of durable enamel paints by heat, normally over 65°C, either in a convection oven or by radiant heat lamps.

vitreous enamelling A glazed surface finish produced by applying powdered glass, dry or suspended in water, which is fused onto metal. This is a true enamel – not enamel paint.

Sources: *The Penguin Dictionary of Building*
Illustrated Dictionary of Building

Roofing

Tiles, slates and shingles
Typical minimum pitches

Bituminous shingles	17°
Cedar shingles	14°
Cedar shakes	20°
Clay tiles – plain	35°
Clay tiles – interlocking	25°
Concrete tiles – plain	35°
Concrete tiles – interlocking	17.5°
Fibre cement slates	20°
Natural slates	22.5°
Stone slates – sandstone and limestone	30°

Note: In areas of high winds and driving rain, these minimum
      pitches may not be advisable.

Roofing slates

Type	Size mm	No./m²	Batten gauge	No./m²	Batten gauge	No./m²	Batten gauge
		50 mm lap		**75 mm lap**		**100 mm lap**	
Princesses	610 × 355	10.06	280	10.55	267	11.05	255
Duchesses	610 × 305	11.71	280	12.28	267	12.86	255
Small Duchesses	560 × 305	12.86	255	13.55	242	14.26	230
Marchionesses	560 × 280	14.01	255	14.76	242	15.53	230
Wide Countesses	510 × 305	14.26	230	15.11	217	15.99	205
Countesses	510 × 255	17.05	230	18.07	217	19.13	205
Wide Viscountesses	460 × 255	19.13	205	20.42	192	21.79	180
Viscountesses	460 × 230	21.21	205	22.64	192	24.15	180
Wide ladies	405 × 255	22.16	177	23.77	165	25.80	152
Ladies	405 × 205	27.56	177	29.56	165	32.09	152

Grade	Thickness	Weight
Best	4 mm	31 kg/m²
Medium Strong	5 mm	35 kg/m²
Heavies	6 mm	40 kg/m²

Source: Alfred McAlpine Slate Ltd

Roofing tiles

	Clay PLAIN	Clay interlocking SINGLE PANTILE	Concrete interlocking DOUBLE ROMAN	Concrete interlocking DOUBLE PANTILE	Concrete interlocking FLAT SLATE
Size mm	265 × 165	380 × 260	418 × 330	420 × 330	430 × 380
Pitch min	35°	22.5°	17.5°	22.5°	17.5°
Pitch max	90°	90°	90°	44°	44°
Headlap min	65 mm	65 mm	75 mm	75 mm	75 mm
Gauge max	100 mm	315 mm	343 mm	345 mm	355 mm
Cover width	165 mm	203 mm	300 mm	296 mm	343 mm
Coverage	60/m²	15.6/m²	9.7/m²	9.8/m²	8.2/m²
Weight @ max gauge	77 kg/m²	42 kg/m²	45 kg/m²	46 kg/m²	51 kg/m²
Weight per 1000	1.27 tonnes	2.69 tonnes	4.69 tonnes	4.7 tonnes	6.24 tonnes

Coverage relates to tiles laid at the maximum gauge. The number of tiles will increase as gauge decreases.
Weights are approximate and relate to tiles laid at maximum gauge. Weights will increase as gauge decreases.

Battens
All tiles may be fixed to 38 × 25 mm battens with supports at maximum 600 mm centres. Battens for plain clay tiles may be reduced to 38 ×19 mm when fixed at 450 mm centres.

Matching accessories
Accessories made in materials to match the tiles include the following: Universal angle ridge tiles, mono ridge tiles, specific angle ridge and hip tiles, ornamental ridge tiles, block-end ridge tiles, cloaked verge tiles, ridge ventilation tiles, ridge gas flue tiles, vent tiles for soil pipes and fan ducts.

uPVC accessories
These include devices for fixing ridge and hip tiles without mortar and for providing under-eaves ventilation and abutment ventilation for lean-to roofs.

Sources: Redland Roofing, Marley Building Materials Ltd

Shingles

Shingles are taper sawn from blocks of western red cedar.

No.1 grade Blue Label is the premium grade for roofs and walls.

Size
The standard size is 400 mm long in varying widths from 75 to 350 mm. The thickness tapers from 3 mm at the head to 10 mm at the butt, or tail, end.

Colour
Reddish-brown, fading to silver-grey when weathered.

Treatment
Shingles are available untreated, tanalized, or with fire retardants. Tanalizing is recommended for external use. Some local authorities may insist on a fire retardant treatment depending on the nature of the location.

Fancy butt
These are shingles with shaped butt ends such as diamond, half round, arrow, fish scale, hexagonal, octagonal etc. These are suitable for pitches over 22°.

Accessories
Pre-formed cedar hip and ridge units 450 mm long, are available which are normally fixed over 150 mm wide strip of F1 roofing felt.

Pitch
14° minimum pitch
14° to 20° maximum recommended gauge   =   95 mm
Over 20° maximum recommended gauge   = 125 mm
Vertical walling maximum recommended gauge = 190 mm

Coverage
Shingles are ordered by the bundle. One bundle covers approximately 1.8 m² @ 100 mm gauge.

Weight

400 mm long @ 95 mm gauge

untreated	8.09 kg/m²
tanalized	16.19 kg/m²
with fire retardant	9.25 kg/m²

Battens

Shingles are fixed to 38 × 19 mm battens with a 6 mm gap between adjacent shingles using silicon bronze nails – two nails to each shingle. Nails are positioned 19 mm in from side edge and 38 mm above the butt line of the course above.

Underlays are not normally recommended except in cases of severe exposure. For warm roofs, counter battens will be required between the shingle batten and the insulation board.

Flashings

Bituminous paint should be applied to metal flashings to avoid contact between shingles and metal and subsequent staining. As an alternative, GRP valleys and flashings may be more suitable.

Source: John Brash & Co Ltd.

Thatch

Water reed

Phragmites communis, grown in British and Continental rivers and marshes. Norfolk reed is the finest thatching material. Water reed thatch is found in East Anglia, the South Coast, S Wales and NE Scotland.

Combed wheat reed

Winter wheat straw, nowadays 'Maris Huntsman', which is passed through a comber. Butt ends are aligned to form face of thatch. Found in the West Country. Sometimes called Devon Reed.

Long wheat straw

Threshed wheat straw, wetted and prepared by hand. Ears and butts are mixed up and a greater length of stem is exposed. Found in central, southern and SE regions of England.

Pitch

Recommended pitch is 50°, minimum 45° and maximum 60°.

Weight

Approximately 34 kg/m².

Netting

This is essential to preserve the thatch from bird and rodent damage. 20 or 22 gauge galvanised wire mesh should last 10 to 15 years.

Sedge

Cladium mariscus is a marsh plant with a rush-like leaf. It is still used in the fens and for ridges to Norfolk reed thatch.

Heather

Calluna vulgaris was once in general use in non-corn growing areas such as Dartmoor and the NE and can still occasionally be seen in Scotland.

Thatching data

	Water reed	Combed wheat reed	Long wheat straw
Length	0.9 m–1.8 m	1.2 m	1.2 m
Coat thickness	300 mm	300–400 mm	400 mm
Coverage	80–100 bundles / 9.3 m² (1 bundle = 300 mm Ø)	1 tonne / 32 m²	1 tonne / 36.6 m²
Lifespan	50–70 years	20–40 years	10–20 years
Battens (38 3 25 mm) centres	255 mm	150–230 mm	150 mm

Sources: *Thatch, A Manual for Owners, Surveyors, Architects and Builders*
The Care and Repair of Thatched Roofs, SPAB

Lead

Lead sheet for the building industry may be either *milled lead sheet* to BS 1178:1982 or *machine cast lead sheet* covered by Agrément Certificates 86/1764 and 91/2662.

Cast lead sheet is also still made by specialist firms using the traditional method of running molten lead over a bed of prepared sand. This is mainly used for replacing old cast lead roofs and ornamental leadwork.

Milled lead sheet is the most commonly available having about 85 per cent of the market. There are no significant differences in the properties, performance or cost between cast and milled lead sheet. Cast lead sheet at first appears slightly darker and less shiny than milled, but is indistinguishable six months after installation.

Thickness
Choice of thickness depends upon use. Additional thickness will cope better with thermal movement, mechanical damage and resist windlift. It will also provide more material for dressing and bossing into shape.

Sizes
Lead sheet is specified by its BS code number or its thickness in millimetres. The range of metric sizes corresponds closely to the former imperial sizes which were expressed in lb/sq.ft. The ends of lead coils may also carry colour markings for easy recognition as shown below.

BS Code no.	Thickness mm	Weight kg/m²	Colour code	Application
3	1.32	14.99	green	soakers
4	1.80	20.41	blue	soakers, flashings
5	2.24	25.40	red	soakers, flashings, gutters, wall and roof coverings
6	2.65	30.05	black	gutters, wall and roof coverings
7	3.15	35.72	white	gutters, roof coverings
8	3.55	40.26	orange	gutters and flat roofs

Sheet size

Lead sheet may be supplied cut to size or as large sheets 2.4 m wide and up to 12 m long.

For flashings, coils are available in code 3, 4 and 5 lead and in widths from 150 to 600 mm in steps of 50 mm, and 3 m or 6 m in length.

Weight

To determine the weight of a piece of lead, multiply the length × width (m) × thickness (mm) × 11.34 = kgs.

Joints
Maximum spacing

BS Code no.	Flat Roof 0-3°		Pitched Roof 10°–60°		Pitched Roof 60°–80°		Wall Cladding	
	Joints with fall	Joints across fall	Joints with fall	Joints across fall	Joints with fall	Joints across fall	Vertical joints	Horizontal joints
4	500	1500	500	1500	500	1500	500	1500
5	600	2000	600	2000	600	2000	600	2000
6	675	2250	675	2250	675	2250	600	2000
7	675	2500	675	2400	675	2250	650	2250
8	750	3000	750	2500	750	2250	700	2250

Parapet and Tapered Gutters

BS Code no.	maximum spacing of drips mm	maximum overall girth mm
4	1500	750
5	2000	800
6	2250	850
7	2700	900
8	3000	1000

Lead – continued

Flashings

To ensure long life flashings should never exceed 1.0 m in length for code 3 lead and 1.5 m in length for codes 4 and 5. Flashings should lap a minimum of 100 mm horizontally. Vertical laps should be a minimum as shown below.

Roof pitch	Lap mm	Roof pitch	Lap mm
11°	359	40°	115
15°	290	50°	100
20°	220	60°	85
30°	150	90°	75

DPCs

Code 4 lead sheet is suitable for most DPCs. This may be increased to code 5 where a 50 mm cavity is exceeded.

Lead DPCs should be covered both sides with bituminous paint to avoid the risk of corrosion from free alkali in fresh Portland cement.

Condensation

In well heated buildings, warm moist air may filter through the roof structure and condense on the underside of the lead covering, leading in the long term to serious corrosion. Ensure that there is ventilation between the timber decking supporting the lead and any insulation.

Corrosion

Lead may be used in close contact with copper, zinc, iron and aluminium. It may be attacked by organic acids from hardwoods and cedar shingles.

Sources: Lead Sheet Association
Lead Development Association
Midland Lead Manufacturers Ltd

Copper roofing

Copper is classified as a noble material. It has a long life (75–100 years), is corrosion resistant and is lightweight and workable. It is more resistant to creep on vertical surfaces than lead and can cover flat or curved surfaces.

Copper for roofing, flashings and DPCs should conform to BS 2870 : 1980.

Copper strip = 0.15 to 10 mm thickness, of any width and not cut to length. It is usually supplied in 50 kg coils. It is cheaper than sheet.

Copper sheet = 0.15 to 10 mm thick flat material of exact length and over 450 mm wide.

Copper foil   = 0.15 mm thick or less.

Normal roofing thickness is 0.6 mm; 0.45 mm is now considered sub-standard. 0.7 mm is used for pre-patinated copper sheet and for sites with exposure to high winds.

Pre-patinated copper was first used in Germany in the late 1980s. 0.7 mm thick copper sheets have a chemically induced copper chloride patina. This produces the blue/green appearance which is more even than the streaky appearance of some naturally induced patinas. The sheet size is limited to 3 m in length so is not suited for long strip roofing.

Longstrip copper roofing

This method was introduced to the UK from the Continent in 1957. Factory or site formed copper trays are attached to a fully supporting deck with standing seams or roll joints. The copper used has a harder temper and special expansion clips at seams allow longitudinal movement. The main advantage is absence of cross joints on sloping roofs and drips on flat roofs, which saves labour and reduces cost. Suitable for pitches from 6° to 90°.

Bay size = 525 mm centres × 10.0 m. In exposed sites bay widths should be reduced to 375 mm centres.

After 10 m in length, 50 mm high drips should be placed across fall.

Weight
0.6 mm @ 525 mm centres = 5.7 kg/m²

Falls
Minimum fall for any copper roof 1 : 60 (17 mm in 1 metre)
Minimum fall for copper gutters   1 : 80 (12 mm in 1 metre)

Parapet gutters
Maximum length of any one sheet is 1.8 m. Thereafter 50 mm minimum deep drips should be introduced. Continuous dripping of rainwater from tiled or slated roofs may perforate gutter linings. Sacrificial strips should be placed in gutters and replaced when worn.

Step flashing
Maximum 1.8 m long with welted joints. Single step flashings, with each end overlapping 75 mm, may be easier to repair where small areas corrode.

Laying

Lay with underfelt of impregnated flax felt with ventilation to space or voids under decking to avoid condensation. Fixings are copper clips (cleats) secured by copper nails or brass screws to decking. Avoid any use of soft solder to prevent electrolytic action. Use mastic between apron flashings and pipes.

DPCs

Copper is highly suitable for DPCs as it is flexible and not attacked by cement mortar. Joints should overlap 100 mm.

Corrosion

Copper can be corroded by sulphur dioxide from chimneys unless stacks rise well clear of roof. Copper will corrode when in contact with damp wood impregnated with some fire retardants and from the run-off from western red cedar cladding. Ammonia (from cats' urine) may cause cracking. Copper will corrode aluminium, zinc and steel if in direct contact or indirect contact from water run-off. Copper may leave green stains on masonry.

Patina

This takes 5–20 years to form, depending on location. It is a thin, insoluble layer of copper salts which protects the underlying material from atmospheric attacks. It is generally green but may look buff or black in soot–laden air.

Traditional copper roofing

There are two traditional methods of copper roofing:

Batten rolls
40 mm high shaped wooden rolls are laid parallel to bay slope. Bay sheets are turned up sides of roll and covered with copper capping strip. Ridge rolls are 80 mm high. Suitable for flat and pitched roofs.

Bay size = 500 mm centres $\times$ 1.8 m.

Standing seams
These are suitable for side joints on roofs which are not subject to foot traffic, and may be used for roofs over 6°. The seams are double welted joints 20–25 mm high.

Bay size = 525 mm centres $\times$ 1.8 m.

Cross joints
At right angles to wood rolls or standing seams. They should be *double* lock cross welts. Above 45° pitch, *single* lock cross welts may be used. Stagger cross joints in adjacent bays to avoid too much metal at seams. On flat roofs, drips 65 mm deep should be introduced at maximum 3 m centres (see Falls above).

Maximum sheet sizes
Sheet sizes should not exceed 1.3 m^2, reduced to 1.10 m^2 where 0.45 mm thick sheet is used.

Sources: Copper Development Association
Broderick Structures Ltd

Aluminium roofing

Aluminium is strong but lightweight and malleable, has a long life and low maintenance. A high proportion of recycled material is used in its manufacture.

The most readily available recommended roofing grade is 1050A, which is 99.5 per cent pure aluminium, with H2 temper. 0 temper (fully soft) is suitable for flashings or intricate shaping. See CP 143 Part 15 1973 (1986) for application.

Aluminium is normally available in 'mill finish' which weathers to a matt grey, staying light in unpolluted areas but darkening in industrial atmospheres. It can also be supplied with a factory applied PVF2 paint in a limited range of colours. Avoid dark, heat-absorbing shades.

Thickness
0.8 mm is recommended roofing gauge.

Sheet width
450 mm standard.

Bay width
Typically 380 mm; longstrip typically 525 mm; batten roll typically 390 mm.

Bay length
Traditional standing seam - 3 m maximum rising to 6 m for roofs pitched above 10°.
Longstrip – 10 m maximum is typical but is available up to 50 m.

Weight
0.8 mm @ 525 mm centres = 2.6 kg/m^2.

Falls
Minimum 1 : 60.

Fixings
All aluminium, including adjacent flashings and gutters.

Aluminium roofing – continued

Joints
Traditional standing seam, longstrip standing seam and batten roll.

Corrosion
Aluminium is corroded by contact with brass and copper. Direct contact with and run-off from lead should be protected with a barrier of bituminous paint. Zinc is sacrificial to aluminium which can lead to premature failure of zinc coated steel fixings. Avoid contact with wood preservatives and acidic timbers by the use of polythene barrier membranes.

Source: Hoogovens Aluminium Building Systems Ltd

Zinc roofing

Zinc is versatile, ductile, economical, has good resistance to atmospheric corrosion and is suitable for marine locations.

During the 1960s zinc alloys replaced commercial zinc for roofing. The material is 99.9 per cent pure zinc alloyed with titanium and copper. There are two types, A and B, which should conform to BS 6561 : 1985. For installation see CP 143 Part 5 : 1964.

Type A
Fine, even grain structure with good resistance to creep and thermal movement. Primarily used for roofing. Available in sheets and coils.

Recommended roofing thicknesses are 0.65, 0.70 and 0.80 mm.

Typical sheet size: 2438 × 914 mm (8′ × 3′) in thicknesses from 0.50 to 1.0 mm.

Typical coil size: 500, 610, 686, 914 and 1000 mm widths up to 21 m long.

Zinc can also be supplied pre-patinated in 0.70 mm thickness with blue-grey colour.

Type B

Rolled to a soft temper and used mainly for flashings – also for coverings to small balconies, canopies, dormer windows and for DPCs. Available in coils.

Typical coil size: 150, 240, 300, 480 and 600 mm widths by 10 m long.

Bay sizes

From 500 to 900 mm.
Typical longstrip bay: 525 mm centres with standing seam and 540 mm centres with batten roll.
Maximum bay length: 10 m.

Weight

0.7 mm @ 525 mm centres = 5.1 kg/m^2.

Falls

Minimum 3° but ponding may occur so 7° is the minimum recommended pitch, particularly for longer bays.

Side joints

Standing seam and batten roll – similar to copper.

Cross joints

Between 3° and 10° – 75 mm high drips.
Between 10° and 25° – single lock welt with additional soldered undercloak.
Between 25° and 90° – single lock welt with 25 mm undercloak and 30 mm overcloak.

Fixings

Nails   = galvanized steel or SS.
Screws   = galvanized or zinc anodized steel or SS.
Clips   = zinc to match roofing type.
Solder   = 60 : 40 lead/tin alloy.
Liquid flux = Bakers fluid or killed spirits of salt.

Zinc roofing – continued

Corrosion
Zinc is non-staining and contact is possible with iron, steel, aluminium, lead and stainless steel. Run-off from unprotected iron and steel may cause staining but no harm. Zinc should not be used directly or indirectly from run-off with copper which will cause corrosion. Zinc may be corroded by contact with western red cedar, oak, sweet chestnut, certain fire retardants and soluble salts in walling materials.

Sources: Zinc Development Association
Metra Non-Ferrous Metals Ltd

Stainless steel roofing

Stainless steel is lightweight, can be pre-formed, has a low co-efficient of expansion, high tensile strength, can be worked at any time of year, is resistant to corrosion attack by condensation, and can match and be used alongside lead. Stainless steel for roofing should conform to BS 1449 Part 2: 1983.

There are two grades normally used for roofing:

Type 304: (Austenitic) Suitable for most UK situations but *not* within 15 miles of the sea or in aggressively industrial atmospheres – 0.38 mm thick.

Type 316: (Austenitic Molybdenum)   Highest grade which is now the standard grade recommended, suitable for all atmospheres – 0.4 mm thick.

Stainless steel is naturally reflective but low reflectivity is achieved by:

Mechanical rolling   -   Rolling sheets under pressure through a set of engraving tools.

Terne coating   -   Hot dipping into lead/tin alloy which weathers to form a mid-grey patina similar to lead.

Sheet width
Coils vary typically 500 mm and 650 mm wide but sometimes still imperial 457 mm (18″) and 508 mm (20″).

Bay width
385 mm and 435 mm centres with standing seams,
425 mm and 450 mm centres with batten rolls.

Bay length
Maximum is normally 9 m but is available up to 15 m.
Over 3 m expansion clips must be used.

Weight
0.4 mm @ 435 mm centres = 4 kg/m^2.

Falls
Minimum 5° up to 90°. 9° minimum recommended for exposed sites.

Joints
Traditional standing seam, longstrip standing seam and batten roll.
Cross joints between   5° and 12° should be lap lock welt.
Cross joints between 13° and 20° double lock welt.
Cross joints between 21° and 90° single lock welt.

Fixings
Stainless steel throughout for all clips, nails and screws.

Corrosion
Resistant to most chemicals. Hydrochloric acid, used to clean masonry, will cause corrosion. Contact with copper may cause staining but otherwise no harm. Migrant rust marks can occur from the sparks of carbon steel cutting/grinding machines. It is not attacked by cement alkalis, acids in timber or run-off from lichens.

Sources: Broderick Structures Ltd
            Lee Steel Strip Ltd

Profiled metal sheet

Profiled metal sheet may be used for both roofing and cladding. Profiling thin metal sheet gives stiffness, providing greater strength. The deeper the profile, the stronger the sheet and greater the span. Bolder profiles cast darker shadows and may therefore be preferred aesthetically. Coated steel is lowest in cost but limited in life to the durability of the finish. Aluminium develops its own protective film but is less resistant to impact. Cladding to lower parts of buildings should be protected by guard rails or other devices. Avoid complex building shapes to simplify detailing. Profiled sheets are quick to erect, dismantle and repair. The most common profile is trapezoidal.

Curved profiled sheet

Radiused corners may be achieved by using crimped profiled sheets. Typical minimum external radius is 370 mm. Non-crimped profiled sheets may be pre-formed to a minimum radius of 3 m which may be useful for barrel vaulting. Ordinary profiled sheets may be curved slightly on site. As a rule of thumb, the depth of the trough in mm gives the maximum curve in metres. Mitred units are available for both internal and external corners with flashings purpose-made to match.

Thickness

0.5 to 1.5 mm.

Sheet width

500 to 1000 mm.

Trough depth

20 to 70 mm for roofing – depths up to 120 mm are normally used for structural decking.

Weight

0.9 mm - 3.7 kg/m^2.

Falls
1.5° (1 : 40) minimum.

Finishes
Hot dip galvanizing, stove and vitreous enamelling, terne coating, mill finish aluminium, PVC and PVF2 colour coatings, composite bitumen mineral fibres etc.

Source: Rigidal Industries Ltd

Flat roofs – non-metallic

A flat roof is defined as having a fall not greater than 10° (1 : 6). BS 6229 : 1982 *Flat roofs with continuously supported coverings* deals with design principles.

Design considerations
A flat roof must be *structurally rigid*, and have substantial and *continuous support* for the membrane, provision for *movement joints, rainwater* disposal, *thermal* design, *condensation* avoidance, *wind* resistance, consideration for roof *penetrations* and appropriate *protection* of the membrane.

Rainwater
Flat roofs should have a minimum fall of 1 : 80. However, to allow for construction tolerances, a design fall of minimum 1 : 50 is desirable.

The fail safe drainage of flat roofs is to fall to external gutters, less good is via scuppers in parapet walls to external RWPs.

Where internal RWPs are planned, position them away from parapet edges where debris will collect and it is difficult to make a watertight seal. Ideally they should be sited at points of maximum deflection.

Avoid only one outlet in a contained roof as this may block, causing water to rise above upstands and cause damage from water penetration or from overloading the structure.

Where roofs meet walls, upstands must be a minimum of 150 mm high. They should be protected with lead, copper or super purity aluminium flashing tucked 30 mm minimum into the wall.

Condensation
Condensation is the major cause of failure leading to blistering and decay. Moisture laden rooms below flat roofs should have good ventilation, extra insulation and vapour control layers which can withstand accidental damage during construction.

Avoid thermal bridges which can result in localized condensation.

Wind
All layers must be properly secured to substrate to resist wind uplift.

Penetration
Keep roof penetration to a minimum. Where available, use proprietary components such as flanged roof outlets and sleeves for cables.

Sunlight
Ultra-violet light will damage bituminous felts, asphalts and some single ply materials. They should be protected with a layer of stone chippings bonded in hot bitumen or a cold bitumen solution. Alternatively, mineral reinforced cement tiles or glass reinforced concrete tiles laid in a thick coating of hot bitumen will provide a good surface for pedestrian traffic.

25 mm thick concrete pavings provide a more stable walking surface and should be bedded on proprietary plastic corner supports which have the advantage of making up irregularities of level and the separation of the promenade surface from the membrane with rapid drainage of surface water.

Light coloured top surfaces and reflective paints reflect the sun's energy but provide only limited protection against damage from ultra-violet light.

Vapour control layer

Proprietary felts incorporating aluminium foil when laid fully supported are the best type of vapour control layer. They are essential in cold and warm roofs but are not required in inverted warm roofs. Over profiled metal decking, two layers bonded together may be required because of lack of continuous support.

Mastic asphalt

Asphalt is a blend of fine and coarse aggregates bonded with bitumen. The ingredients are heated and blended in batches and either delivered hot in bulk or cast into blocks for re-heating on site.

Roofing grade asphalts are described in BS 6925 : 1988 and BS 6577. For specification and application of asphalt roofing see CP 144 : Part 4 : 1970.

Recent developments include the addition of polymers which claim to make the material more flexible. These are not yet covered by a British Standard.

Asphalt is laid over a *separating layer* of inodorous black felt to BS 747 type 4A(i), and laid in two layers of a combined thickness of 20 mm. Application in two layers allows the joints to be staggered. The final surface is trowelled to produce a bitumen rich layer which is then dressed with fine sand to mask surface crazing in cold weather. This should then be protected with chippings or pavings. See **Sunlight** above.

Bituminous felt

Formerly roofing felts were made of rag, asbestos or glass fibre cores coated with bitumen. Over the last 15 years or so, most felts have been made with cores of polyester fleece which give increased stress resistance. BS 747 : 1977 (1986) has been amended to include this type. See CP 144 Part 3 for specification and application.

Newer felts are often made with polymer modified bitumen producing greater flexibility and better performance.

Roofing felts are applied in two or more layers, bonded in hot bitumen, and bonded by gas torch or by means of a self-adhesive layer incorporated onto one side of the felt.

First layer felts, often perforated, bind directly to the substrate.

Intermediate felts are smooth faced for full bonding.

Top layer felts may have the top surface prepared for site-applied protection such as chippings.

Cap sheet felts, designed to be left exposed without further protection, incorporate a surface coating of mineral chippings or metal foil.

Single ply membranes

Developed in Europe and the USA, these are now increasingly available in the UK (as yet not covered by a British Standard), and are made of plastics, synthetic rubber-based materials and some modified bitumen materials.

There are thermoset and thermoplastic type plastics:

Thermoset includes all synthetic rubbers. These have fixed molecular structures which cannot be reshaped by heat or solvents and are joined by adhesives.

Thermoplastic materials are those whose molecular structure is not permanently set and welds may be formed by heat or solvents. Welding is more satisfactory than glueing but requires greater skill.

Sheets may be attached mechanically to the substrate with screw fasteners and disc washers set in seams or by welding membrane to disc washers fixed to substrate. On inverted warm roofs, the membrane is loose laid and ballasted.

Some single ply materials may not be used in conjunction with expanded polystyrene insulation.

Sources: *Flat Roofing – A Guide to Good Practice*

Glass

Clear float glass   A high quality annealed glass, transparent and free from distortion with a bright polished surface. Can be cut to order, toughened, laminated, acid-etched, sand-blasted, bevelled, screen printed, decorated with lead and coloured film and silvered for mirrors.

Thicknesses	2, 3, 4, 5, 6, 8, 10, 12, 15, 19 and 25 mm
Standard sizes	From 920 × 2140 to 3210 × 6000 mm
Weight	4 mm 10 kg/m²; 6 mm 15 kg/m²;
	8 mm 20 kg/m²; 10 mm 25 kg/m²

Textured glass   Rolled cast glass, one surface of which has a specific surface treatment to form textures including rough cast, ribs, dots, linear patterns and floral decorations. They vary in obscuration which is rated from 1 (least) to 5 (most). Can be toughened or laminated.

Thicknesses	4 mm and 6 mm
Maximum size	1320 × 2140 mm

Screen printed glass   Ceramic ink designs printed onto float glass which is subsequently heated to give a durable finish suitable for internal and external use. White ink is most commonly used – other colours to order, limited to one colour per sheet of glass. Typical standard designs are small 2 and 3.5 mm Ø dots and 10 mm stripes. Screen printing can provide aesthetic and technical control of heat and light transmission and privacy. Can be applied to glasses 6 to 12 mm thick.

Maximum printed area 1800 × 3600 mm

Glass for mirrors   Specially selected clear or body tinted float glass coated on the back with silver nitrate, copper and two coats stove enamelled paint.

Thicknesses	3, 4 and 6 mm
Maximum size	3210 × 6000 mm

Surveillance mirrors   Clear float or laminated clear float glass with silver reflecting coating providing undetected surveillance and high quality one-way vision to achieve complete privacy. Coating must be fixed on the observer's side. Suitable for internal use.

Thicknesses   6 mm clear float or 6.4 mm laminated clear float
Maximum size   2100 × 3210 mm

Fire resistant glass

Pilkingtons make four fire resisting glasses: two grades of wired glass and two grades of laminated glass. The former were known as 'Georgian' wired glass. As a cost guide, the price rises in the following order: Pyroshield, Pyroshield Safety, Pyrodur, Pyrostop.

Pyroshield   A glass with a 13 mm square steel mesh sandwiched in its centre during manufacture. When exposed to fire, the glass fractures but is held in place by the wire mesh. Because of the mesh the glass is instantly recognizable as a fire resistant glass. It is suitable for fire doors and windows and for overhead or inclined glazing where the risk to people from falling broken glass needs to be avoided. It has 80 per cent light transmittance and can be laminated to other glass. Available in clear and textured forms. Readily available and easily cut.

Fire ratings   Designated Class Ext AA and classified as
                        Class O for spread of flame
                        Integrity 30 minutes minimum
Pyroshield Clear   6 mm thick, 1980 × 3300 mm maximum size
Pyroshield Texture 7 mm thick, 1980 × 3700 mm maximum size
Weight   6 mm thick, 16.6 kg/m^2
                     7 mm thick, 16.7 kg/m^2

Pyroshield Safety   A fire and impact safety glass combining good fire resistance with a consistent level of impact safety. It is the only monolithic wired glass to meet the requirements of Part N and Part B of the Building Regulations. Similar in appearance to the Pyroshield glasses except that the gauge of the wire in the mesh is thicker. It has 80 per cent light transmittance and is available in clear and textured forms.

Fire ratings	Designated Ext AA and classified Class O for surface spread of flame Integrity 30 minutes minimum, higher depending on glazing method
Impact Rating	Class C to BS 6206 : 1981
Pyroshield Safety Clear	6 mm thick, 1985 × 3300 mm maximum size
Pyroshield Safety Texture	7 mm thick, 1985 × 3500 mm maximum size
Weight	6 mm thick, 16.6 kg/m^2 7 mm thick, 16.7 kg/m^2

Pyrodur   A glass made up of three layers of float glass with one intumescent and one ultra-violet interlayer. It can be used externally and internally. Suitable for fire doors and screens where a non-insulating glass is acceptable. With its 87 per cent light transmittance it provides totally clear and unobstructed vision. On exposure to fire the intumescent layer turns opaque. Supplied cut to size.

Fire ratings	Integrity 30 minutes; insulation 16 minutes
Impact Rating	Class B to BS 6206 : 1981
Size	10 mm thick, 1400 × 2000 mm maximum size tested
Weight	25 kg/m^2

Fire resistant glass – continued

Pyrostop   Float glass with intumescent layers as follows:

15 mm – Four layers of glass with three intumescent layers
21 mm – Five layers of glass with four intumescent layers
44 mm – 15 mm and 21 mm Pyrostop sheets double glazed with 8 mm space bar
50 mm – Two 21 mm Pyrostop sheets double glazed with 8 mm space bar

These are suitable for internal use only. An external grade is available which consists of the above products with an additional glass layer and UV filter interlayer laminated onto the outside face of the glazing. Up to 88 per cent light transmittance. May be laminated to other glasses. Supplied cut to size.

Fire ratings	15 mm = 60 minutes integrity; 30 minutes insulation
	21 mm = 60 minutes integrity; 60 minutes insulation
Impact rating	Class B to BS 6206 : 1981
Sizes	15 mm, 1600 × 2000 mm maximum size tested
	21 mm, 1600 × 2200 mm maximum size tested
Weight	15 mm = 36 kg/m^2
	21 mm = 48 kg/m^2

Source: Pilkington United Kingdom Ltd

Safety glass

Requirement N1 of the Building Regulations concerns glazing in critical locations. In such places glass should either (1) break safely, (2) be robust, i.e. adequately thick, or (3) be permanently protected. See p. 190.

Glass which is deemed to break safely must conform to BS 6206 : 1981.

Toughened and laminated glass can meet these requirements.

Toughened glass

Toughened glass is normal annealed glass subjected to heating and rapid cooling. This produces high compression in the surface and compensating tension in the core. It is about 4–5 times stronger than annealed glass and is highly resistant to thermal shock. When it breaks it shatters into relatively harmless pieces. It *cannot* be cut, drilled or edgeworked after toughening. Any such work must be done prior to toughening. The 'strain' pattern of toughening, i.e. horizontal bands about 275 mm apart, may be noticed in bright sunlight. Can be made to incorporate designs for decoration or obscuration.

Thicknesses   4 to 19 mm
Maximum sizes 2550 × 1550 mm; 2720 × 1270 mm
Minimum size   305 × 200 mm

Laminated glass

Laminated glass is made from two or more panes of various glasses with interlayers of polyvinyl butyral bonded between each pane. Normal thickness is 3 ply, i.e. two panes of glass and one interlayer. On impact the glass adheres to interlayers.

Unlike toughened glass it can be cut, drilled and edgeworked after manufacture. Screen printed designs can be incorporated during manufacture.

Anti-Bandit glasses have thicker interlayers and are designed to resist manual attack.

Bullet Resistant glasses are made from thicknesses from 20 mm up. They are designed to meet specific bullets from 9 mm automatics up to 5.56 mm military rifles. They can also provide protection against bomb blast.

Thicknesses   From 4.4 mm to 45 mm
Maximum size   3200 × 2000 mm depending on glass used

Environmental control glasses

Environmental control glasses are divided into two types – Solar Control glasses and Low Emissivity (Low E) glasses.

Solar Control glass is used primarily where the need to limit solar heat gain is greatest as in warm climates, and Low E glasses are more appropriate for cool climates where good heat insulation is paramount.

By choosing a combination of these glasses in double glazing, even greater environmental control can be achieved.

As a guide to cost the price of these glasses rises in roughly the following order: Antisun, Reflectafloat, Eclipse, Suncool Classic & Low Reflection, Pilkington K, Kappafloat, Suncool High Performance.

All the glasses, with the exception of Kappafloat, can be supplied in toughened or laminated form. This should be specified where glass may be thermally at risk or where required by the Building Regulations for glazing in hazardous areas. See p. 190.

Solar control glass

Antisun float glasses are body tinted grey, bronze, blue or green throughout their thickness and offer low to medium solar control in a relatively economic way. They have very low reflection and may be used for single and double glazing.

Thicknesses	Blue 6 mm; green 4,6 and 10 mm; bronze and grey 4, 6, 10 and 12 mm
Maximum sizes	Blue 3300 × 2440 mm; green, bronze and grey 3210 × 6000 mm

Eclipse glasses are a range of reflective medium performance solar control glasses available with blue/green, bronze, grey or silver durable coatings. These coatings may be glazed to the exterior or interior of buildings providing different colour reflections. May be single or double glazed.

Thickness	6 mm
Maximum size	3300 × 5180 mm

Reflectafloat glass is a medium performance reflective solar control glass with a bright silver appearance which can be used to achieve privacy. May be single or double glazed.

Thickness	6 mm
Maximum size	3000 × 5100 mm

Suncool Classic   A range of high performance reflective solar control float glasses with durable coatings applied to clear or tinted substrates. In reflection the colours are blue, silver, bronze, green or grey. They are excellent at reducing solar heat transmittance. May be single or double glazed.

Thicknesses	6 mm as standard; 10 and 12 mm to special order
Maximum size	From 2000 × 3000 mm to 2500 × 3600 mm depending on colour and type

Suncool Low Reflection   Glasses with high solar control and very low external reflection which is useful where dazzle could be a problem. Available in green, blue, bronze and grey. May be single or double glazed.

Thickness	6 mm
Maximum size	Green, bronze and grey 3500 × 2000 mm; blue 3000 × 2000 mm

Suncool High Performance   This range combines high light transmission and high solar control performance with the highest level of thermal insulation. Only suitable for double glazing. The colours – silver, gold, green, blue, bronze, grey, neutral – vary in reflectivity.

Thicknesses   6 mm as standard; 10 and 12 mm to special order
Maximum unit size 2400 × 3600 mm approximately

Low emissivity glass (Low E)

Pilkington K   A float glass with a transparent low emissivity coating applied to one surface during manufacture. This coating allows heat from the sun to enter the building but significantly reduces heat loss from inside the building, thus providing good thermal insulation and reducing condensation and cold down-draughts. It looks almost the same as clear float glass and has high light transmission. Normally used as an inner pane of double glazing with the coating facing into the cavity. It can also be used as single glazing in the inner sash of secondary double glazing.

Thicknesses   4 and 6 mm
Maximum size   3210 × 6000 mm

Kappafloat   was the predecessor of *Pilkington K* and has many of the properties described above with a slightly higher U-value. The coating is applied *after* the float glass is manufactured and therefore cannot be toughened or laminated. However, Kappafloat coatings may be applied to toughened or laminated glass. Not suitable for single glazing.

Thicknesses   6, 8 and 10 mm
Maximum size   6 mm   – 3600 × 2200 mm
                     8 and 10 mm – 3210 × 2100 mm

Environmental control glass properties

Examples of double glazed units with a second pane of 6 mm float glass and 12 mm airgap compared with double glazed units with two panes of clear float glass.

		Maximum* unit sizes annealed / toughened mm	Light % trans-mittance	Light % reflect-tance	Solar radiant heat % trans-mittance	Shading co-efficient	U-Value W/m²K
Solar control glass	Clear Float 6 mm	2400 × 4000 2000 × 4000	76	14	72	0.82	2.8
	Antisun 6 mm Bronze	2400 × 4000 2000 × 4000	44	7	49	0.57	2.8
	Eclipse 6 mm clear	2400 × 4000 2000 × 4000	39	42	49	0.56	2.8
	Reflectafloat 6 mm 33/53 silver	2000 × 4000 2000 × 3300	30	44	44	0.50	2.8
	Suncool Classic 6 mm 20/34	2400 × 3600 2000 × 3500	18	23	25	0.29	2.5
	Suncool Low Reflection 6 mm 21/42 grey	2100 × 3210 2000 × 3500	19	5	29	0.34	2.6
	Suncool High Performance 6 mm neutral	2400 × 3600 2000 × 3500	52	9	44	0.50	1.7
Low E glass	Pilkington K 6 mm	2400 × 4000 2000 × 4000	73	16	69	0.79	1.9
	Kappafloat 6 mm neutral	2200 × 3600 2000 × 3600	74	12	62	0.72	1.8

* Maximum sizes are for guidance only and are **not** recommended glazing sizes. Upper figure is for annealed glass, lower figure for toughened glass.

Screen glasses

A range of laminated glasses designed to provide impact safety together with different environmental performance characteristics. Available in varying thicknesses and combinations of annealed, toughened and heat strengthened glass which can be single or double glazed.

Audioscreen   Designed for situations where noise levels need to be reduced. Annealed or toughened laminates with sound insulation ratings from 37 to 45 db for internal or external use.

Thicknesses   7, 9, 11 and 17 mm
Maximum size   2100 × 3500 mm

Lightscreen   A range of light diffusing translucent white laminates for internal and external use. Diffuses light more evenly across insides of buildings. Reduces glare and can provide privacy. Suitable for museums, art galleries and roof glazing where reduction of direct glare and sunlight may be beneficial. Two standard grades, TW70 and TW40 giving 70 per cent and 40 per cent light transmission respectively.

Thickness   8 mm
Maximum size   2100 × 3500 mm

UV screen   will reduce or eliminate UV radiation whilst transmitting a good deal of light. Useful for situations where fabrics or works of art may be damaged by ultra-violet light. Three grades available, UV0, UV3 and UV20.

Thickness   8 mm
Maximum size   2100 × 3500 mm

Safety screen   Screens made up of non-coated glasses in annealed, toughened or heat strengthened form incorporated into 3 or 5 ply laminates with a total thickness not exceeding 25 mm. All satisfy the requirements of BS 6208 : 1981 as a safety glass. Together with high impact resistance, they will withstand high wind loads. Patterned and body tinted glasses can be used. Suitable for low level safety glazing, roof glazing and swimming pools. All manufactured to size.

Thicknesses   7, 8, 9, 10, 11 and 17 mm

Maximum size   2100 × 3500 mm float
                  2140 × 1320 mm patterned

Source: Pilkington United Kingdom Ltd

Glass blocks

Glass blocks are now no longer made in the UK but are imported from Germany and Italy. Metric and imperial sizes are made, imperial being used not only for new work but also for renovation and the US market.

Metric sizes	115 × 115 × 80 mm; 190 × 190 × 80 and 100 mm; 240 × 240 × 80 mm; 240 × 115 × 80 mm; 300 × 300 × 100 mm.
Imperial sizes	6″ × 6″ × 3⅛″ and 4″; 8″ × 8″ × 3⅛″ and 4″; 8″ × 4″ × 3⅛″ and 4″; 8″ × 6″ × 3⅛″.
Colours	Clear as standard; bronze, blue, turquoise, pink, green, grey
Patterns	Waves, chequers, ribs, sand blasted, etc.
Specials	Fixed louvre ventilator (190 mm sq), corner blocks, bullet resistant, end blocks with one side mitred for unframed edges to free standing panels.
Radii	Minimum internal radii for curved walls for block widths as follows : 115 mm = 650 mm; 6″(146 mm) = 1200 mm; 190 mm =1800 mm; 240 mm = 3700 mm
Weight	80 mm thick = 100 kg/m^2, 100 mm thick = 125 kg/m^2
U-values	80 mm thick = 2.9 W/m^{2}K; 100 mm thick = 2.5 W/m^{2}K
Light transmission	Clear blocks = 80%; bronze = 60% approx.
Fire rating	Class O – fixing systems for both half-hour and one-hour fire rating
Sound insulation	37–42 db over 100–3150 Hz

Structure   Glass blocks are self-supporting but not load bearing.

Mortar jointed panels should not exceed 6 m (3 m for fire resisting panels) in any direction, nor be greater than 18.5 m².

Fixing   Glass blocks are generally fixed on site but can be prefabricated in panels. The normal joint is 10 mm but can be wider to suit dimensional requirements.

Blocks are laid in wet mortar with 6 or 8 mm Ø SS reinforcing bars fixed horizontally or vertically, normally about every other block. Joints are then pointed up.

Silicone sealants are applied at perimeters.

Intumescent mastics are applied to internal and external perimeter joints for fire resisting panels.

Source: Luxcrete Ltd

Timber

Timber sustainability

The world's forests are under threat from illegal logging, clearance for agricultural expansion and poor management. However, timber can be a most energy efficient material. A tree grows to maturity in the space of one human lifetime, whereas stocks of oil, fossil fuels and minerals take millennia to produce and are therefore not *renewable* resources. The growth of trees fixes carbon and actually reduces the amount of CO_2 in the atmosphere. This advantage is only realised in well-managed forests where trees are replaced. Timber has seven times less embodied energy (by weight) than that of steel and 29 times less than aluminium, as it needs no heat for manufacture and extraction is relatively cheap compared to mining. How do architects obtain information from suppliers as to whether timber comes from renewable resources?

The **Forest Stewardship Council** (FSC) was founded in 1993 and is an international non-profit and non-governmental organization. It is an association of environmental and social groups, timber trade organizations and forestry professionals from around the world. Its objectives are to provide independent certifiers of forest products and to provide consumers with reliable information about these materials.

It evaluates, accredits and monitors timber all round the world, whether it is tropical, temperate or boreal (northern). Certification is the process of inspecting forests to check they are being managed according to an agreed set of principles and criteria. These include recognition of indigenous people's rights, long-term economic viability, protection of biodiversity, conservation of ancient natural woodland, responsible management and regular monitoring. Timber from FSC-endorsed forests will be covered by a 'chain-of-custody-certificate'.

Consult the FSC for their lists of suppliers and certified timber and wood products.

Sources: Forest Stewardship Council, Friends of the Earth Forests Forever, *The Culture of Timber*

Timber nomenclature

'Softwood' and 'Hardwood' are botanical terms and do not necessarily reflect the density of the species. Softwoods are coniferous (cone-bearing) trees of northern climates and are relatively soft with the exception of Pitch Pine and Yew (670 kg/m^3). Hardwoods are deciduous trees and vary enormously in density from Balsa (110 kg/m^3) to Lignum Vitae (1250 kg/m^3).

Moisture

Moisture content of newly-felled trees can be 60 per cent and higher. Air drying will reduce the moisture content to approximately 18 per cent. Further kiln drying can reduce the moisture content to six per cent.

Recommended average moisture content for timbers from BS 1186 : Part 1

External joinery		16°
Internal joinery	Buildings with intermittent heating	15°
	Buildings with continuous heating from 12–16°C	12°
	Buildings with continuous heating from 20–24°C	10°

Durability

This relates to fungal decay. It is expressed in the five durability classes described below and numbered in the tables on pp.254–5 and 256–8. Sapwood of all species is non-durable and should not be used in exposed situations without preservative treatment.

1 =	very durable	- more than 25 years
2 =	durable	- 15–25 years
3 =	moderately durable	- 10–15 years
4 =	non-durable	- 5–10 years
5 =	perishable	- less than 5 years

Classes of timber for joinery

These are effectively appearance classes and make no reference to durability and workability, stability or surface absorbency. The four classes characterize the quality of timber and moisture content after machining, at the time it is supplied to the first purchaser. They describe the presence (or absence) of knots, splits, resin pockets, sapwood, wane, straightness of grain, exposed pith, rot, joints (in long timbers), plugs or filler (of knots).

Class CSH   Clear softwood and hardwood – i.e. free from knots or other surface defects. Difficult to obtain in softwoods with the possible exception of selected Douglas fir, hemlock, parana pine and western red cedar.

Class 1   This is suitable for both softwood and hardwood components, particularly small mouldings such as glazing bars and beads.
Also for joinery which will receive a clear finish.

Class 2   Suitable for general purpose softwood joinery and laminated timber. Commonly used for window casements.

Class 3   As class 2 but with greater latitude in knot size and spacing.

Timber sizes

Softwoods and hardwoods are usually available in sizes as shown in the tables on p.253 and p.259.

European softwoods are generally supplied in 1.8 m lengths in increments of 300 mm up to about 5.7 m.

North American softwoods are normally supplied in 1.8 m lengths up to 7.2 m in 600 mm increments. Other lengths to special order up to a maximum of 12.0 m.

Hardwoods which are imported in log form may be cut to specified sizes and are available in 19, 25, 32, 38, 50, 63 and 75 mm thicknesses; widths from 150 mm up and lengths from 1.8 m to typically 4.5 m and sometimes 6 m.

Softwood – standard sawn sizes (mm)

Thickness	25	38	50	75	100	125	150	175	200	225	250	300	
12	•	•	•	•	•		•						
16			•	*	*	*	*						
19	•	•	•	*	*	*	*						
22				*	*	*	*						
25	•	•	•	*	*	*	*	*	*	*	*	*	These
32				*	*	*	*	*	*	*	*	*	sizes
36				*	*	*	*						generally
38		•	•	*	*	*	*	*	*	*			from
44				*	*	*	*	*	*	*	*	*	Europe
47				*	*	*	*	*	*	*	*	*	
50			•	*	*	*	*	*	*	*	*	*	
63				*	*	*	*	*	*	*			
75			•	*	*	*	*	*	*	*	*	*	
100				*			*		*		*	*	These
150							*		*			*	sizes
200									*				generally
250											*		from
300												*	N America

• = sizes that may be available from stock or sawn from larger standard sizes
* = sizes laid down in BS 4471 : 1996

Reduction from sawn sizes by planing

Structural timber	3 mm up to 100 mm
	5 mm over 100 mm
Joinery and cabinet work	7 mm up to 35 mm
	9 mm over 35 mm
	11 mm up to 150 mm
	13 mm over 150 mm.

Softwoods

Species	Place of origin	Appearance	Density kg/m³	Durability class	Veneer	Uses (remarks)
Cedar of Lebanon* *Cedrus Libani*	Europe UK	light brown	580	2	✓	garden furniture, drawer linings (aromatic smell)
Douglas Fir *Pseudotsuga menziesii*	N America UK	light, reddish brown	530	3	✓	plywood, construction (long lengths), joinery, vats
Hemlock, western *Tsuga heterophylla*	N America	pale brown	500	4		construction (large sizes), joinery (uniform colour)
Larch, European *Larix decidua*	Europe	pale, reddish	590	3	✓	boat planking, pit props, transmission poles
Larch, Japanese *Larix kaempferi*	Europe	reddish brown	560	3		stakes, construction
Parana Pine *Araucaria angustifolia*	S America	golden brown and red streaks	550	4	✓	interior joinery, plywood (may distort)
Pine, Corsican *Pinus nigra maritima*	Europe	light yellow-brown	510	4		joinery, construction
Pine, maritime *Pinus pinaster*	Europe	pale brown to yellow	510	3		pallets, packaging
Pine, pitch *Pinus palustris*	South USA	yellow-brown to red-brown	670	3		heavy construction, joinery
Pine, radiata *Pinus radiata*	S Africa Australia	yellow to pale brown	480	4		packaging, furniture
Pine, scots *Pinus sylvestris*	UK	pale yellow-brown to red-brown	510	4		construction, joinery
Pine, yellow *Pinus strobus*	N America	pale yellow to light brown	420	4		pattern-making, doors, drawing boards
Spruce Canadian *Picea* spp	Canada	white to pale yellow	450	4		construction, joinery

Species	Place of origin	Appearance	Density kg/m³	Durability class	Veneer	Uses (remarks)
Spruce, sitka *Picea sitchensis*	UK	pinkish-brown	450	4		construction, pallets, packaging
Spruce, western white *Picea glauca*	N America	white to pale yellow-brown	450	4		construction (large sizes), joinery
Western Red Cedar *Thuja plicata*	N America	reddish-brown	390	2	✓	exterior cladding, shingles, greenhouses, beehives
Whitewood, European *Picea abies* and *Abies alba*	Europe Scandinavia USSR	white to pale yellow-brown	470	4	✓	interior joinery, construction, flooring
Yew *Taxus baccata*	Europe	orange-brown to purple-brown	670	2	✓	furniture, cabinetry, turnery (good colour range)

* = limited availability

Source: Trada Technology Ltd

Hardwoods

Species	Place of origin	Appearance	Density kg/m³	Durability class	Veneer	Uses (remarks)
Afrormosia *Pericopsis elata*	W Africa	light brown, colour variable	710	1	✓	joinery, furniture, cladding
Agba *Gossweilero dendron balsamiferum*	W Africa	yellow-brown	510	2	✓	joinery, trim, cladding (may exude gum)
Ash, European *Fraximus exelsior*	UK Europe	pale white to light brown	710	5	✓	interior joinery (may be bent), sports goods
Balsa * *Ochroma pyramidale*	S America	pinky-white	160	5		insulation, buoyancy aids, architectural models
Beech, European *Fagus sylvatica*	UK Europe	pale pinkish brown	720	5	✓	furniture (bends well), flooring, plywood
Birch, European * *Betula pubescens*	Europe Scandinavia	white to light brown	670	5	✓	plywood, furniture, turnery (bends well)
Cherry, European * *Prunus avium*	Europe	pink-brown	630	3	✓	cabinet making (may warp), furniture
Chestnut, sweet * *Castanea sativa*	Europe	honey-brown	560	2	✓	joinery, fencing (straight grained)
Ebony * *Diospyros* spp	W Africa India	black with grey stripes	1110	1	✓	decorative work, inlaying, turnery (small sizes only)
Elm, European * *Ulmus* spp	Europe UK	reddish-brown	560	4	✓	furniture, coffins, boats (resists splitting)
Gaboon * *Aucoumea klaineana*	W Africa	pink-brown	430	4	✓	plywood, blockboard
Greenheart *Ocotea rodiaei*	Guyana	yellow-olive green to brown	1040	1		heavy marine construction, bridges etc. (very large sizes)

Species	Place of origin	Appearance	Density kg/m³	Durability class	Veneer	Uses (remarks)
Hickory * *Carya* spp	N America	brown to red-brown	830	4		tool handles, ladder rungs, sports goods (bends well)
Iroko *Chlorophora excelsa*	W Africa	yellow-brown	660	1	✓	joinery, work-tops, construction
Keruing *Dipterocarpus* spp	SE Asia	pink-brown to dark brown	740	3		heavy and general construction, decking, vehicle flooring
Lignum Vitae * *Guaicum* spp	Central America	dark green-brown	1250	1		bushes, bearings, sports goods (small sizes only)
Lime, European * *Tilia* spp	UK Europe	yellow-white to pale brown	560	5		carving, turnery, bungs, clogs (fine texture)
Mahogany, African *Khaya* spp	W Africa	reddish-brown	530	3	✓	furniture, cabinetry, joinery
Mahogany, American *Swietenia macrophylla*	Brazil	reddish-brown	560	2	✓	furniture, cabinetry, boats, joinery (stable, easily worked)
Maple, rock *Acer saccharum*	N America	creamy-white	740	4	✓	flooring, furniture, turnery (hardwearing)
Meranti, dark red *Shorea* spp	SE Asia	medium to dark red-brown	710	3	✓	joinery, plywood (uniform grain)
Oak, American red *Quercus* spp	N America	yellow-brown with red tinge	790	4	✓	furniture, interior joinery (bends well)

Hardwoods – continued

Species	Place of origin	Appearance	Density kg/m³	Durability class	Veneer	Uses (remarks)
Oak, European *Quercus robur*	UK Europe	yellow to warm brown	690	2	✓	construction, joinery, flooring, cooperage, fencing (bends well)
Obeche *Triplochiton scleroxylon*	W Africa	white to pale yellow	390	4	✓	interior joinery, furniture, plywood (very stable)
Plane, European * *Platanus hybrida*	Europe	mottled red-brown	640	5	✓	decorative work, turnery, inlays
Ramin *Gonystylus* spp	SE Asia	white to pale yellow	670	4	✓	mouldings, furniture, louvre doors (easily machined)
Rosewood * *Dalbergia* spp	S America India	purplish-brown with black streaks	870	1	✓	interior joinery, cabinetry, turnery, veneers
Sapele *Entandophragma cylindricum*	W Africa	red-brown with stripe figure	640	3	✓	interior joinery, door veneers, flooring
Sycamore * *Acer pseudoplatanus*	Europe UK	white to creamy yellow	630	5	✓	furniture, panelling, kitchen ware (does not taint or stain)
Teak *Tectona grandis*	Burma Thailand	golden brown	660	1	✓	furniture, joinery, boats (chemical and termite resistant)
Utile *Entandophragma utile*	W Africa	reddish-brown	660	2	✓	joinery, furniture, cabinetry
Walnut, European * *Juglans regia*	Europe UK	grey-brown with dark streaks	670	3	✓	furniture, turnery, gun stocks (decorative)

* = limited availability

Hardwood – standard sawn sizes (mm)

Thickness	50	63	75	100	125	150	175	200	225	250	300
19			*	*	*	*	*				
25	*	*	*	*	*	*	*	*	*	*	*
32			*	*	*	*	*	*	*	*	*
38			*	*	*	*	*	*	*	*	*
50				*	*	*	*	*	*	*	*
63						*	*	*	*	*	*
75						*	*	*	*	*	*
100						*	*	*	*	*	*

* = sizes laid down in BS 5450 : 1977.

Reduction from sawn sizes by planing

Structural timber	3 mm up to	100 mm
	5 mm for	101–150 mm
	6 mm for	151–300 mm
Flooring, matchings	5 mm up to	25 mm
	6 mm for	26–50 mm
	7 mm for	51–300 mm
Wood trim	6 mm up to	25 mm
	7 mm for	26–50 mm
	8 mm for	51–100 mm
	9 mm for	101–105 mm
	10 mm for	151–300 mm
Joinery and cabinet work	7 mm up to	25 mm
	9 mm for	26–50 mm
	10 mm for	51–100 mm
	12 mm for	101–150 mm
	14 mm for	151–300 mm

Softwood mouldings

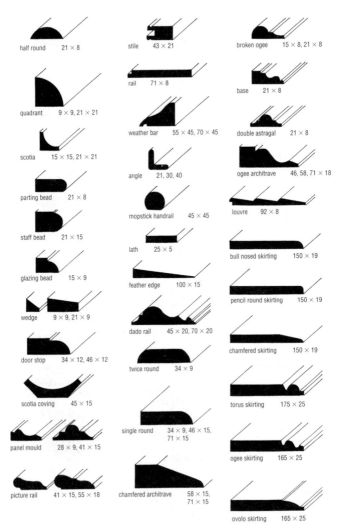

half round   21 × 8

quadrant   9 × 9, 21 × 21

scotia   15 × 15, 21 × 21

parting bead   21 × 8

staff bead   21 × 15

glazing bead   15 × 9

wedge   9 × 9, 21 × 9

door stop   34 × 12, 46 × 12

scotia coving   45 × 15

panel mould   28 × 9, 41 × 15

picture rail   41 × 15, 55 × 18

stile   43 × 21

rail   71 × 8

weather bar   55 × 45, 70 × 45

angle   21, 30, 40

mopstick handrail   45 × 45

lath   25 × 5

feather edge   100 × 15

dado rail   45 × 20, 70 × 20

twice round   34 × 9

single round   34 × 9, 46 × 15,
                  71 × 15

chamfered architrave   58 × 15,
                        71 × 15

broken ogee   15 × 8, 21 × 8

base   21 × 8

double astragal   21 × 8

ogee architrave   46, 58, 71 × 18

louvre   92 × 8

bull nosed skirting   150 × 19

pencil round skirting   150 × 19

chamfered skirting   150 × 19

torus skirting   175 × 25

ogee skirting   165 × 25

ovolo skirting   165 × 25

Some sections are available in a range of sizes.
The dimensions given are those most often available.

Hardwood mouldings

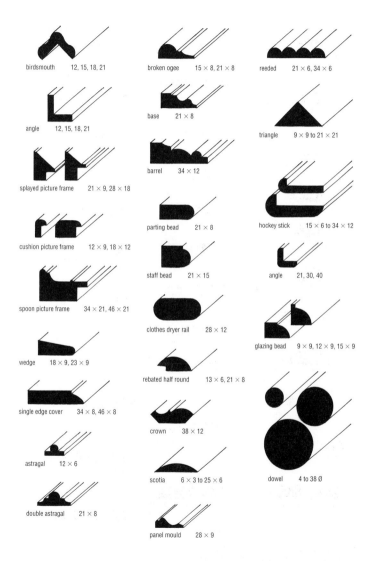

birdsmouth   12, 15, 18, 21

angle   12, 15, 18, 21

splayed picture frame   21 × 9, 28 × 18

cushion picture frame   12 × 9, 18 × 12

spoon picture frame   34 × 21, 46 × 21

wedge   18 × 9, 23 × 9

single edge cover   34 × 8, 46 × 8

astragal   12 × 6

double astragal   21 × 8

broken ogee   15 × 8, 21 × 8

base   21 × 8

barrel   34 × 12

parting bead   21 × 8

staff bead   21 × 15

clothes dryer rail   28 × 12

rebated half round   13 × 6, 21 × 8

crown   38 × 12

scotia   6 × 3 to 25 × 6

panel mould   28 × 9

reeded   21 × 6, 34 × 6

triangle   9 × 9 to 21 × 21

hockey stick   15 × 6 to 34 × 12

angle   21, 30, 40

glazing bead   9 × 9, 12 × 9, 15 × 9

dowel   4 to 38 Ø

Wood veneers

QUARTER CUT veneers are cut at right angles to the growth rings in the logs. The variations in colour brought about by summer/winter growth produce a straight grain effect. This is thought to be an advantage in veneers such as sapele.

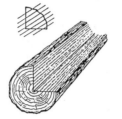

CROWN CUT/FLAT CUT veneers are produced by slicing through logs, giving a less straight grained veneer with more figure and in general a more decorative finish.

ROTARY CUT is made by mounting a log on a lathe and rotating it against a sharp fixed knife. The cut follows the annular growth rings producing a bold variegated grain. Rotary cut veneer is exceptionally wide.

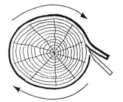

BURR/BURL VENEERS are made from the enlarged trunk of certain trees, particularly walnut. The grain is very irregular with the appearance of small knots grouped closely together. Small sections of this veneer are normally joined together to form a larger sheet.

Source: James Latham plc

Wood rotting fungi

Dry rot *Serpula lacrimans*
This is the most damaging of fungi. Mainly attacks softwoods and typically occurs in wood embedded in damp masonry. It needs wood with only 20% moisture content and thrives in dark, humid conditions and so is seldom seen externally. It is able to penetrate bricks and mortar and thus can transport moisture from a damp source to new woodwork.

Fruit body	Tough, fleshy pancake or bracket. Yellow ochre turning to rusty-red with white or grey margins.
Mycelium (fungal roots)	Silky white sheets, cotton wool-like cushions or felted grey skin showing tinges of yellow and lilac. Strands sometimes 6 mm thick, becoming brittle when dry.
Damage	Darkens wood with large cuboidal cracking and deep fissures. Wood lightweight and crumbly. No skin of sound wood. Wood may be warped and give off distinctive musty mushroomy smell.

Wet rots
These can only grow on timber with a 40–50 per cent moisture content and tend not to spread much beyond the source of dampness.

Coniophora puteana (cellar fungus)
A brown rot occurring in softwoods and hardwoods. Most common cause of decay in woodwork soaked by leaking water.

Fruit body	Rare in buildings. Thin greenish olive-brown plate. Spores on minute pimples.
Mycelium	Only present in conditions of high humidity. Slender thread-like yellowish becoming deep brown or black.
Damage	Darkens wood, small cuboidal cracks, often below sound veneer.

Wood rotting fungi – continued

Fibroporia vaillantii   (mine fungus)
A brown rot which attacks softwood, particularly in high temperature areas.

Fruit body	Irregular, white, cream to yellow lumpy sheets or plates with numerous minute pores.
Mycelium	White or cream sheets of fern-like growths.
Damage	Resembles dry rot in cuboidal pieces but wood lighter in colour and cracks less deep.

Phellinus contiguus
A white rot which attacks softwoods and hardwoods and is frequently found on external joinery.

Fruit body	Only found occasionally. Tough, elongated, ochre to dark brown, covered in minute pores.
Mycelium	Tawny brown tufts may be found in crevices.
Damage	Wood bleaches and develops stringy fibrous appearance. Does not crumble.

Donkioporia expansa
A white rot which attacks hardwood, particularly oak, and may spread to adjacent softwoods. Often found at beam ends bedded in damp walls and associated with death watch beetle.

Fruit body	Thick, hard, dull fawn or biscuit coloured plate or bracket. Long pores, often in several layers.
Mycelium	White to biscuit felted growth, often shaped to contours in wood. Can exude yellow-brown liquid.
Damage	Wood becomes bleached and is reduced to consistency of whitish lint which will crush but does not crumble.

Asterostroma

A white rot usually found in softwood joinery such as skirting boards.

Fruit body	Thin, sheet-like, without pores rather like mycelium.
Mycelium	White, cream or buff sheets with strands which can cross long distances over masonry.
Damage	Wood is bleached and becomes stringy and fibrous.
	No cuboidal cracking and does not crumble.

Treatment

Timber suffering from fungal or woodworm damage should only be treated if really necessary. Very often the damage is old, as when the sapwood has been destroyed but the remaining heartwood is sufficient for structural stability.

Many defects can be cured by eliminating the source of the damp and improving ventilation. The use of unjustified treatment is contrary to the Control of Substances Hazardous to Health (COSHH) Regulations and is not acceptable.

The person or company applying the treatment could be liable to prosecution.

However, when there is no alternative to chemical treatment, the following action should be undertaken:

Identify fungus. Rapidly dry out any moisture sources and improve ventilation.

Remove all affected timber (about 400 mm from visible signs for dry rot) and ideally burn on site.
Avoid distributing spores when handling.

Treat all remaining timbers with approved fungicide. Replace with pre-treated timber.

Woodworm

Wood boring insects do not depend on damp and humid conditions, although certain species prefer timber which has been decayed by fungi.

The life cycle of a woodworm is egg, larva, pupa and adult. First signs of attack are the exit holes made by the adults who emerge to mate and usually die after reproduction.

The following insects can all cause serious damage and the death watch and longhorn beetle can cause structural damage. Other beetles only feed on damp wood rotted by fungi and, since they cannot attack sound dry wood, remedial action to control wood rot will limit further infestation.

Common furniture beetle   *(Anobium punctatum)*
Attacks both softwoods and European hardwoods and also plywood made with natural glues. It is the most widespread beetle and only affects sapwood if wood rot is present. Commonly found in older furniture, structural timbers, under stairs, cupboards and areas affected by damp.

Beetle 2–6 mm long, exit hole 1–2 mm, adults emerge May–September.

Wood boring weevils
(Pentarthrum huttonii and *Euophryum confine)*
Attacks decayed hard and softwoods in damp situations, typically poorly ventilated cellars and wood in contact with wet floors and walls.

Beetle 3–5 mm long, exit hole 1.0 mm with surface channels, adults emerge at any time.

Powder post beetle   *(Lyctus brunneus)*
Attacks tropical and European hardwoods, not found in softwoods. Veneers, plywood and blockboard are all susceptible.

Beetle 4–7 mm long, exit hole 1–2 mm.

Death watch beetle   *(Xestobium rufovillosum)*

Attacks sapwood and heartwood of partially decayed hard-woods and occasionally adjacent softwoods. Often found in old churches with oak and elm structures. Typically found in areas prone to dampness such as wall plates, ends of joists, lintels and timbers built into masonry.

Beetle 6–8 mm long, exit hole 3 mm, adults emerge March–June.

Longhorn beetle   *(Hylotrupes bajulus)*

Attacks softwood, particularly in roof timbers. May be over-looked in early stages as there are few exit holes. Scraping noises audible on hot days with large infestations. Prevalent only in Surrey and SW London. Outbreaks should be reported to BRE Timber & Protection Division.

Beetle 10–20 mm long, exit hole 6–10 mm oval, adults emerge July–September.

Treatment

Fresh exit holes and bore dust on or below timbers are signs of active infestation, although vibrations may dislodge old bore dust. Chemical treatment however may not be necessary. See paragraph on Treatment on p. 265.

Identify beetle and treat timbers with appropriate insecticidal spray, emulsion or paste to destroy adults and unhatched eggs on the surface of the wood and larvae before they develop into pupae. Solvent-based products penetrate timber very effectively but have health and safety problems associated with them. Some water-based products claim to be as effective but more environmentally friendly.

If associated with fungal decay, treat as for wood rot and use a dual-purpose remedy (i.e. anti rot and beetle). Do not use dual purpose products where woodworm is present in timbers which are dry and expected to remain so.

Source: *Recognising Wood Rot and Insect Damage in Buildings*

Wood boring beetles

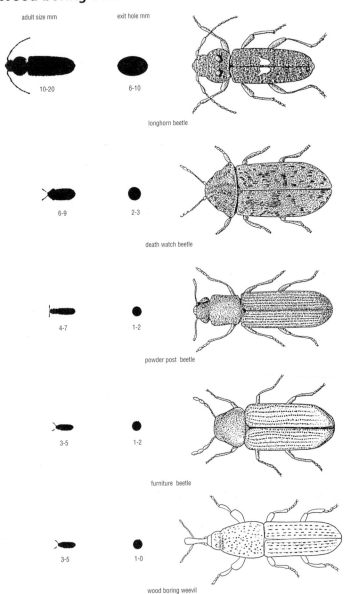

adult size mm   exit hole mm

10-20   6-10

longhorn beetle

6-9   2-3

death watch beetle

4-7   1-2

powder post beetle

3-5   1-2

furniture beetle

3-5   1-0

wood boring weevil

Building boards

Chipboard

Particle board with a variety of woodchips bonded with resin adhesives.

No chipboard is completely moisture resistant and should not be used externally.

Six classes identified in BS 5669 Part 2 : 1989

C1   = general purpose use   C3 = moisture resistant
C1A = slightly better quality C4 = moisture resistant
         for furniture   flooring quality
C2   = flooring quality   C5 = moisture resistant
                                          structural quality

Sheets can be supplied wood veneer and melamine faced; with low formaldehyde rating, or bonded to polystyrene for insulated flooring.

Thicknesses	12, 15, 18, 22, 25, 28, 30 and 38 mm.
Sheet sizes	1220 × 2440 mm, 1830 × 2440 mm,
	1220 × 2745 mm, 1830 × 3050 mm,
	1220 × 3050 mm, 1830 × 3660 mm
	also
	600 × 2440 mm for 18 and 22 mm flooring

Wood veneer and melamine faced shelves

Thickness	15mm
Widths	152 (6″), 229 (9″), 305 (12″), 381 (15″),
	457 (18″), 533 (21″), 610 (24″), 686 (27″),
	762 (30″); 914 mm (36″)
Lengths	1830 (6′) and 2440 mm (8′)

Source: CSC Forest Products Ltd

Blockboard

Composite board with one or two veneers applied to solid core of timber blocks 7 mm–30 mm wide, also available with decorative wood or laminate veneers, commonly 18 mm thick.

Thicknesses   13, 16, 18, 22, 25, 32, 38 and 45 mm
Sheet sizes   1220 × 2440 mm; 1525 × 3050 and 3660 mm; 1830 × 5200 mm

Source: James Latham plc

Hardboard

Thin, dense boards with one very smooth face and mesh textured reverse. Grainless, knotless, and will not easily split or splinter. It can be bent, is easy to machine, has high internal bond strength for glueing and good dimensional stability. Two types available:

Standard hardboard   = general internal linings and door facings
Oil tempered hardboard = structural purposes (higher strength and moisture resistance), flooring overlays

Thicknesses   3.2, 4.8 and 6.0 mm
Sheet sizes   1220 × 2440 and 3050 mm

Also available:
Perforated hardboard with
4.8 mm Ø holes @ 19 mm centres × 3.2 mm thick and
7.0 mm Ø holes @ 25 mm centres × 6.0 mm thick

Hardboard with painted finishes.

Source: Masonite CP Ltd

Laminboard

A composite board with veneers applied to a core of narrow timber strips (as opposed to wider blocks in blockboard). It is heavier, flatter and more expensive than blockboard but is less likely to warp.

Thicknesses   13, 16, 19, 22, 25, 32, 38 and 44 mm
Sheet sizes   1220 × 2440 mm, 1525 × 3050 and 3660 mm.

MDF   (Medium Density Fibreboard)

Homogenous board of softwood fibres bonded with synthetic resins producing a very dense, fine textured uniform material which can be machined to great accuracy. Normal grades are not moisture resistant but moisture resistant grades are available. Low and zero formaldehyde, flame retardant and integrally coloured boards are also available.

Thicknesses 6, 9, 12, 15, 18, 22, 25 and 30 mm (smaller and larger thicknesses also made by a few manufacturers).
Sheet sizes 1220 × 2440 mm 1525 × 2440 mm 1830 × 2440 mm
1220 × 2745 mm 1525 × 2745 mm 1830 × 3660 mm
1220 × 3050 mm 1525 × 3050 mm

Medium hardboard

A board with a density between that of wood fibre insulation board and standard hardboard. It has good thermal and insulation properties with a fine finish. Can be cold and steam bent. Moisture resistant and flame retardant grades available. Used for notice boards, ceilings, wall linings, shop fittings, display work and pin boards.

Thicknesses   6.4, 9.5 and 12.7 mm
Sheet size   1220 × 2440 mm

Source: Williamette Europe Ltd

OSB   (Oriented Strand Board)

Made from softwood strands, approximately 75 mm long, placed in layers in different directions, bonded and compressed together with exterior grade water resistant resins. A 'green' product made from thinnings from managed plantations. Process utilises 95 per cent of the wood, discarded bark being used for fuel or horticulture. Cheaper than plywood, strong in both directions, with a uniform and decorative appearance.

Two grades available, one suitable for formwork, site hoardings and crating, the other for sheathing, flooring and decorative panels.

Thicknesses   6, 8, 9, 11, 15, 18, 22 and 25 mm
Sheet sizes   1200 × 2400 mm; 1220 × 2440 mm;
          590 × 2400 mm and 2440 mm for
          9 mm thick t & g flooring

Source: CSC Forest Products Ltd

Matchboarding

Timber boards, tongued and grooved on opposite sides. Joints can be plain butt joints as for floorboards or moulded with 'V' or quirk (rounded) shoulders for wall cladding.

Typical sizes of matchboards

Nominal size mm	Laid width mm	Finished thickness mm
12.5 × 100	80	10
19 × 75	55	15
19 × 100	80	15
19 × 150	130	15
25 × 75	55	20
25 × 100	80	20
25 × 150	130	20

Plywood

Made from softwood and hardwood veneers placed at right angles, or sometimes 45°, to one another. The veneers are strong in the direction of the grain, weak in the other. Thus structural plywoods have odd numbers of layers so that the grain to the outside faces lies in the same direction. Adhesives used are described as WBP (weather and boil proof) for external or arduous conditions. BR (boil resistant), MR (moisture resistant) and INT (interior) are progressively less resistant.

Plywoods are graded according to species and country of origin and are effectively as follows:

Veneer with minimal imperfections as peeled.
Veneer with imperfections plugged or filled.
Veneer with imperfections which have not been repaired.

Thicknesses	0.8, 1.0, 1.2, 1.5 mm (aircraft specification); 2, 2.5, 3, 4, 5, 6, 6.5, 9, 12, 15, 18, 21, 24 and 27 mm
Sheet sizes	1220 × 1220 mm 1525 × 610 mm (t & g)
	1220 × 2440 mm 1525 × 1525 mm
	1220 × 3050 mm 1525 × 2440 mm
	1220 × 3660 mm 1525 × 3050 mm
	1270 × 1270 mm 1525 × 3660 mm

Source: James Latham plc

Plasterboard

Boards with a core of aerated gypsum plaster bonded between two sheets of strong paper which should comply with BS 1230 Part 1 : 1985.

There are different grades for dry lining and wet plaster. Dry lining boards have tapered edges to allow for jointing tapes.

Boards are available backed with foil, polystyrene, polyurethane foam and woodwool. Others have more moisture resistant and fire resistant cores.

Thicknesses	9.5, 12.5, 15 and 19 mm (25–50 mm for boards backed with insulation)	
Sheet sizes	400 × 1200 mm	600 × 1800 mm
		600 × 2400 mm
	900 × 1200 mm	1200 × 2400 mm
	900 × 1800 mm	1200 × 2700 mm
	900 × 2400 mm	1200 × 3000 mm

Source: British Gypsum

Calcium silicate board

Asbestos-free board mainly used for structural fire protection. Cellulose fibres dispersed in water are mixed with lime, cement, silica and fire protective fillers to form a slurry. Water is then removed from the slurry under vacuum to form boards which are transferred to high pressure steam autoclaves for curing. Denser boards are hydraulically compressed before curing. Boards can be easily cut to size and drilled for screw fixing. 9 mm and 12 mm thick boards are available with rebated edges for seamless flush jointing. Boards may be decorated or left untreated.

Thicknesses	6, 9, 12, 15, 20, 22, 25, 30, 35, 40, 45, 50, 55 and 60 mm
Sheet sizes	1220, 1830, 2440, 3050 mm long × 610 and 1220 mm wide
Fire Classification	Class 0 for surface spread of flame
Fire Protection	From 60 to 240 minutes depending on product

Source: Cape Casil

Plastics

Plastics – commonly used in building

Plastics are organic substances mainly derived from by-products of coal-gas manufacture and refining of mineral oil. These are manipulated to form long-chain molecules on which the plasticity and rigidity of the material of the products made from them depend. They are made up of three main groups:

- **thermoplastics**, such as polythene, vinyls and nylon, where the structure is not permanently set and which can therefore be joined by heat or solvents.
- **thermosetting plastics**, such as phenol formaldehyde, melamine and fibreglass, which have fixed molecular structures that cannot be re-shaped by heat or solvents and are joined by adhesives.
- **elastomers**, such as natural rubber, neoprene and butyl rubber, which have polymers in which the helical molecular chains are free to straighten when the material is stretched and recover when the load is released.

Plastics – industrial techniques

glass reinforced plastic (**GRP**) Synthetic resin reinforced with glass fibre, used for rooflights, wall panels, etc.

injection moulding Similar to die casting for moulding thermoplastics. Plastic is melted and then forced under pressure into a cooled moulding chamber.

plastic laminate Decorative laminate made up of paper or fabric impregnated with melamine or phenolic resins and bonded together under pressure to form a hard-wearing, scratch-resistant finish used primarily for work surfaces.

solvent welding A permanent joint made between thermoplastics by smearing both sides with an appropriate solvent before joining together.

vacuum forming Making components by evacuating the space between the sheet material and the die so that forming is effected by atmospheric pressure.

Plastics – abbreviations in general use

Abbreviation	Plastic	Uses
ABS	Acrylonitrile butadiene styrene	cold water pipes
CPE	Chlorinated polyethylene	water tanks
CPVC	Chlorinated polyvinyl chloride	hot water and waste pipes
EPDM	Ethylene propylene di-monomer	gaskets, single ply roofing
EPS	Expanded polystyrene	plastic foam for insulation
ETFE	Ethyl tetra fluoro ethylene	film for foil roof cushions
EVA	Ethylene vinyl acetate	weather protective films
GRP	Glass-reinforced polyester (fibreglass)	cladding, panels, mouldings
HDPE	High density polyethylene	flooring, piping
HIPS	High impact polystyrene	ceilings, mirrors
LDPE	Low density polyethylene	bins, pipes, fittings
MF	Melamine-formaldehyde	laminated plastics, adhesives
PA	Polyamide (nylon)	electrical fittings, washers, ropes
PB	Polybutylene	pipe fittings
PC	Polycarbonate	anti-vandal glazing
PE	Polyethylene	electrical insulation, flooring, piping
PF	Phenol-formaldehyde (Bakelite)	electrical fittings, door furniture
PMMA	Polymethyl methacrylate (Perspex)	sanitary ware, transparent sheet
PP	Polypropylene	electrical insulation, piping
PS	Polystyrene	insulation, suspended ceilings
PTFE	Polytetrafluoroethylene	pipe jointing, sealing tape
PU	Polyurethane	insulation, paints, coatings
PVA	Polyvinyl acetate (latex emulsion)	emulsion paint, bonding agents
PVC	Polyvinyl chloride	floor and wall coverings
PVB	Polyvinyl butyral	laminated glass
PVF	Polyvinyl fluoride	protective films
UF	Urea-formaldehyde	glues, insulation
UP	Unsaturated polyester	paint, powder coatings, bituminous felt
UPVC	Unplasticised polyvinyl chloride	rainwater, soil and waste pipes, roof sheeting

Nails and screws

Nails

panel pin		round wire nail	
hardboard panel pin		purlin nail	
lath nail		lost head nail	
plasterboard nail		cut floorboard brad	
gimp pin for upholstery		cut clasp nail for heavy carpentry	
cut lath nail		double head shutter nail for temporary fixing	
cedar shake nail		masonry nail	
carpet tack		helical threaded nail for corrugated sheet	
sprig for fixing glass to timber frames		annular nail for boats and external joinery	
escutcheon pin		convex head nail for corrugated sheet	
clout nail for roofing, felt and fencing		chisel point nail for fixing pipes to masonry	
large clout nail for roofing felt			
clout head peg for roof tiling			

Wood screws

countersunk	
raised head	
raised countersunk	
dome head	
coach screw	
cross head	

Machine screws and bolts

countersunk	
raised countersunk	
round	
binder pan	
pan	
cheese	
fillister	
mushroom	

Source: *Handbook of Fixings and Fastenings*

Standard wire gauge (SWG)
in millimetres and inches

SWG	mm	inches	SWG	mm	inches
1	7.62	0.300	16	1.63	0.064
2	7.00	0.276	17	1.42	0.056
3	6.40	0.252	18	1.22	0.048
4	5.89	0.232	19	1.02	0.040
5	5.38	0.212	20	0.914	0.036
6	4.88	0.192	21	0.813	0.032
7	4.47	0.176	22	0.711	0.028
8	4.06	0.160	23	0.610	0.024
9	3.66	0.144	24	0.559	0.022
10	3.25	0.128	25	0.508	0.020
11	2.95	0.116	26	0.457	0.018
12	2.64	0.104	27	0.417	0.016
13	2.34	0.092	28	0.376	0.015
14	2.03	0.080	29	0.345	0.014
15	1.83	0.072	30	0.315	0.012

Paints

Colour

The *colour spectrum* is made up of colour refracted from a beam of light, as through a glass prism or as seen in a rainbow. The bands of colour are arranged according to their decreasing wavelength (6.5×10^{-7} for red to 4.2×10^{-7} for violet), and are traditionally divided into seven main colours: red, orange, yellow, green, blue, indigo and violet. When arranged as segments of a circle, this is known as the *colour circle*. The *primary* colours are red, yellow and blue, as these cannot be mixed from other colours. The *secondary* colours are orange, green and purple, and the *tertiary colours* are produced by adding a primary colour to a secondary colour.

Complementary colours are pairs of colours on opposite sides of the circle, which when mixed together make browns and greys. The term *hue* indicates a specific colour, defined in terms of, say, redness or blueness, but not lightness or darkness. *Tone* is the lightness or darkness of a colour. Adding black, white or grey to a hue reduces its intensity.

Colour systems

British Standards Colour System BS: 4800 1989. Colours are defined by a three-part code consisting of hue, greyness and weight. Hues are divided into twelve equal numbers, from 02 (red/purple) to 24 (purple), with an additional 00 for neutral whites, greys and blacks. The greyness is described by five letters: (A) grey; (B) nearly grey; (C) grey/clear; (D) nearly clear and (E) clear. Weight, a subjective term, describes both lightness and greyness, so each letter is followed by number from 01 to 58. Thus the colour 'heather' 22 C 37 is made up of:

22 (violet) C (grey/clear) 37 (medium weight)

NCS Natural Colour System. The Natural Colour System (NCS), generally referred to in the UK as '*Colour Dimensions*', was developed by the Scandinavian Colour Institute in 1978.

It is a colour language system that can describe any colour by notation, and is based on the assumption that human beings are able to identify six basic colours – white W; black S (note *not* B); yellow Y; red R; blue B and green G. These are arranged in a *colour circle*, with yellow, red, blue and green marking the quadrants. These segments are divided into 10 per cent steps, so that orange can be described as Y 50 R (yellow with 50 per cent red). To describe the shade of a colour there is the NCS *triangle*, where the base of the triangle is a grey scale marked in 10 per cent steps from white W to black S. The apex of the triangle represents the pure colour and is similarly marked in 10 per cent steps. Thus a colour can be described as 1080-Y50R for an orange with 10 per cent blackness, 80 per cent chromatic intensity at yellow with 50 per cent red. This system allows for a much finer subdivision of colours than the BS system.

RAL Colour Collection. This system is used within the building industry for defining colours of coatings such as plastics, metals, glazed bricks and some paints and lacquers. It was established in Germany in 1925 and developed over the years, is now designated RAL 840-HR, and lists 194 colours. Colours are defined by four digits, the first being the colour class: 1 yellow; 2 orange; 3 red; 4 violet; 5 blue; 6 green; 7 grey; 8 brown and 9 black. The next three digits relate only to the sequence in which the colours were filed. An official name is also applied to each standard RAL colour, e.g. RAL 6003 olive green.

RAL Design System. This system has 1688 colours arranged in a colour atlas based on a three-dimensional colour space defined by the co-ordinates of hue, lightness and chroma. The colours are coded with three numbers; thus reddish/yellow is 69.9 7.56 56.5. It is similar to the Natural Colour System except that it is based on the mathematical division of the whole visible wavelength spectrum, which is then divided into mostly 10 per cent steps. The system can be easily used by computer programs to formulate colours.

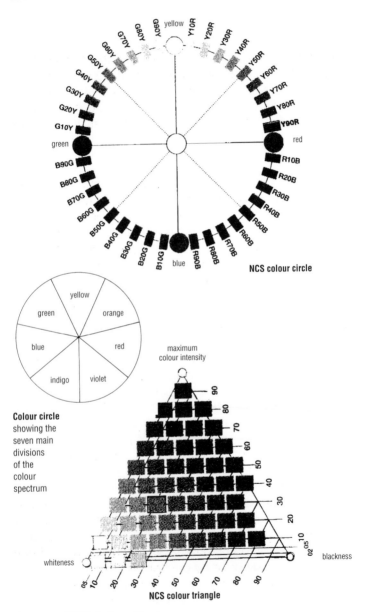

NCS colour circle

Colour circle
showing the
seven main
divisions
of the
colour
spectrum

maximum
colour intensity

whiteness

blackness

NCS colour triangle

Source: NCS Colour Centre

Painting

Preparation. Careful preparation is vital if the decorative finish applied is to succeed and be durable. It is important to follow instructions about preparing substrates, atmospheric conditions and drying times between coats. Ensure that the right product is specified for the task, and that primers and subsequent coats are compatible.

Paints

Paints basically consist of pigments, binder, and a solvent or water. Other ingredients are added for specific uses.

Solvent-based paints are now considered environmentally unsound and are increasingly being supplanted by water-based alternatives. These are less glossy and more water-permeable than oil paints, but are quick-drying, odour-free, and tend not to yellow with age.

Primers offer protection to the substrate from corrosion and deterioration, and give a good base for undercoats.

Undercoats, which are often just thinner versions of the finishing coat, provide a base for the topcoats.

Topcoats provide the durable and decorative surface, and come in gloss, satin, eggshell and matt finishes.

In addition to the paints listed overleaf there are specialist paints such as: *flame-retardant* paints, which emit non-combustible gases when subjected to fire; *intumescent coatings*, which expand to form a layer of insulating foam for structural steel; *multi-colour* paints, which incorporate coloured flecks, or two-part systems which use a special roller for the top coat to reveal partially the darker colour of the first coat; *silicone water-repellent* paints for porous masonry; *bituminous* paints for waterproofing metals and masonry; and *epoxy-ester coatings* to resist abrasion, oil and detergent spills.

Paints – typical products

Primers	Use*	Base*	Description
Zinc phosphate acrylic	M	WB	for all metals inside and out, quick drying, low odour
Red oxide	M	SB	replaces red lead and calcium plumbate for ferrous metals
Etching	M	SB	factory pre-treatment for new galvanized metal
Mordant solution	M	WB	pre-treatment of galvanized metal
Micaceous iron oxide	M	SB	for marine and industrial steelwork, resists pollution and high humidity
Acrylated rubber	M, Ms	BS	for all metals, plaster and masonry, resists moisture
Wood primer	W	SB	non-lead primer for all woods inside and out
Wood primer/undercoat	W	WB	high opacity, quick-drying primer and undercoat
Aluminium wood primer	W	SB	good for resinous woods and as sealer for creosoted and bituminous surfaces
Alkali-resistant	P	SB	for dry walls under SB finishes, seals stains and fire damage
Plaster sealer	P	WB	for dry porous interior surfaces, e.g. plasterboard
Stabilizing primer	Ms	SB	to seal powdery and chalky surfaces
Undercoats			
Exterior flexible	W	SB	long-lasting, flexible, good opacity for exterior wood
Undercoat	all	SB	for use inside and out under solvent-based finishes
Preservative basecoat	W	SB	for new and bare wood to protect against blue stain and fungal decay
Finishes			
High gloss	all	SB	alkyd high gloss for all surfaces inside and out
Satin, eggshell, flat	W, M, P	SB	alkyd paints in three finishes for interior use
Vinyl emulsion	P	WB	matt, soft sheen and silk finishes for interiors
Masonry – smooth	Ms	WB	contains fungicide, for dry masonry, rendering, concrete etc.
Masonry – textured	Ms	WB	fine granular finish, for dry masonry etc
Masonry – all seasons	Ms	SB	flexible, smooth and good for applying in cold conditions
Epoxy floor	Ms, C	WB	two-pack mid-sheen paint for interior masonry and concrete floors
Floor	W, C	WB	quick-drying, for interior concrete and wood floors
Ecolyd gloss	W, M, Ms	SB	high quality, mirror-finish gloss, low solvent content
Protective enamel	M	SB	glossy, protective, quick-drying, for machinery
Exterior UPVC	PVC	WB	for redecoration of weathered UPVC surfaces
Acrylated rubber coating	M, Ms	SB	for steelwork and masonry inside and out, good against condensation
Aluminium	W, M	SB	heat resisting to 260°C, for metals and wood
Timber preservative	W	SB	coloured, water-repellent finish for sawn timber, fences, sheds etc.
Protective wood stain	W	SB	water-repellent, mould-resistant, light-fast translucent colours
Exterior varnish	W	SB	transparent gloss finish for exterior wood
Interior varnish	W	WB	tough, quick drying, durable clear polyurethane finish
Aquatech basecoat	W	WB	flexible satin finish for bare and new wood
Aquatech woodstain	W	WB	flexible satin coloured finish, resists peeling, blistering
Diamond glaze	W	WB	clear lacquer for interior wood surfaces subject to hard wear

*C = concrete; M = metal; Ms = masonry; P = plaster; SB = solvent-based; W = wood; WB = water-based.

Source: ICI Paints

Paint covering capacity

Approximate maximum areas
for smooth surfaces of average porosity

			m²/litre
Preparation	Fungicidal wash		30
	Stabilizing primer		12
	Etching primer		19
	Timber preservative	– solvent based	10
	Timber preservative	– water based	12
Primers	Wood primer	– solvent based	13
	Wood primer	– aluminium	16
	Wood primer	– microporous	15
	Wood primer undercoat	– water based	12
	Metal primer	– solvent based	6
	Metal primer	– water based	15
	Metal primer	– zinc phosphate	6
	Acrylated rubber primer		5
Finishes	Undercoat	– solvent based	16
	Emulsion	– matt	15
	Emulsion	– vinyl silk	15
	Matt finish	– solvent based	16
	Eggshell finish	– solvent based	16
	Eggshell finish	– water based	15
	Microporous gloss	– solvent based	14
	High gloss	– solvent based	17
	Non-drip gloss	– solvent based	13
	Wood stain	– solvent based	25
	Exterior varnish	– solvent based	16
	Interior varnish	– solvent based	16
	Masonry paint	– smooth	10
	Masonry paint	– textured	6
	Acrylated rubber		6

Source: ICI Paints

Wallpaper coverage for walls and ceilings

Approximate number of rolls required

Walls	Measurement around walls (m)	Height of room above skirting (m)						
		2.3	2.4	2.6	2.7	2.9	3.1	3.2
	9.0	4	5	5	5	6	6	6
	10.4	5	5	5	5	6	6	6
	11.6	5	6	6	6	7	7	8
	12.8	6	6	7	7	7	8	8
	14.0	6	7	7	7	8	8	8
	15.2	7	7	8	8	9	9	10
	16.5	7	8	9	9	9	10	10
	17.8	8	8	9	9	10	10	11
	19.0	8	9	10	10	10	11	12
	20.0	9	9	10	10	11	12	13
	21.3	9	10	11	11	12	12	13
	22.6	10	10	12	12	12	13	14
	23.8	10	11	12	12	13	14	15
	25.0	11	11	13	13	14	14	16
	26.0	12	12	14	14	14	15	16
	27.4	12	13	14	14	15	16	17
	28.7	13	13	15	15	15	16	18
	30.0	13	14	15	15	16	17	19

Ceilings	Measurement around room (m)	no. rolls
	12.0	2
	15.0	3
	18.0	4
	20.0	5
	21.0	6
	24.0	7
	25.0	8
	27.0	9
	28.0	10
	30.0	11
	30.5	12

Notes:
Standard wallpaper roll is 530 mm wide × 10.06 m long (21″ × 33′0″)
One roll will cover approximately 5 m² (54 ft²) including waste

Addresses

RIBA companies

Royal Institute of British Architects
66 Portland Place, London W1N 4AD
email: admin@inst.riba.org
www.riba.org

tel: 020 7580 5533
fax: 020 7255 1541

RIBA Companies Ltd
1-3 Dufferin Street, London EC1Y 8NA
email: admin@ribac.co.uk
www.ribac.co.uk

tel: 020 7496 8300
fax: 020 7374 8300

RIBA Information Services
1-3 Dufferin Street, London EC1Y 8NA
email: admin@ris.gb.com
www.ris.gb.com

tel: 020 7496 8383
fax: 020 7374 8200

RIBA Office Library Service
4 Park Circus Place, Glasgow G3 6AN
email: library@inst.riba.com
www.ris.gb.com

tel: 0141 332 6501
fax: 0141 332 6693

RIBA Publications
56 Leonard Street, London EC2A 4JX
email: sales@ribabooks.com
www.ribabookshop.com

tel: 020 7251 0791
fax: 020 7608 2375

NBS Services
The Close, Newcastle upon Tyne NE1 3RE
email: admin@ribsservices.co.uk
www.nbsservices.co.uk

tel: 0191 232 9594
fax: 0191 232 5714

Technical Indexes Ltd
Willoughby Road, Bracknell RG12 8DW
email: marketing@techindex.co.uk
www.techindex.co.uk

tel: 01344 426311
fax: 01344 424971

RIBA Bookshops

London	66 Portland Place W1N 4AD	tel: 020 7251 0791
Belfast	2 Mount Charles BT2 1NZ	tel: 028 9032 3760
Birmingham	Margaret Street B3 3SP	tel: 0121 233 2321
Leeds	8 Woodhouse Sq. LS3 1AD	tel: 0113 245 6250
Manchester	113 Portland Street M1 6FB	tel: 0161 236 7691

Associations, Institutes and other information sources

Ancient Monuments Society
St Anne's Vestry Hall, 2 Church Entry,   tel: 020 7236 3934
London EC4V 5HB   fax: 020 7329 3677
Architects Registration Board (ARB)
8 Weymouth Street, London W1N 3FB   tel: 020 7580 5861
email: info@arb.org.uk   www.arb.org.uk   fax: 020 7436 5269
Architectural Association (AA)
36 Bedford Square, London WC1B 3ES   tel: 020 7636 0974
email: info@aaschool.ac.uk   www.aaschool.ac.uk fax: 020 7414 0782
Arts Council of England
14 Great Peter Street, London SW1P 3NQ   tel: 020 7333 0100
email: joebloggs@artscouncil.org.uk   fax: 020 7973 5590
www.artscouncil.org.uk
Barbour Index plc
New Lodge, Drift Road, Windsor SL4 4RQ   tel: 01344 884121
email: mso@barbour-index.co.uk   fax: 01344 884113
www.barbour-index.co.uk
Brick Development Association (BDA)
Woodside House, Winkfield, Windsor SL4 2DX   tel: 01344 885651
email: admin@brick.org.uk   www.brick.org.uk   fax: 01344 890129
British Board of Agrément (BBA)
PO Box 195, Bucknalls Lane, Garston,   tel: 01923 665300
Watford WD2 7NG   fax: 01923 665301
email: mail@bba.star.co.uk   www.bbacerts.co.uk
British Cement Association (BCA)
Century House, Telford Avenue,   tel: 01344 762676
Crowthorne RG45 6YS   fax: 01344 761214
email: admin@bca.org.uk   www.bca.org.uk
British Constructional Steelwork Association Ltd (BCSA)
4 Whitehall Court, London SW1A 2ES   tel: 020 7839 8566
email: postroom@bcsa.org.uk   www.bcsa.org.uk fax: 020 7976 1634
British Research Establishment (BRE)
Bucknalls Lane, Garston, Watford WD2 7JR   tel: 01923 664000
email: enquiries@bre.co.uk   www.bre.co.uk   fax: 01923 664787
British Standards Institution (BSI)
389 Chiswick High Road, London W4 4AL   tel: 020 8996 9000
email: info@bsi.org.uk   www.bsi.org.uk   fax: 020 8996 7001
Building Centre
26 Store Street, London WC1E 7BT   tel: 020 7692 4000
email: mann@buildingcentre.co.uk   fax: 020 7580 9641
www.buildingcentre.co.uk
Building Centre Bookshop
26 Store Street, London WC1E 7BT   tel: 020 7692 4040
email: bookshop@buildingcentre.co.uk   fax: 020 7636 3628
www.buildingcentre.co.uk
Cadw – Welsh historic monuments
Crown Buildings, Cathays Park, Cardiff CF10 3NQ tel: 029 2050 0200
email: cadw@wales.gsi.gov.uk   fax: 029 2082 6375
www.cadw.wales.gov.uk

Centre for Accessible Environments
60 Gainsford Street, London SE1 2NY   tel: 020 7357 8182
email: cae@globalnet.co.uk   www.cae.org.uk   fax: 020 7357 8183
Centre for Alternative Technology (CAT)
Machynlleth SY20 9AZ   tel: 01654 703409
email: mail.order@cat.org.uk   fax: 01654 703409
Chartered Institution of Building Services Engineers (CIBSE)
Delta House, 222 Balham High Road,   tel: 020 8675 5211
London SW12 9BS   fax: 020 8675 5449
email: secretary@cibse.org   www.cibse.org
Chartered Institute of Building (CIOB)
Englemere, Kings Ride, Ascot SL5 7TB   tel: 01344 630700
email: reception@ciob.org.uk   www.ciob.org.uk   fax: 01344 630777
Civic Trust
17 Carlton House Terrace, London SW1Y 5AW   tel: 020 7930 0914
email: pride@civictrust.org.uk www.civictrust.org.uk fax: 020 7321 0180
Commission for Architecture & the Built Environment (CABE)
7 St James Square, London SW1Y 4JU   tel: 020 7839 6537
email: enquiries@cabe.org.uk   www.cabe.org.uk   fax: 020 7839 8475
Construction Industry Council (CIC)
26 Store Street, London WC1E 7BT   tel: 020 7637 8692
email: cic@cic.org.uk   www.cic.org.uk   fax: 020 7580 6140
Copper Development Association
224 London Road, St Albans AL1 1AQ   tel: 01727 731200
email: copperdev@compuserve.com   fax: 01727 731216
www.cda.org.uk
Countryside Council for Wales
Plas Penrhof, Penrhof Road, Bangor LL57 2LQ   tel: 01248 385500
www.ccw.gov.uk   fax: 01248 355782
Department for Culture, Media and Sport (DCMS)
2 Cockspur Street, London SW1Y 5DH   tel: 020 7211 6000
www.culture.gov.uk
Department for Transport, Local Government & the Regions (DTLR)
Eland House, Bressenden Place, London SW1E 5DU tel: 020 7944 3000
www.dtlr.gov.uk
Disabled Living Foundation
380 Harrow Road, London W9 2HU   tel: 020 7289 6111
email: advice@dlf.org.uk   www.dlf.org.uk   fax: 020 7266 2922
English Heritage
23 Saville Row, London W1X 1AB   tel: 020 7973 3000
email: info@rchme.co.uk   fax: 020 7973 3001
www.english-heritage.org.uk
English Nature
Northminster House, Peterborough PE1 1UA   tel: 01733 455000
email: enquiries@english-nature.org.uk   fax: 01733 568834
www.english-nature.org.uk
Federation of Master Builders
14 Great James Street, London WC1N 3DP   tel: 020 7242 7583
email: contact@fmb.org.uk   www.fmb.org.uk   fax: 020 7404 0296

Forests Forever

26 Oxenden Street, London SW1Y 4EL	tel:	020 7839 1891
www.forestsforever.org.uk	fax:	020 7839 6594

Forest Stewardship Council (FSC)

Unit D, Station Buildings, Llanidloes SY18 6EB	tel:	01686 413916
email: fsc-uk@fsc-uk.demon.co.uk	fax:	01686 412176
www.fsc-uk.demon.co.uk		

Friends of the Earth Ltd

26 Underwood Street, London N1 7JQ	tel:	020 7490 1555
email: info@foe.co.uk www.foe.co.uk	fax:	020 7490 0881

Glass and Glazing Federation (GGF)

44 Borough High Street, London SE1 1XB	tel:	020 7403 7177
email: info@ggf.org.uk www.ggf.org.uk	fax:	020 7357 7458

Guild of Architectural Ironmongers

8 Stepney Green, London E1 3JU	tel:	020 7790 3431
email: ironmongers@compuserve.com	fax:	020 7790 8517
www.gai.org.uk		

Health and Safety Executive (HSE)

2 Southwark Bridge, London SE1 9HS	tel:	020 7717 6000
www.hse.gov.uk	fax:	020 7717 6717

Heating & Ventilating Contractors Association

ESCA House, 34 Palace Court, London W2 4JG	tel:	020 7313 4900
email: contact@hvca.org.uk www.hvca.org.uk	fax:	020 7727 9268

Historic Buildings & Monuments for N. Ireland

5-33 Hill Street	tel:	028 9054 3037
Belfast BT1 2LA	fax:	028 9054 3111
www.nics.gov.uk//ehs		

Historic Scotland

Longmore House, Salisbury Place, Edinburgh EH9 1SH	tel:	0131 668 8707
www.historic-scotland.gov.uk	fax:	0131 668 8669

HMSO – see Stationery Office

Institution of Civil Engineers (ICE)

1 Great George Street, London SW1P 3AA	tel:	020 7222 7722
www.ice.org.uk	fax:	020 7222 7500

Institution of Electrical Engineers (IEE)

Savoy Place, London WC2R 0BL	tel:	020 7240 1871
email: postmaster@iee.org.uk www.iee.org.uk	fax:	020 7240 7735

Institution of Mechanical Engineers

1 Birdcage Walk, London SW1H 9JJ	tel:	020 7222 7899
email: enquiries@imeche.org.uk	fax:	020 7222 4557
www.imeche.org.uk		

Institution of Structural Engineers (ISE)

11 Upper Belgrave Street, London SW1X 8BH	tel:	020 7235 4535
email: mail@instructe.org.uk	fax:	020 7235 4294
www.instructe.org.uk		

Landscape Institute

6 Barnard Mews, London SW11 1QU	tel:	020 7738 9166
email: mail@l-i.org.uk www.l-i.org.uk	fax:	020 7738 9134

Lead Development Association International

42 Weymouth Street, London W1N 3LQ	tel:	020 7499 8422
email: enq@ldaint.org	fax:	020 7493 1555
www.ldaint.org		

Lead Sheet Association
Hawkwell Business Centre, Pembury,   tel: 01892 822773
Tunbridge Wells TN2 4AH   fax: 01892 823003
email: leadsa@globalnet.co.uk
www.leadroof.com

Lighting Industry Federation (LIF)
207 Balham High Road, London SW17 7BQ   tel: 020 8675 5432
email: info@lif.co.uk   www.lif.co.uk   fax: 020 8673 5880

Ministry of Agriculture, Fisheries and Food (MAFF)
3 Whitehall Place, London SW1A 2HH   tel: 020 7270 3000
www.maff.gov.uk   fax: 020 7270 8125

National Building Specification Ltd (NBS)
Mansion House Chambers, The Close,   tel: 0191 232 9594
Newcastle upon Tyne NE1 3RE   fax: 0191 232 5714
email: info@nbsservices.co.uk
www.nbsservices.co.uk

National Trust
36 Queen Anne's Gate, London SW1H 9AS   tel: 020 7222 9251
www.nationaltrust.org.uk   fax: 020 7222 5097

Ordnance Survey
Romsey Marsh, Maybush, Southampton SO16 4GU tel: 023 8079 2792
email: enquiries@ordsvy.gov.uk   fax: 023 8079 2452
www.ordsvy.gov.uk

Planning Appeals Commission (N. Ireland)
Park House, 87 Great Victoria Street,   tel: 028 9024 4710
Belfast BT2 7AG   fax: 028 9031 2536
email: info@pacni.gov.uk   www.pacni.gov.uk

Planning Inspectorate (England)
Room 11/09 Tollgate House, Houlton Street,   tel: 0117 987 8075
Bristol BS2 9DJ   fax: 0117 987 8139

Planning Inspectorate (Wales)
Crown Buildings, Cathays Park,   tel: 029 2082 5670
Cardiff CF10 3NQ   fax: 029 2082 5150

Royal Incorporation of Architects in Scotland (RIAS)
15 Rutland Square, Edinburgh EH1 2BE   tel: 0131 229 7545
www.rias.org.uk   fax: 0131 228 2188

Royal Institute of British Architects (RIBA) (see also p. 287)
66 Portland Place, London W1N 4AD   tel: 020 7580 5533
email: admin@inst.riba.org   www.riba.org   fax: 020 7255 1541

Royal Institution of Chartered Surveyors (RICS)
12 Great George St, Parliament Square,   tel: 020 7222 7000
London SW1P 3AD   fax: 020 7334 3800
www.rics.org

Royal Town Planning Institute (RTPI)
26 Portland Place, London W1N 9BE   tel: 020 7636 9107
email: online@rtpi.org.uk   www.rtpi.org.uk   fax: 020 7323 1582

Scottish Executive Inquiry Reporters Unit (SEIRU)
2 Greenside Lane, Edinburgh EH1 3AG   tel: 0131 244 5649
email: seiru@Scotland.gov.uk   www.seiru.gov.uk fax: 0131 244 5680

Scottish Natural Heritage
12 Hope Terrace, Edinburgh EH9 2AS   tel: 0131 447 4784
www.snh.org.uk   fax: 0131 446 2279

Society for the Protection of Ancient Buildings (SPAB)
37 Spital Square, London E1 6DY   tel: 020 7377 1644
email: info@spab.org.uk   www.spab.org.uk   fax: 020 7247 5296
Stationery Office (formerly HMSO)
PO Box 29, Norwich NR3 1GN   tel: 0870 600 5522
email: book.enquiries@theso.co.uk   fax: 0870 600 5533
www.itsofficial.net
Stationery Office bookshops (see TSO)
Stone Federation Great Britain
56 Leonard Street, London EC2A 4JX   tel: 020 7608 5094
www.stone-federationgb.org.uk   fax: 020 7608 5081
Timber Trade Federation
26 Oxendon Street, London SW1Y 4EL   tel: 020 7839 1891
email: ttf@ttf.co.uk   www.ttf.co.uk   fax: 020 7930 0094
Town and Country Planning Association (TCPA)
17 Carlton House Terrace, London SW1Y 5AS   tel: 020 7930 8903
email: tcpa@tcpa.org.uk   www.tcpa.org.uk   fax: 020 7930 3280
TRADA Technology Ltd
Stocking Lane, Hughenden Valley.   tel: 01494 563091
High Wycombe HP14 4ND   fax: 01494 565487
email: information@trada.co.uk
www.tradatechnology.co.uk
TSO (The Stationery Office) shops
123 Kingsway, London WC2B 6PQ   tel: 020 7242 6393
68 Bull Street, Birmingham B4 6AD   tel: 0121 236 9696
9 Princess Street, Manchester M60 8AS   tel: 0161 834 7201
16 Arthur Street, Belfast BT1 4GD   tel: 028 9023 8451
18 High Street, Cardiff CF1 2BZ   tel: 029 2039 5548
71 Lothian Road, Edinburgh EH3 9AZ   tel: 0870 606 5566
Water Regulations Advisory Service (WRAS)
Fern Close, Pen-y-fan Industrial Estate   tel: 01495 248454
Oakdale NP11 3EH   fax: 01495 249234
Water Research Centre plc
PO Box 16, Henley Road, Medmenham,   tel: 01491 571531
Marlow SL7 2HD   fax: 01491 579094
Which?
PO Box 44, Hertford X, SG14 1SH   tel: 01992 822800
email: which@which.net   www.which.net   fax: 020 7830 8585
Zinc Development Association (ZDA)
42 Weymouth Street, London W1N 3LQ   tel: 020 7499 6636
email: enq@zda.org   fax: 020 7493 1555

Manufacturers – referred to in the text

ACP Concrete Ltd
Risehow Industrial Estate, Flimby,   tel: 01900 814659
Maryport CA15 8PD   fax: 01900 816200
Avon Manufacturing Ltd
PO Box 42, Montague Road, Warwick CV34 5LS   tel: 01926 496331
email: avonman.warwick@virgin.net   fax: 01926 400291
Autopa Ltd
Triton Park, Brownsover Road, Rugby CV21 1SG   tel: 01788 550556
email: info@autopa.co.uk   www.autopa.co.uk   fax: 01788 550265
Banham Patent Locks Ltd
233 Kensington High Street, London W8 6SF   tel: 020 7622 5151
email: security@banham.com   www.banham.com   fax: 020 7376 1232
Brash, John & Co Ltd
The Old Shipyard, Gainsborough DN21 1NG   tel: 01427 613858
email: info@johnbrash.co.uk   fax: 01427 810218
www.johnbrash.co.uk
British Gypsum
East Leake, Loughborough LE12 6JT   tel: 08705 456123
www.british.gypsum.bpb.com   fax: 08705 456356
Broderick Structures Ltd
Forsyth Road, Sheerwater, Woking GU21 5RR   tel: 01483 750207
                                                           fax: 01483 750209

Buckingham Nurseries
Tingewick Road, Buckingham MK18 4AE   tel: 01280 813556
email: enquiries@bucknur.com   fax: 01280 815491
Cape Casil Systems Ltd
Iver Lane, Uxbridge UB8 2JQ   tel: 01895 463400
www.capecasil.com   fax: 01895 259262
Caradon Catnic Ltd
Pontygwindy Estate, Caerphilly CF8 2WJ   tel: 029 2033 7900
                                                           fax: 029 2086 3178

Caradon Jones Ltd
Whittington Road, Oswestry SY11 1HZ   tel: 01691 653251
                                                           fax: 01691 658623

Caradon Plumbing Solutions; Stelrad
PO Box 103, National Avenue,   tel: 01482 498402
Kingston-upon-Hull HU5 4JN   fax: 01482 498664
Chubb Physical Security Products
PO Box 61, Wednesfield Road,   tel: 01902 455111
Wolverhampton WV10 0EW   fax: 01902 351961
email: info@chubb-safes.com
www.chubb-safes.com
Concord Sylvania
Avis Way, Newhaven BN9 0ED   tel: 01273 515811
                                                           fax: 01273 611101

Corus: tubes and pipes
PO Box 101, Welson Road, Corby NN17 5UA   tel: 01536 402121
www.corusgroup.com   fax: 01536 404111

Cox Building Products
Ickfield Way Industrial Estate, Tring HP23 4RF   tel: 01442 824222
email: enquiries@coxdome.co.uk   fax: 01442 820550
CSC Forest Products Ltd
Station Road, Cowie, Stirling FK7 7BQ   tel: 01786 812921
www.cscfp.com   fax: 01786 815622
Duplus Domes Ltd
370 Melton Road, Leicester LE4 7SL   tel: 0116 261 0710
email: sales@duplus.co.uk   www.duplus.co.uk   fax: 0116 261 0539
GE Lighting Europe
42 Wood Street,Kingston KT1 1UZ   tel: 020 8626 8500
www.gelighting.com   fax: 020 8727 4495
Glynwed Brickhouse
Brickhouse Lane, West Bromwich B70 0DY   tel: 0121 520 6171
                                                      fax: 0121 521 4551

Hoogovens Aluminium Building Systems Ltd
Haydock Lane, Haydock, St Helens WA11 9TY   tel: 01942 295500
email: enquiries@hoogovens.co.uk   fax: 01942 272136
www.hoogovens.co.uk
Ibstock Building Products Ltd
Leicester Road, Ibstock LE67 6HS   tel: 01530 261999
email: marketing@ibstock.co.uk   fax: 01530 264324
www.ibstock.co.uk
ICI Paints Division
Wexham Road, Slough SL2 5DS   tel: 01753 550000
www.dulux.com   fax: 01753 578218
Ideal-Standard Ltd
National Avenue, Kingston-upon-Hull HU5 4HS   tel: 01482 346461
email: brochures@ideal.standard.co.uk   fax: 01482 445886
www.ideal.standard.co.uk
JELD-WEN UK Ltd
Watch House Lane, Doncaster DN5 9LR   tel: 01302 394000
www.jeld-wen.co.uk   fax: 01302 787383
Latham, James plc
Leeside Wharf, Mount Pleasant Hill, London E5 9NG tel: 020 8806 3333
www.lathams.co.uk   fax: 020 8806 6464
Lee Strip Steel Ltd
Meadow Hall, Sheffield S9 1HU   tel: 0114 243 7272
www.avestasheffield.com   fax: 0114 243 1277
Luxcrete Ltd
Premier House, Disraeli Road, Park Royal,   tel: 020 8965 7292
London NW10 7BT   fax: 020 8961 6337
Marley Building Materials Ltd
Station Road, Coleshill, Birmingham B46 1HP   tel: 01675 468400
email: mbm@mbm.marley.co.uk   fax: 01675 468485
www.marley.co.uk
Masonite CP Ltd
Jason House, Kerry Hill, Horsforth, Leeds LS18 4JR   tel: 0113 258 7689
www.masonite.com   fax: 0113 259 0015

McAlpine Slate, Alfred Ltd
Penrhyn Quarry, Bethesda, Bangor LL57 4YG   tel: 01248 600656
email: slate@alfred.mcalpine.com   fax: 01248 601171
www.amslate.com
Metra Non-Ferrous Metals Ltd
Pindar Road, Hoddesden EN11 0DE   tel: 01992 460455
    fax: 01992 451207

Midland Lead Manufacturers Ltd
Woodville, Swadlincote DE11 8ED   tel: 01283 224555
email: sales@midlandlead.co.uk   fax: 01283 550284
NCS Colour Centre
71 Ancaster Green, Henley-on Thames, RG9 1TS   tel: 01491 411717
email: info@ncscolour.co.uk www.ncscolour.co.uk   fax: 01491 411231
Osram Ltd
PO Box 17, East Lane, Wembley HA9 7PG   tel: 020 8904 4321
www.osram.co.uk   fax: 020 8901 1222
Philips Lighting Ltd
420 London Road, Croydon CR9 3QR   tel: 020 8689 2166
www.philips.com   fax: 020 8665 5703
Pilkington United Kingdom Ltd
Prescot Road, St Helens WA10 3TT   tel: 01744 692000
email: info@pilkington.com   www.pilkington.com   fax: 01744 613044
Premdor
Hargreaves Road, Groundwell Industrial Estate,   tel: 01793 708200
Swindon SN2 5AZ   fax: 01793 708290
www.premdor.com
Pressalit Ltd
Riverside Business Park, Dansk Way, Leeds Road,   tel: 01943 607651
Ilkley LS29 8JZ   fax: 01943 607214
Range Cylinders Ltd
Tadman Street, Wakefield WF1 5QU   tel: 01924 376026
    fax: 01924 203428

Redland Roofing Systems Ltd
Regent House, Station Approach, Dorking RH4 1TG   tel: 01306 872000
email: roofing@redland.co.uk www.Redland.co.uk   fax: 01306 872111
Rigidal Industries Ltd
Blackpole Trading Estate, Worcester WR3 8ZJ   tel: 01905 750500
email: mailbox@rigidal.co.uk   www.rigidal.co.uk   fax: 01905 750555
Ruberoid Building Products Ltd
Tewin Road, Welwyn Garden City AL7 1BP   tel: 01707 822222
email: rbp-wgc@ruberoid.co.uk www.ruberoid.co.uk   fax: 01707 375060
Tarmac Topblock Ltd
Cannock Rd, Featherstone,   tel: 01902 305060
Wolverhampton WV10 7HP   fax: 01902 384542
www.topblock.co.uk
Titan Plastech
Barbot Hall Industrial Estate, Mandham Road,   tel: 01709 538300
Rotherham S61 4RJ   fax: 01709 538301
Ubbink (UK) Ltd
Borough Road, Brackley NN13 7TB   tel: 01280 700211
www.ubbinkrega.com   fax: 01280 705332

Velux Company Ltd
Woodside Way, Glenrothes, East Fife KY7 4ND   tel: 01592 772211
email: enquiries@velux.co.uk   www.velux.co.uk   fax: 01592 771839
Vent-Axia Ltd
Fleming Way, Crawley RH10 2NN   tel: 01293 526062
email: info@vent-axia.com   www.vent-axia.com   fax: 01293 552552
Williamette Europe Ltd
Maitland House, Warrior Square,   tel: 01702 619044
Southend-on-Sea SS1 2JY   fax: 01712 617162
email: sales@williamette.europe.com
www.williamette.europe.com
Xpelair Ltd
Morley Way, Peterborough PE2 9JJ   tel: 01733 456189
email: info@redring.co.uk   www.redring.co.uk   fax: 01733 310606
Zehnder Ltd
Unit 6, Invincible Road, Farnborough GU14 7QU   tel: 01252 515151
email: sales@zehnder.co.uk   www.zehnder.co.uk   fax: 01252 522528

Sources

Activities and Spaces: Dimensional Data for Housing Design Noble, J. (ed) 1983 The Architectural Press

AJ Handbook of Architectural Ironmongery Underwood, G. and Planck, J. 1977 The Architectural Press

Barbour Index '00 Barnes, C. (ed) 2000 Barbour Index plc

Building & Structural Tables Blake, F. H. 1947 Chapman & Hall

Building a Sustainable Future 1998 DETR

Building Construction McKay, W.B.M. 1963 Longman

Building for Energy Efficiency 1997 CIC

The Building Regulations Explained & Illustrated Powell-Smith, V. and Billington, M. J. 1995 Blackwell Science

Building Regulations 1991 Approved Documents DETR 1991–2000 The Stationery Office

The Care and Repair of Thatched Roofs Brockett, P. 1986 SPAB

The Culture of Timber McCartney, K. 1994 University of Portsmouth

Dampness in Buildings Oxley, T. A. and Gobert, E. G. 1994 Butterworth-Heinemann

Designing for Accessibility 1999 Centre for Accessible Environments

Easibrief Haverstock, H. 1998 Miller Freeman

Fireplace Design and Construction Baden-Powell, C. 1984 Longman

Flat Roofing – A Guide to Good Practice March, F. 1983 Tarmac Building Products Ltd

The Good Wood Guide Counsell, S. 1996 Friends of the Earth

A Guide to Planning Appeals The Planning Inspectorate 1997 DoE

A Guide to the Security of Homes Central Office of Information 1986 HMSO

Sources – continued

Handbook of Fixings and Fastenings Launchbury, B. 1971 Architectural Press

Hillier Designer's Guide to Landscape Plants 1999 Hillier Romsey

Home Security & Safety Good Housekeeping Guide 1995 Ebury Press

Illustrated Dictionary of Building Marsh, P. 1982 Longman

Lighting for people, energy efficiency & architecture 1999 DETR

Listing Buildings – The work of English Heritage 1997 English Heritage

The Macmillan Encyclopaedia Isaacs, A. (ed) 1986 Macmillan

Managing construction for health and safety, **CDM Regulations 1994** Approved Code of Practice 1995 Health & Safety Commission

Materials for Architects and Builders Lyons, A. R. 1997 Hodder Headline Group

Mathematical Models Cundy, H. M. and Rollett, A. P. 1981 Tarquin Publications

Metric Handbook Adler, D. 1998 Architectural Press

Party Wall etc. Act: explanatory booklet 1997 DoE

The Penguin Dictionary of Building Maclean, J. H. and Scott, J. S. 1995 Penguin Books

Planning: A Guide for Householders Central Office of Information 1996 DoE

Recognising Wood Rot & Insect Damage in Buildings Bravery, A. F. 1987 DoE

The Right Hedge for You (leaflet) 1999 DETR

Safety in the Home DoE (leaflet) 1976 HMSO

Series 'A' Design Data CIBSE Guide 1980 CIBSE

Space in the Home Metric Edition DoE 1968 HMSO

Spaces in the Home – Bathrooms and WCs DoE 1972 HMSO

Spaces in the Home – Kitchens and laundering spaces DoE 1972 HMSO

Specification '94 Williams, A. 1994 Emap Architecture
Stone in Building Ashurst, J. and Dimes, F. 1984 Stone Federation
Thatch: A Manual for Owners, Surveyors, Architects and Builders West, R. C. 1987 David & Charles
Tomorrow's World McLaren, D., Bullock, S. and Yousuf, N. 1998 Friends of the Earth
Tree Planting Year 1973 circular 99/72 DoE
Water Conservation in Business 1999 DETR
Water Supply (Water Fittings) Regulations 1999 DETR
What Listing Means – A guide for Owners and Occupiers 1994 Dept of National Heritage
The Which? Book of Plumbing and Central Heating Holloway, D. 1985 Consumers' Association
Whitaker's Concise Almanack Marsden, H. (ed.) 1996 J. Whitaker & Sons Ltd
WRAS Water Regulations Guide Water Regulations Advisory Scheme (WRAS)

CIC   = Construction Industry Council
DoE   = Department of the Environment (now DETR)
DETR = Department of the Environment, Transport & the Regions
HMSO = Her Majesty's Stationery Office (now the Stationery Office)
SPAB = Society for the Protection of Ancient Buildings

Index

Notes

Notes

Notes

Notes

Notes